Case Studies in Infant Mental Health

Case Studies in Infant Mental Health:
Risk, Resiliency, and Relationships

Joan J. Shirilla &
Deborah J. Weatherston, *Editors*

ZERO
TO
THREE®

Washington, D.C.

Published by:
ZERO TO THREE
2000 M Street NW, Suite 200
Washington, DC 20036-3307
(202) 638-1144
Toll-free for orders: (800) 899-4301
Fax: (202) 638-0851
Web: http://www.zerotothree.org

Cover design: Will Works, Parkton, Maryland
Text design and composition: Susan Lehmann, Washington, D.C.

Library of Congress Cataloging-in-Publication Data
Case studies in infant mental health: risk, resiliency, and relationships /
Joan J. Shirilla, Deborah J. Weatherston, editors.
    p. cm.
    Includes bibliographical references.
ISBN 0-943657-57-1 (pbk.)
1. Infants—Mental health. 2. Infant psychiatry.
I. Shirilla, Joan J., 1951- II. Weatherston, Deborah.
RJ502.5 .C37   2002
618.92'89—dc21   2002004005

First Edition First Printing (April 2002)
ISBN 0-943657-57-1
Printed in the United States of America

Suggested citations:
Book citation:
Shirilla, J. J., & Weatherston, D. J. (Eds.). (2002). *Case studies in infant mental health:
Risk, resiliency, and relationships.* Washington, DC: ZERO TO THREE.
Chapter citation:
Oleksiak, C. (2002). Risk and resiliency: Failure to thrive in the first year of life. In J. J.
Shirilla & D. J. Weatherston (Eds.), *Case studies in infant mental health: Risk, resiliency,
and relationships* (pp. 41-50). Washington, DC: ZERO TO THREE.

For Holly

2/28

107458

This case study book was completed with the award of a grant from The Gerber Foundation to the Infant Mental Health Program at the Merrill-Palmer Institute of Wayne State University, Detroit, Michigan. The editors and authors wish to express their gratitude for the Foundation's longstanding commitment to the well-being of infants and their families.

 is a national nonprofit organization whose mission is to promote the healthy development of our nation's infants and toddlers by supporting and strengthening families, communities, and those who work on their behalf. We are dedicated to advancing current knowledge; promoting beneficial policies and practices; communicating research and best practices to a wide variety of audiences; and providing training, technical assistance, and leadership development.

Foreword

This volume is a wonderful collection of case studies as well as a thoughtful and useful discussion of the nature and heart of infant mental health practice. It is well worth reading and pondering by both beginning and experienced practitioners. Contributors beautifully capture the remarkable experience of working with babies and those who are caring for them. In doing so, they allow us to readily join in the complicated journey each family and practitioner make together.

Throughout the book run an explicit, deep appreciation and an understanding of the work of Selma Fraiberg. Indeed, this volume should be considered a direct descendant of The Child Development Project, which Selma Fraiberg began in Ann Arbor, Michigan, in 1973, and which I joined a year later. It is poetically proper, as well as logical, that this book should emerge from the Merrill-Palmer Institute and that so many of the contributors are leaders in the Michigan Association for Infant Mental Health. Mrs. Fraiberg would love it. She was born and raised in Detroit, got her social work degree from Wayne State University, and Michigan was always her true home.

To understand these case studies as the well-deserved tribute to Selma Fraiberg that they are, one must understand that Selma Fraiberg was a remarkable woman. She was a thoughtful and critical integrator of knowledge, read passionately, and pursued her interests with vigor and imagination. Along the way she produced a number of wonderful and creative ideas. Among them was one that was truly seminal, and it is because of it that this particular volume exists. That idea had its own interesting origins.

In 1960, Selma Fraiberg and Gerald Freedman were asked, in their roles as consultants to the family service society of New

Orleans, to design a program for blind children ages 3 to 14. As it was to evolve, the agency asked just the right people. Mrs. Fraiberg was a social worker and psychoanalyst, and Dr. Freedman was a neurologist and psychoanalyst. How could one design such a program, they wondered, if one didn't know what is different about the early development of a child with visual deficits from that of a sighted child? And how much might we learn about the development of sighted children from this contrasting perspective?

Mrs. Fraiberg and Dr. Freedman were disturbed by the atypical patterns they saw among children with visual deficits—for example, stereotyped movements, odd mannerisms, and a lack of differentiation of self and other. Equally concerning were what they felt were notably tenuous connections of these children to others. A thorough literature search revealed their assessments as typical of other researchers. However, newly emerging literature suggested that blindness itself was probably not the factor predisposing these children to worrisome developmental patterns. Rather, issues of emotional stimulation and incentives for development played a major role.

Careful interviewing and fastidious filming and observation of the babies were the beginning of what was to be a long, interesting journey for Mrs. Fraiberg. In 1963, the two researchers moved to different universities. Their mutual interest in the topic continued, but along separate paths. Mrs. Fraiberg continued her observational studies and, in 1965, received a grant to expand her efforts. The families selected for the research and also those referred who could not be part of the research protocol were visited at home for purposes of guidance, with the understanding that what was learned would be shared with the families as it seemed useful. The families within the research group were also observed and filmed.

Beginning in 1960, Mrs. Fraiberg and her colleagues engaged in a lively and remarkable exchange of knowledge and ideas with a dazzling group of psychologists and psychiatrists who were similarly intrigued with the exquisitely detailed study of early development. This cast of players included (in order of appearance) Sibylle Escalona, Peter Wolff, Therese Gouin Decarie, Jean Piaget, Eric Lenneberg, Rene Spitz, Sally Provence, Robert Emde, David Metcalf, Mary Ainsworth, Arthur Parmelee, Justin Call, Daniel Stern, and Ken Robson. The soberness of their deliberations and the joy in each other's company in this context was enormously productive. Mrs. Fraiberg reported that Piaget threw his beret in the air and cheered when he saw, on film, one of the blind children achieving stage six on his scale of development (demonstrating, by searching for it, that he understood that something out of his awareness existed)—an achievement that is a challenge to develop without vision.

These studies made an enormous contribution to the under-standing of the development of blind infants and illuminated understanding of the development of sighted infants as well. This new knowledge, coupled with the extremely successful intervention with the young blind infants and their families, provoked Mrs. Fraiberg's seminal idea. It went something like this:

If beginning as early as possible is so successful in preventing prob-lems with these families and these babies, why wouldn't it be possible to work in a similar way where there are other impediments to an infant's development? It should not matter whether the impediments stem from a different source intrinsic to the baby or from impediments within the parents.

Mrs. Fraiberg reached this conclusion because she understood that early experience is crucial to development. She pointed to her work with blind babies and their families as the defining impetus that led to the establishment of The Child Development Project in Ann Arbor, Michigan, in 1973. This was the first program that took as its sole focus work with infants and parents *together*, in order to improve and enhance the overall ego development of the baby in whatever ways seemed necessary.

Since 1973, programs for infants, toddlers, and families have steadily proliferated. They all have the goal of supporting and enhancing the children's development in a positive way. They also see an improvement in aspects of the child's home environment as being of primary relevance to this goal. But how this is understood and implemented, and how the service is designed and delivered, varies enormously. The State of Michigan, in the form of a very far-sight-ed Betty Tableman, chose to support interested mental health prac-titioners from community mental health agencies across the state to receive training from The Child Development Project. This resulted in an unusually effective dissemination of interest and skills. Practi-tioners in Michigan have remained closely tied to the original pres-ence and impact of The Child Development Project, even as the project itself moved to the University of California, San Francisco, in 1979. This volume reflects these enduring connections.

The work described in these 12 case studies embraces many of the essential elements of The Child Development Project in a splendid way. One of the most striking and valuable aspects of these collected stories is their realistic untidiness. We are able to hear the true voices of many different people, whether baby, toddler, parent, or practitioner. The stories have not been conceptualized or edited into some homogeneous way of presentation, of being, or of seeing. This diversity reflects the world of this therapeutic work as it truly is—unpredictable, untidy, careful, reflective, modest, and devoted to the shepherding of a process that is not primarily one's own. The stories represent uniqueness —as they should. No baby, no parent, no practitioner is like any other. And no prescriptive way of being or doing can be assumed to be efficacious in relation to everyone, by anyone. No practitioner can be the same with each family and be effective. And no two practitioners will be the same.

Still, the underlying themes are always familiar. They are organized around people's feelings about themselves and others in the past and in the present. We all cloak ourselves in many-layered disguises created by the need to protect, assert, and create a self that can somehow manage. As a result, it is not easy to understand the important meanings of a parent's words or behavior, nor is it easy to discern how our own messages are heard. It is the baby who can be counted upon to be the most straightforward, whose behavior tells the clearest story. But even babies grow more complicated quickly.

Competent practitioners are no less complicated than parents, but the thread they try to weave themselves around is their responsibility for creating as useful and effective a therapeutic relationship as possible. Although this effort will be different for each practitioner in each circumstance, it is always based on being sensitively alert to discovering who is feeling what, communicating what, and why. As practitioners, we create stories with families we see that will follow no particular, predictable course, but they will represent the best story we can tell together. Sometimes the story will end too soon. Always it will have life to contend with.

The privilege of working with families in so important and intimate a way is one we always continue to experience, appreciate, and remember. The responsibility we feel is never casual, even as we recognize its practical and reasonable limits. As practitioners, we are responsible for what we do and how we are, but not for what the families do. We try not to get confused about that.

We know that we cannot always do our work well without the help of a colleague, a consultant, or a supervisor, someone who will listen and think and aid us in locating and beginning to unsnarl some tangle that interferes with how we want and need to be—a person who can help us understand something about someone with whom we are working (the parent or the baby) in a way that we have not been able to. This collection of case studies speaks to all of this and more.

The stories and the questions that follow each of them provoke us again and again to appreciate sameness and difference, and also to wonder what we might have done differently in those circumstances and why. Do we have a differing sense, in a particular instance, of what a mother's actions or words mean? Is there a moment when our sense of a baby's need would have provoked a different intervention? Some questions reverberate through many stories, and infant/family work in general. How do you hold the empathy for parent and child in balance so that neither is sacrificed to the other—so that our concern for one does not lead to lack of sufficient awareness and understanding of the other, or that both are not endangered by our strong wish to help them be together? This balance is like walking an emotional tightrope with the need for constant awareness of exactly where you are. How do you keep appropriate advocacy for a family with an outside entity delicate enough not to be (or seem) defensive or belligerent? Can you do *for* a parent and *with* a parent simultaneously? How do you avoid a sense of being exploited? When does it happen? How do you factor in your own moods and your life's vicissitudes?

Some of these questions need to be answered each time we work with a baby and family. There are no specific programmed, prescriptive ways to do any of the things we will need to do. In addition to our being appropriately trained and knowledgeable, our best and steadfast compass is knowing ourselves and something about how to be; that will, of course, not always look or feel the same. These case studies raise all of these questions and more, and help us think about answers.

Doing this kind of work is truly a mutual adventure, each and every time. One is always curious and interested, often surprised, and always learning. I still remember very vividly, sitting around the conference table at The Child Development Project in 1974, trying, with my new colleagues, to figure out what we were doing. We knew *why* we were doing it, but we were grappling with *how* we should do it, and how we would know if we were being successful. This process is a continuous one. All of us engaged in this work strive to be ever better able to realize and articulate what the essential shapes our interventions can take and why.

In reading these case studies, those who have done this work for some time will meet many old familiar, internal friends and enemies, and some new ones. For those less experienced, these stories are a wonderful way to get experience that someone else has earned for you. Whether alone or with a group, whether thinking or thinking and discussing, you will garner from this collection valuable insights into the complexities, pains, and pleasures of this incredible and wonderful work.

Jeree Pawl
San Francisco, California
January 2002

Acknowledgments

This book reflects the work of many people who have generously shared their understanding of infancy, early parenthood, and relationship development with practitioners in Michigan for the past 30 years. We begin with the pioneering work of Selma Fraiberg, her staff, and early trainees at The Child Development Project at the University of Michigan in Ann Arbor, Michigan, from 1969-1980. Many babies, toddlers, and their families benefited from her early studies and insights about the first 3 years of life that led to the development of infant mental health services. Several generations have benefited from her understanding that healthy emotional development occurs within the context of close human relationships.

We are deeply indebted to Betty Tableman, who extended Selma Fraiberg's devotion to infant mental health service and training to the public arena of the community mental health system, beginning in 1973, and continuing throughout her tenure as the Director of Prevention Services for the Michigan Department of Community Mental Health until 1995. Thanks also to Jeff Goldblatt and Sherita Falvay who continued to support the construction of infant mental health services through the state system.

We would also like to acknowledge those who have been with us since the inception of our book. First, Barbara Getz, Executive Director of the Gerber Foundation and Mid-Career Fellow at ZERO TO THREE. Her encouragement strengthened our commitment and enabled us to receive generous funding from the Gerber Foundation of Fremont, Michigan. Without their support we would have been unable to undertake this project. Emily Fenichel, Associate Director of ZERO TO THREE, offered initial support and immediate enthusiasm that enabled us to move ahead and helped us always to hold in mind the importance of this project.

We also wish to thank the many parents and infants who worked courageously with infant mental health specialists in their communities and allowed their stories to be told here. It is through their courage that we are able to share the lessons we have learned.

The contributors are especially thankful to the following senior clinicians who guided and supported their work: Bill Schafer, Ph.D.; Barry Wright, Ph.D.; Tom Horner, Ph.D.; Kathleen Baltman, M.A.; Melissa Kaplan Estrin, Ph.D.; B. Kay Campbell, Ph.D.; Doug Davies, Ph.D.; Arlene Gendelman, M.A.; and Deborah Weatherston, Ph.D.

The development of a collection of case studies is a daunting task that requires the cooperation and enthusiasm of many people. Additionally, Wayne State University's Merrill-Palmer Institute provided a home for the project. We acknowledge Merrill-Palmer, with special thanks to Reta Collins and Rose Foster for their clerical support and computer expertise. We also wish to acknowledge the skillful copyediting of Sally Chichester, Maria Brown, Lauren Beck, and Gina Skurchak.

Each author of these case studies is a leader in the infant mental health field who works tirelessly as both a clinician and an advocate for the well-being of infants and their families. They have helped shape quality intervention on behalf of at-risk families with very young children in the State of Michigan. We are grateful for their kindness and their friendship. Each colleague's willingness to write about his or her work, after hours and often on weekends, required time, energy, and commitment. Their steadfast commitment to excellence was apparent as they considered our ideas, accepted suggestions, and worked to revise the text. Their talents were always clear to us. We remain inspired by their words and in awe of their work.

Finally, as editors and contributors, we are grateful for the time we have had to work on this project together for the past 2 years. With offices across the hall from each other, we were able to plan and write together, listen to each other, share our uncertainties, and laugh together. From this collaboration we strengthened our friendship and renewed our commitment to promoting healthy emotional development in infants, toddlers, and their families.

Joan J. Shirilla &
Deborah J. Weatherston, Editors

Preface

The 12 detailed case studies in this volume illustrate infant mental health practice as conceived originally, more than 25 years ago, by Selma Fraiberg and her colleagues in Ann Arbor, Michigan, and implemented in a wide variety of settings that serve infants, young children, and their families. Contributing authors are trained infant mental health specialists with backgrounds in social work, psychology, education, child and family development, and special education and are working in home-visiting/family support programs, early intervention, child welfare, and Early Head Start, as well as child guidance and mental health settings. Infant mental health specialists use concrete assistance, emotional support, developmental guidance, early relationship assistance and support, advocacy, and infant-parent psychology to strengthen the development and well-being of infants and young children within secure and stable parent-child relationships. Of additional importance, infant mental health practice is complementary to such other treatment approaches as, for example, occupational and play therapies.

Michigan has long had a strong commitment to the training of professionals from multiple disciplines to work with infants, toddlers, and their families. The Michigan Association for Infant Mental Health, established in 1977, has supported clinical meetings, annual conferences, and training opportunities to promote professional and interdisciplinary competencies. Three universities— Wayne State University, Michigan State University, and the University of Michigan—have developed unique training programs in infancy and infant mental health. From this strong infant mental health service and training tradition in Michigan, the idea developed to provide case study materials for professionals to consider when preparing to work or when working with infants, toddlers, and families. We wanted to acknowledge the work that has been done in Michigan and share some of the lessons learned over the years about effective infant mental health practice.

Each author was chosen because of exemplary work with infants and families. Each case study describes the infant mental health specialist's direct work with young children and families, the supervision and consultation that support the specialist, and the specialist's interaction with the larger service system. The variety further illustrates service delivery in rural communities, small towns, large towns, and cities. The studies involved families living in shelters, housing projects, apartments, and more affluent suburbs. To protect confidentiality, the families' names and certain other identifying details have been changed in these narratives. Discussion questions at the end of each chapter are designed to guide self-reflection or group study. It is our hope that these case studies generate interest in the field of infant mental health and wonder about the capacities each infant, parent, and practitioner has to forge relationships that lead to strength and change.

Contents

Introduction to the Infant Mental Health Program

Deborah J. Weatherston

More than a quarter-century ago, Selma Fraiberg, one of the founding Board members of ZERO TO THREE, and her colleagues in Ann Arbor, Michigan, crafted an extraordinary approach to strengthening the development and well-being of infants and young children within secure and stable parent-child relationships. Fraiberg called the practice "infant mental health." "Infant" referred to children under 3 years of age. "Mental" included social, emotional, and cognitive domains. "Health" referred to the well-being of young children and families.

Fraiberg described new knowledge about early development and relationships as "a treasure that should be returned to babies and their families as a gift from science" (Fraiberg, 1980, p. 3). In the early 1970s, knowledge about the first 3 years of life was expanding rapidly, in the laboratories of developmental psychologists, in neonatal nurseries and pediatric clinics, and in Fraiberg's own work with blind infants and with emotionally vulnerable infants and parents.

Under Fraiberg's careful direction, social workers, psychologists, nurses, and psychiatrists—seasoned practitioners and student interns—worked together at The Child Development Project in Ann Arbor, Michigan, to translate new knowledge into practice through the Infant Mental Health (IMH) approach. Parent and infant were seen together, most frequently in their own homes, for early identification of risk and treatment to reduce the likelihood of serious developmental failure and relationship disturbance. Each practitioner returned to "the source," the home where an infant and parent lived, to observe, firsthand, the infant or toddler within the context of the emerging parent-child relationship. Sitting beside the parent and infant at the kitchen table or on the floor or on a sofa, the IMH practitioner watched and listened carefully in effort to understand the capacities of the child and family, the risks they faced, and the ways in which the practitioner might be helpful to the infant or toddler and family.

IMH represented a dramatic shift in focus in clinical practice as it existed at the time. Attention to the baby, the parent, and the early developing parent-child relationship required a comprehensive and intensive approach. Services included concrete assistance, emotional support, developmental guidance, early relationship assessment and support, infant-parent psychotherapy, and advocacy. These dimensions of service (see Table 1) continue to define IMH practice in many settings.

The IMH Specialist: Beliefs, Skills, and Clinical Strategies

The early IMH practitioners were social workers, psychologists, nurses, and psychiatrists. Within their various disciplines, many had been trained in a psychodynamic or relationship-based approach to mental health treatment for adults and children, which they adapted to meet the needs of infants, toddlers, and their parents. In recent years, attention to infancy, early relationship development, and parental mental health has become part of the training of practitioners in other disciplines—for example, early childhood education, occupational therapy, and physical therapy. Consequently, it may be most helpful to define the IMH specialist not as a member of a particular discipline, but rather as someone with a distinct set of core beliefs, skills, training experiences, and clinical strategies who incorporates a comprehensive, intensive, and relationship-based approach to working with young children and families.

In its *Guidelines for Infant Mental Health Practice* (Stinson, Tableman, & Weatherston, 2000), the Michigan Association for Infant Mental Health listed the following basic beliefs that support and sustain IMH specialists as they work with infants and families:

- Optimal growth and development occur within nurturing relationships.
- The birth and care of a baby offer a family the possibility of new relationships, growth, and change.
- What happens in the early years affects the course of development across the life span.
- Early developing attachment relationships may be distorted or disturbed by parental histories of unresolved losses and traumatic life events ("ghosts in the nursery") (Fraiberg, Adelson, & Shapiro, 1975).
- The therapeutic presence of an IMH specialist may reduce the

Table 1 Infant Mental Health Services

Concrete assistance

A family's urgent and immediate need for food, formula, medical care, and housing must be met if parents are going to be able to feed, protect, and nurture their young children. The IMH specialist understands that if a family is hungry, they must be fed and if they need medical care, they must be taken care of. Parents cannot adequately meet their infants' basic needs until their own basic needs are met. Such assistance offers a powerful metaphor for the help that a specialist will be able to give to support parents in caring for their infants and in reducing risks of failure in families.

Emotional support

An IMH specialist offers emotional support to families who face immediate crises related to the care of their children. The specialist pays careful attention to the expressed concerns, e.g., the birth of a sick baby, the death of a child, the abandonment of a parent, the hospitalization of a baby. The specialist is observant of the parent's neediness for consistent care and thoughtful response to the care that a baby needs, the trauma of hospitalization, and the adjustments required when there is a significant loss. She acknowledges the parent's needs and strengths, showing compassion for the situation and empathy in response to the crisis. The specialist's consistent presence and availability offer reassurance to the family. Words communicate reassurance and steady support, reducing the family's distress. Within the context of a therapeutic relationship, the specialist helps parents to turn their attention to the care requirements of their infants and to begin to heal.

Developmental guidance

The IMH specialist offers information to the parent that is specific to the baby's development and needs for care. In the course of observing the infant or toddler carefully, the specialist encourages parents to notice what the child is doing and what developmental tasks might come next. The specialist invites the parent to share in the understanding of the baby, to ask questions about the baby's development, and to celebrate milestones as they are reached. The specialist offers experiences that encourage positive interaction and playful exchange. In some instances, the specialist speaks for the baby, drawing attention to particular wants or developmental needs. Modeling may also be appropriate, guiding parents in caregiving activities or showing parents how to relate in a different way. Developmental guidance supports and strengthens parent-child interaction and response. All of the specialist's efforts reinforce what the parent is able to do for the infant to encourage mutual pleasure and purposeful response. For many parents who are unprepared for the care of a baby or isolated from family and friends, the guidance of the IMH specialist is crucial for the infant's or toddler's optimal care.

Early relationship assessment and support

IMH specialists offer parents multiple opportunities to build and use their relationship with the practitioner to nurture, protect, steady, and enhance their understanding about their babies. Specialists observe interactions of parents and infants together, noticing what is happening "in the moment," inviting parents' comments, and reinforcing what is going well. The use of videotape for guided interaction is a particularly useful strategy when supporting overburdened parents in their developing relationships with young children (McDonough, 1993). As specialists and parents grow comfortable with one another, they are able to talk about the infant's contributions to the relationship, pleasurable and painful, and discuss other relationships, past and present, that make the care of the infant problematic or possible.

Advocacy

IMH specialists often speak for those who cannot, the infants or the parents who have not found their voices. The specialist may need to speak for the baby's need to be fed or put in a safe spot or the parent's need for a food bank or a roof over her head. Specialists may have to help families negotiate systems by finding child care, accompanying parents to the welfare office, or articulating the need for a special infant assessment. In other instances, specialists may have to testify on behalf of a child's right to remain with a parent, the need for immediate placement in foster care, or the parent's right to visit the infant weekly with full therapeutic support. It is a daunting task to know when and how to speak effectively on behalf of infants and families enrolled for IMH services.

Infant-parent psychotherapy

The presence of the infant is clearly vital to the practice of infant-parent psychotherapy. The infant or toddler fuels the specialist's understanding, serving as an energizing focus for the intervention. The parent's feelings in the presence of the infant or toddler are often intense and complex. Their expression within the safety of the specialist's relationship offers the possibility of thoughtful exploration about parenthood and the infant's or toddler's continuing needs for care. The parent's perceptions and representations of the infant or toddler are often more available in the presence of the infant for therapeutic consideration and response. Aware that the infant or toddler evokes myriad thoughts and feelings, the specialist offers parents many opportunities to recover and understand the feelings that threaten to interrupt the development of a positive and enduring relationship with their child.

Negative experiences and unresolved losses may gravely affect the parent's capacity to attend to or fall in love with the baby and alter the relationship as it develops in the infant's first years. Neglectful or abusive care in infancy or childhood, interruptions or removal from the home, early trauma, and broken or conflicted family relationships may deepen the pain of early parenthood and lead to another generation of failure. Parents may not be able to hold or feed their babies, talk to or offer appropriate playthings to excite or arouse their curiosity. They may not be able to set limits that are appropriate or keep their children safe. Infant-parent psychotherapy offers parents many opportunities to have and express their emotions surrounding earlier traumas, reducing the risk of inadequate care and of repeated failure or dysfunction in this new relationship.

risk of relationship failure and offer the hopefulness of warm and nurturing parental responses.

These tenets help specialists to understand their role, cherish each encounter with young children and caregivers, think deeply about the meaning that each interaction has for the infant and the parent, and plan interventions in partnership with families. These beliefs also guide the practice of IMH consultation to infant/family programs.

Qualitative summaries of IMH home-visiting services include a rich store of case study materials that describe interventions with parent(s) and infant or toddler together, for short-term or long-term work together (Fraiberg et al., 1975; Fraiberg, Shapiro, & Adelson, 1976; Fraiberg & Adelson, 1977; Fraiberg, 1980; Blos & Davies, 1993; Pawl, 1995; Weatherston, 1995). These studies reveal basic skills and strategies that are fundamental to effective and compassionate IMH home-visiting work. Interviews with experienced IMH consultants, supervisors, and practitioners in Michigan confirm the centrality of these strategies to competent and reflective practice (Weatherston, 2000). These skills and strategies include

1. building relationships and using them as instruments of change;

2. meeting with the infant and parent together throughout the period of intervention;

3. sharing in the observation of the infant's growth and development;

4. offering anticipatory guidance to the parent that is specific to the infant;

5. alerting the parent to the infant's individual accomplishments and needs;

6. helping the parent to find pleasure in the relationship with the infant;

7. creating opportunities for interaction and exchange between parent(s) and infant or parent(s) and practitioner;

8. allowing the parent to take the lead in interacting with the infant or determining the "agenda" or "topic for discussion";

9. identifying and enhancing the capacities that each parent brings to the care of the infant;

10. wondering about the parent's thoughts and feelings related to the presence and care of the infant and the changing responsibilities of parenthood;

11. wondering about the infant's experiences and feelings in interaction with and relationship to the caregiving parent;

12. listening for the past as it is expressed in the present—inquiring and talking;

13. allowing core relational conflicts and emotions to be expressed by the parent—holding, containing, and talking about them as the parent is able;

14. attending and responding to parental histories of abandonment, separation, and unresolved loss as they affect the care of the infant, the infant's development, the parent's emotional health, and the early developing relationship;

15. attending and responding to the infant's history of early care within the developing parent-infant relationship;

16. identifying, treating, and/or collaborating with others, if needed, in the treatment of disorders of infancy, delays and disabilities, parental mental illness, and family dysfunction; and

17. remaining open, curious, and reflective.

All of these strategies contribute to the parent's understanding of the infant, the awakening or repair of the early developing attachment relationship, and the parent's capacity to nurture and protect a young child. They form a critical conceptual base for the IMH specialist to consider and use in order to understand and work with families effectively.

The skills and strategies described in points 1 through 9 and 17, above, are not unique to the IMH specialist. Relationship-building, informal and formal observation of a young child's development, guided interaction and parental support, and reflection are skills that all infant/family practitioners who work from a relationship perspective use and value. However, points 10 through 16, above, are more clearly specific to the IMH specialist and may help to distinguish IMH practice from other forms of infant and family services. These seven strategies attend to the emotional health and development of both parent and child. They focus clearly on relationships, past and present, and the complexities that many parents encounter when nurturing, protecting, and responding to the emotional needs of young children. Finally, these strategies require holding, the creation of a safe and nurturing context in which a parent and specialist may think deeply about the care of the infant, the emotional health of the parent, the multiple challenges of early parenthood, and possibilities for growth and change.

These seven strategies characterize the work of IMH specialists across disciplines and at multiple service levels, from prevention and early identification of risks to intensive assessment and treatment of serious emotional disturbances or jeopardized relationships. The IMH specialist uses these clinical strategies as she works with infants, toddlers, and families who come to her attention because of concerns about the child's development or behavior, parental factors, situational stress, or multiple risks to child and family. The following section describes in more detail how the IMH specialist attends to emotional experience and emotional needs.

Attending to the Emotional Experience and Needs of Infants, Toddlers, and Families

IMH specialists pay attention to the emotional experience of each infant or toddler and each parent. They ask, "What is it like to be this baby? What is it like to be this parent?" In the course of intervention, the IMH specialist pays attention to the infant's expression of rage or flattened affect or the failure to cry out when hungry, tired, or wet. The IMH specialist wonders what the baby's experience is of a particular caregiving interaction or relationship. Carefully attuned to the infant's expression of emotion, the IMH specialist works at understanding the meaning of the infant's communications and guides the parent in understanding this, too.

Similarly, the IMH specialist is very attentive to the parent's emotional state. She notices the parent's rough handling of her baby when he needs a diaper changed. She notices shifts in the parent's affect, the disgust she cannot hide, or the absence of affection. The specialist watches quietly and wonders, to herself, what makes the handling of the baby so difficult. She allows herself to connect with the parent's intense and conflicted emotion. She is both repelled and filled with empathy for the parent's pain. The specialist keeps a very sharp eye on her own emotional responses as a guide to what is happening in the moment between parent and child. She may speak to what she sees and feels, and wonder what the parent is experiencing. She may notice and address the parent's change in mood, the struggle around caring for the baby, and the parent's wish to run away.

She may empathize with the parent's difficulty in having to care for the baby alone. She may ask the parent what she is experiencing as she holds, feeds, or diapers her child. She may inquire about the care of other babies or the loss of an older child. She may offer empathy in abundance and acknowledge the painful struggle she feels as she sits beside the mother and her child. There are many possible responses, and there is never a script. What the IMH specialist understands is the importance of remaining open to the emotion expressed in the parent's handling of her infant or toddler and the challenge to remain emotionally available as she frames her response.

Present relationships. The IMH specialist who is able to recognize, hold, and tolerate the emotions expressed by both infant and parent offers a context in which a parent may talk openly about the infant's care. As the specialist makes it possible for the parent to feel and also express a range of emotions in her presence, she will invite the parent to talk, and she will listen intently. Parents offer stories about the pregnancy, labor, and delivery, the feelings encountered in the early care of the baby, and their early relationship. Mothers offer stories about boyfriends who have abandoned them or husbands who have left them. They offer stories about family members who are abusive and friends who disappoint them. The IMH specialist is careful to follow the parent's lead, not deepening the pain, but allowing the emotion surrounding these events and relationships to be expressed as a parent is able.

The infant or toddler, dependent on a parent for protection and nurturing, is a powerful participant within an IMH intervention. The infant shows the specialist what life is like in this particular household—what is going well for the family as well as the risks. The specialist observes how the infant seeks attention or makes needs and wants known. The specialist watches who cares for, plays with, or responds to the baby. Of equal interest is the infant's behavior and response. "Why is the care of this baby so difficult? What is the role of the infant in the difficulties or the parent's despair?" These, and questions like these, guide the specialist who sits at the kitchen table and observes parent and child together, listening as stories of caregiving, past and present, unfold.

Indeed, it is the infant who allows a story to be told. The way in which a parent handles the baby, gestures of care, and playful interactions (or the absence of interaction) suggest to the specialist what the capacities are and what some of the conflicts might be. For example, the parent may cuddle the baby comfortably and stroke his arm as he falls asleep. The specialist sees how easily the parent responds to the baby's need for a nap and comments on the parent's ability to read the baby's cues correctly. Alternatively, the parent may leave the baby to cry in a darkened room while she cleans the kitchen. She responds at last, fixing a bottle and propping it. The baby sucks greedily, and the parent observes angrily, "She'll eat me out of house and home if I let her." The specialist wonders what has happened to put such distance between the two. What demands does the baby make? What does the baby contribute to the difficulty between them? The specialist also wonders how lonely and hungry the parent is. How many of her own needs are met and by whom? The specialist asks, "What have the first weeks with the baby at home been like for you? Who has been here to help you? Would it be helpful to talk about this?" Their relationship begins.

Past relationships. The IMH specialist may wonder who the baby represents to the parent—for example, an abusive father, an abandoning mother, or a sister who required attention and care. In the example above, the specialist wondered if the parent had cared for other young children. "Have you ever taken care of a baby before?" she asked. The young mother had. "I was the 'mother' to three younger brothers by the time I was 8 years old," she said, tearfully. An important story of another mother and other babies began to be told.

The infant may also represent the parent as a small child. Faced with the neediness of a very small infant, the parent may feel all over again her own helplessness and re-enact, quite unconsciously, neglectful or inconsistent or teasing patterns representative of her own early care. Alert to the struggle, the IMH specialist wonders what other baby may have been neglected or hurt, abandoned or teased. The earlier traumas may never have been spoken about before. Within the context of the relationship with the IMH specialist, aspects of early care may be more safely re-experienced, feelings attached to them expressed, and memories shared. By separating the past from the present, the specialist and parent try hard to reach an understanding that will protect against repeating a hurtful cycle of care. Both will be alert to the possibility of a new relationship between parent and infant that is positive and secure.

To the extent that the IMH specialist understands a parent's history of relationship and care, she will understand the parent's ability (or inability) to nurture and protect her child. Parents who have had many negative life experiences and disturbed or unresolved relationship losses may not respond to their infants or toddlers with sensitivity, consistency, or warmth. It is the IMH specialist's task to attend and respond to parental histories of abandonment, neglect, separation, and loss. The IMH specialist offers a safe place for the experience and expression of emotions surrounding intensely painful events and relationship experiences. For many parents, the experience with the IMH specialist is the first time they have shared their confusion or anger, disappointment or grief with someone who has a capacity for compassionate response.

The IMH specialist learns to be strong and compassionate as she listens to many difficult stories. It is not unusual for parents to disclose details of early and continuous abuse, neglectful parental care, abandonment by a parent, removal to foster care, the death of an older child, the birth of a baby with special needs. Parents who are able to mourn their losses or express their anger and despair within the context of a nurturing and responsive relationship with the IMH specialist may become clearer about their early history and, as a consequence, more emotionally available and appropriately responsive to their infant—less angry, less depressed.

Reflective functioning. The IMH specialist who attends to the emotional needs of infants and families must remain alert to his or her own emotional health. Most IMH specialists learn to use the supervisory relationship to reflect on the complex emotional realities of overburdened families and infants at risk. In the process, the IMH specialist grows increasingly aware of personal responses, too. Longings for relationship, memories, hopes, and wishes are continuously evoked in the presence of infants and parents who are negotiating conflicted early relationships. The IMH specialist may be affected deeply by individual infants and families enrolled; she needs to have time to discuss what is seen and heard.

Commitment to emotional health. A unique and powerful focus that an IMH specialist brings to the intervention experience is the commitment to the emotional health of infants and parents as they develop in relationship to one another in the first years of life. Why is this so important? As William Schafer (1991), a seasoned IMH practitioner and training consultant, observes:

> . . . During the first eighteen months of life a child constructs a lasting internal vision of what human relationships are, how they work, what to expect from them, and what to offer in return. . . . What gets set in early life is one's deepest beliefs about human relationships. These determine how a person goes about learning, profiting from experience, using help, and parenting one's own children. (p. 1)

To the extent that an IMH specialist is able to understand, support, and sustain parents in interacting and responding sensitively to their infants' or toddlers' emotional needs, an overarching and significant goal will have been reached (Cramer, 1998; Lieberman & Paul, 1993; Lieberman & Zeanah, 1999; Weatherston & Tableman, 1989).

Beyond Infant and Parent: IMH Consultation to Birth-to-3 and Family Programs

IMH specialists are often called upon to provide developmental and clinical consultation to individuals and agencies working with children from birth to 3 and their families. As consultants, IMH specialists bring knowledge about infancy, early parenthood relationship development, and strategies for change. They have experience in carrying out developmental observations and assessments with sensitivity and regard for the uniqueness of each infant or toddler and parent referred. They have experience in providing clinical services to a variety of infants and families, and they understand the strategies required when responding to families at multiple risk. In addition to the skills and clinical strategies of IMH practice, the IMH consultant needs:

- an ability to observe and listen carefully;
- a willingness to work hard at establishing and strengthening strong and meaningful relationships with individuals and consulting groups;
- a respect for continuity and predictability, sensitivity and responsiveness as integral to effective consultation with early intervention practitioners/groups;
- an ability to invite another person to tell what he saw/heard/felt/experienced when caring for an infant or toddler, talking with a parent, visiting a home, working with a parent and infant together, determining eligibility for services, running a teen parent-infant group, etc.; and
- an ability to provide a context in which people feel safe and secure, able to think about their work with families and able to reflect appropriately on their own emotional responses.

The IMH consultant may be asked to meet with an individual practitioner to discuss a particular developmental or clinical concern. In this instance, the consultation may be limited to one or two meetings or until the questions are resolved. The consultant may be asked to meet regularly with a group of child and family practitioners for training and case discussion for a year. Regardless of the group size, frequency of meetings, or length of service to the individual or group, IMH consultants understand the importance of relationship building to enhance each practitioner's developmental and clinical skills. They work hard at establishing and strengthening meaningful relationships with individuals and consultation groups. They know that practitioners—newly developing and experienced—need opportunities to ask questions and talk about the infants, toddlers, and families with whom they work. The consultant provides a context within the consultant-practitioner relationship where it is safe to do this.

Consultants encourage practitioners to bring the details of their observations about a particular baby, alone or in interaction with someone, and to talk about what they see. In the process, they are invited to think about the capacities of an infant or toddler, the uniqueness of a particular infant-parent pair, and the intricacies of relationship work. The consultant may ask questions to guide the consultation process; for example, "What did you notice about the baby's developmental capacities? What did you see him do?"; "What does the baby bring to the newly developing relationship with his mother? What kind of care does the toddler demand?"; "What about the parent? How interested or responsive does she seem to be? How able is the parent to pay attention to the toddler's needs?"; or "How do they interact with one another? How satisfying does the interaction seem to be?" As practitioners learn to observe and listen more closely, they grow more sensitive to a range of risks (Wright, 1986). At the same time, they grow more aware of their own emotions and responses to the very difficult work that they do.

The consultant is challenged to keep an eye on the affective experience of each practitioner throughout each consultation and give permission to talk within the group. The consultant might ask what practitioners are thinking about as they present their work. Many thoughts and feelings may wash over them as they begin to reflect more deeply, often for the first time, on what they see in a particular family, what they experience as they are present with the family, and what they are feeling now. Aware of the emotion that the practitioner offers or silently shares, the consultant may ask if this is something a practitioner would like to talk more about. This approach invites the practitioner to connect with the emotion, yet allows the practitioner to remain in control. In addition to supporting the practitioner, this offers an example of thoughtful responding when working with parents, too.

In the process of discussing a particular infant, parent, or home visit, the IMH specialist often reflects on her own thoughts about infancy and early parenthood, relationships past or present, and her own emotional response to complex and challenging work. IMH consultation invites practitioners to be reflective about the services they provide to infants and families, and about themselves.

IMH consultation brings many rewards. Practitioners from multiple disciplines and agencies learn to sit quietly, to watch the baby, and to follow the infant's and parent's lead. They learn to listen more carefully in order to hear what a parent wants to say. They learn about each infant's or toddler's contribution to the relationship and the importance of each parent's emotional response. They learn about the power and importance of emotional expression within the context of trusting relationships, in their work with families, and within the consultation experience. They grow increasingly confident in understanding infants and parents, appreciating the dynamics of interaction, and containing the feelings expressed or aroused.

The Training of an IMH Specialist

As we have seen, IMH is a field dedicated to understanding and treating children from birth to 3 years of age within the context of family, caregiving, and community relationships. The field is broad and interdisciplinary, embracing professionals from many disciplines, including social work; child welfare; education; speech-language, occupational, and physical therapies; child and family development; psychology; nursing; pediatrics; and psychiatry. IMH specialists may be trained at the bachelor's, master's, doctoral, and/or post-doctoral levels. Training programs may include academic or community inservice programs of specialized study.

Each specialist develops knowledge and skills that are specific to the discipline in which they are prepared—for example, developmental assessment protocols, techniques for clinical interviews, referral and collaboration, or treatment planning. In addition, IMH professionals develop a knowledge base and competencies that are quite specific to the optimal development of infants and toddlers within the context of nurturing relationships—for example, knowledge of attachment and early development, infant and family observation for the purpose of early assessment and care, the identification of disorders in infancy, and strategies for intervention with parent and child. It is the overlay of specialized studies, opportunities for skill-building, and supervised service experiences with children birth to 3 and their families that contribute to the optimal development of an IMH professional (Eggbeer & Fenichel, 1990).

In sum, IMH practice, as originally developed by Selma Fraiberg and her young staff, is indeed a gift returned to parents and infants in the form of thoughtful observation, careful listening, and empathic response. The strategies that characterize the work of an IMH specialist are embedded in the belief that development occurs within the context of relationships, past and present. To the extent that the IMH practitioner and consultant offer opportunities for relationships to flourish, the gift is multiplied, 10-fold.

References

Blos, P., & Davies, D. (1993). Extending the intervention process: A report of a distressed family with a damaged newborn and a vulnerable preschooler. In E. Fenichel & S. Provence (Eds.), *Development in jeopardy* (pp. 51-92). Madison, CT: International Universities Press, Inc.

Cramer, B. (1998). Mother-infant psychotherapy: A widening scope in technique. *Infant Mental Health Journal, 19*(2), 151-167.

Eggbeer, L., & Fenichel, E. (1990). *Preparing practitioners to work with infants, toddlers and their families.* Arlington, VA: National Center for Clinical Infant Programs.

Fraiberg, S. (1980). *Clinical studies in infant mental health.* New York: Basic Books.

Fraiberg, S., & Adelson, E. (1977). An abandoned mother, an abandoned baby. *Bulletin of the Menninger Clinic, 41*, 162-180.

Fraiberg, S., Adelson, E., & Shapiro, V. (1975). Ghosts in the nursery: A psychoanalytic approach to the problems of impaired infant-mother relationships. *Journal of the American Academy in Child Psychiatry, 14*, 397-421.

Fraiberg, S., Shapiro, V., & Adelson, E. (1976). Infant-parent psychotherapy on behalf of a child in a critical nutritional state. *Psychoanalytic Study of the Child, 31*, 461-491.

Lieberman, A., & Pawl, J. (1993). Infant-parent psychotherapy. In C. Zeanah (Ed.), *Handbook of infant mental health* (pp. 427-442). New York: Guilford Press.

Lieberman, A., & Zeanah, C. (1999). Contributions of attachment theory to infant-parent psychotherapy and other interventions with infants and young children. In J. Cassidy & P. Shaver (Eds.), *Handbook of attachment* (pp. 555-574). New York: Guilford Press.

McDonough, S. (1993). Interaction guidance: Understanding and treating early infant-caregiver relationship disturbances. In C. Zeanah, Jr. (Ed.), *Handbook of infant mental health* (pp. 414-426). New York: Guilford Press.

Pawl, J. (1995). The therapeutic relationship as human connectedness: Being held in another's mind. *Zero to Three, 15*(4), 3-5.

Schafer, W. (1991). Planning as an attachment experience. *The Infant Crier.* East Lansing: Michigan Association for Infant Mental Health.

Stinson, S., Tableman, B., & Weatherston, D. (2000). *Guidelines for infant mental health practice.* East Lansing: Michigan Association for Infant Mental Health.

Weatherston, D. (1995). She does love me, doesn't she? *Zero to Three, 15*(4), 6-10.

Weatherston, D. (2000). *Infant mental health practice: Parents' and practitioners' voices.* Unpublished doctoral dissertation, Detroit, MI: Wayne State University.

Weatherston, D., & Tableman, B. (1989). *Infant mental health services: Supporting competencies/reducing risks.* Lansing, MI: Department of Mental Health.

Wright, B. (1986). An approach to infant-parent psychotherapy. *Infant Mental Health Journal, 7*(4), 247-263.

Learning to See Her Son:
A Baby and His Mother

Gregory A. Proulx

Summary

An isolated young mother is referred to an infant mental health (IMH) program by a hospital social worker because it was reported that she was not following recommendations for feeding her 6-month-old son, who is failing to gain weight. Of additional concern, an older child had been removed from the home for neglect. The IMH specialist, relatively new to the field, works hard to establish a working relationship with the mother that is based on non-judgmental listening and respect, rather than uninvited "solutions." Supported by reflective supervision and group consultation, the IMH specialist realizes that effective intervention is not a matter of technique alone; equally important are the clinician's sensitivity to what is happening around him and his understanding of his reactions to it. During their yearlong therapeutic relationship with the IMH specialist, the toddler begins to thrive and his mother realizes that her child needs and loves her, and that she can meet his needs.

Uncertain Beginnings

My first meeting with Rebecca, the single mother of two sons, was on a dull, gray day. The shades were drawn in the dimly lit living room of the old house where the family lived. In the adjacent dining room were two automobile tires, a broken bicycle, a broken lamp on a beat-up chair, a pile of newspapers, a stack of boxes, and an ironing board. There was no dining room table. Six-month-old Curtis sat next to his mother on the worn living room sofa, bundled in a car seat. He was an attractive but small baby, with a wisp of blond hair and a perfectly round face. He was quiet, displaying a pensive, almost worried look.

Rebecca and Curtis had been referred to our IMH program by a social worker from the regional hospital, where a respected neonatologist and the hospital dietitian were treating him for nonorganic failure to thrive. The social worker expressed concern that Rebecca was "resisting" their recommendation that she feed Curtis at regular intervals with a fortified infant formula. The social worker worried that Curtis's condition had been exacerbated by two serious ear infections during the past 4 months, one of which had required hospitalization. The social worker complained, "I don't think Curtis's mother really cares about him. She only visited once during the whole week he was on the ward. And you know, her first son got taken away from her because of neglect."

On our first visit, I told Rebecca that I was there to listen, to try to find the best way to help Curtis grow, and to act as her assistant in this process. Rebecca began speaking almost immediately of her unpredictable relationship with Curtis's father, Steve. She complained, "He's never around when I need him." She also spoke of her distrust of hospital staff who "would not listen when I tried to tell them that Curtis made it really hard to feed him. He won't be still."

As I drove away that day, I felt alone, overwhelmed, emotionally empty, and uncertain. The gloomy weather and the shadows of Rebecca's home intensified the experience. I wondered, "How in the world would I help this mother and this infant? What am I going to say or do that will make a difference? She has some of the most respected professionals in the area providing treatment to her son."

During our weekly session, I conveyed my feelings of helplessness to my supervisor. We reviewed the family history provided by the hospital. My supervisor listened very carefully to how I described my experience of meeting Rebecca and Curtis. She wondered how Rebecca might understand the people and relationships in her life. Sensing my uncertainties, she observed, "This surely was an overwhelming situation." She suggested that I try holding on to what I would see and hear. "Be patient," she advised.

Listening and Wondering

When I met with Rebecca the following week, Curtis was lying on his tummy on a blanket. Toys were carefully arranged around him on the living room floor. He cooed and reached for a squeaky duck. Rebecca moved busily about the room, picking up clothes and clutter. When she left the room, Curtis's gaze followed her. He began to fuss at her absence. Rebecca returned with a diaper and began to change him on the floor. He quieted and focused on her. She talked to him as she worked. "Your momma does everything for her little mouse. Those bad people think I'm not feeding you right. They just don't know. They just don't listen." She helped him roll back over to his tummy and moved his duck within reach. He grabbed it, examined it, vocalized, and put it in his mouth. Overall, his behavior—his hand-eye coordination, inspection of objects, vocalizations, and rolling over—seemed on track developmentally.

Rebecca returned to sit next to me on the sofa. There seemed to be an edge of anxiety in her voice as she spoke further of her situation. She seemed to be uncertain about whether I would really listen to her, or if I would turn out to be just another person who would tell her what she needed to do. Rebecca was afraid of "the system." After all, Children's Protective Services had removed her first son from her care because, she explained, "They didn't think I was a fit mother. When they thought I needed help cleaning my house, they sent workers over from a local parenting program to show me how. They changed things all around. Nicky was just 3 months old then. I never asked them to start coming over. At first, I thought it was kind of cool, having free help. But then they started seeing me as bad." I nodded, saying, "You must be even more worried than ever now, with Curtis's getting all of this attention." She answered, "Yeah, I never asked for all *this* help either."

Rebecca and I talked for another hour. To gather information, I asked questions, in as gentle and nonjudgmental a manner as I could. I wondered if Rebecca would put me in the same category as those uninvited "helpers."

I asked Rebecca how she was making ends meet. She said that she had a part-time job and that her parents helped out with food and baby supplies. "Do you have someone you can trust to watch Curtis?" I continued. "Yes," she answered, "But I'm getting really frustrated. My mom takes care of him, but she doesn't follow my instructions, like how and when to feed him. Last week she let her sister take Curtis to the store without asking me first. That made me so mad." I felt the urge to shift into my problem-solving mode and to suggest a different child care arrangement. Then an equally strong feeling came over me, reminding me that she was not asking for a solution. I held these feelings for a moment and said, "It must be very frustrating when people won't listen and respect your feelings."

Caring and Holding

Before leaving, I told Rebecca that I was trying to listen to her very carefully and would continue to do so if she would permit me to visit again. She agreed. I expressed an interest in visiting during one of Curtis's mealtimes so that I could understand this experience better. A visit was set for the following week.

Rebecca was not home when I arrived. Within the clinical context, I generally interpret "no-shows" as being directly related to how a person is feeling—either about what happened on a previous visit (for example, "I shared too much, I need to hide" or "What we talked about made me feel anxious"), or what they expect to feel on a visit to come (for example, "I can't trust anyone," "I'll be hurt," or "If I'm not home, I won't get hurt"). From what I already knew about Rebecca, I guessed that she might be expecting to be disappointed by yet another person who wouldn't listen. She might assume that if she were not home for our scheduled visit, I would not come back again, proving that I, like other "helpers," wasn't interested in listening to her. This sequence would confirm her well-developed model of how people do not care and do not listen. But I persisted, believing that I might begin to erode this model by demonstrating consistency and caring. I left a handwritten note expressing concern for Rebecca's and Curtis's well-being, saying that I had been thinking of them and specifying another time for a visit.

When we met again—after another no-show and another note from me—Rebecca was visibly distressed. She told me the doctor threatened that, if Curtis did not gain an ounce per week for the next 8 weeks, he would make a referral to the local Children's Protective Services office.

She said, "I tried to tell the doctor that I was doing all I could. I even went over, step-by-step, what I was doing, how I was fixing up the formula. I tried to tell him that Curtis would not be still when I try to give him his bottle. He squirms all over the place. It gets interrupted. Sometimes we can get started again right away, but sometimes Curtis won't take it. I tried to tell him that. He just said, 'You have to make sure he is eating. If you can't make sure of that, then we'll have to find someone who can.'" She began to cry. "Why won't anyone listen?"

Curtis slept throughout this visit. I was unable to watch or support the feeding process. I was transfixed by Rebecca's story, feeling that she was being treated unfairly. I badly wanted to jump in and fix the situation, to make everyone understand the truth. I sensed, though, that I would not be heard if I directly confronted the other professionals working with Rebecca and Curtis. I thought that they would see me as overinvolved and lacking in judgment. When I discussed all this with my supervisor, she encouraged me to be patient, to continue holding on to what I was feeling and seeing, and to keep listening.

Holding—as the term is used in IMH practice—involves being aware of feelings (our own and those of the family), understanding affective aspects of communication, formulating sensitive and empathetic responses, and connecting to the family by articulating understanding. It is very difficult to hold what we feel and see in the midst of complex and confusing circumstances and relationships. It takes great self-awareness, control, and mindfulness of the moment to absorb the impact of another's feelings and organize an empathetic response. More often, we get swept up in the moment, moved by the experience of powerful emotions; we are dumbstruck. This is why reflective clinical supervision is such an essential part of IMH practice: It allows the IMH specialist to explore his or her feelings about the work and examine critical information about the family and their feelings. In supervision, the IMH specialist can work on how he is in relation to the family. As Pawl (1995) points out, it is "how" and "who" we are that ultimately determine the effectiveness of our interventions.

The Story Deepens

On my next visit, Rebecca was composed and calm. Curtis was again placed cozily between us on the sofa, his cherubic face peering out at the world. Rebecca asked, "Can I tell you about how all of this started?" I said, "Yes, of course." She began to talk about Curtis's first hospitalization. It was following a routine baby check-up at the doctor's office, when Curtis was 3 months old. Rebecca was just beginning to get over her self-doubt about caring for this new baby. The anxiety came rushing back, however, when the doctor noticed that Curtis had an ear infection. "Why didn't I know this?" she thought. Curtis's weight was also dipping below the fifth percentile on the growth chart that the doctor kept but had never showed her before. Rebecca wanted Curtis to be treated for his ear infection, but her heart sank when the doctor ordered Curtis to be admitted to the hospital because he was underweight.

In the hospital, Curtis began to gain weight faster and more consistently than at home. Rebecca said that she had visited once and then did not return. She said, "The nurses and that social worker were talking about me. They thought that I was a bad mom because of Curtis's health condition and what happened in the past with Nicky. They think it's all my fault. I felt awful. I couldn't drag myself back there. But I know they talked about me even more, then. They thought I didn't care about Curtis because I didn't visit and stay with him. But I didn't go because of what they were saying." Rebecca sounded furious. I mustered a response, acknowledging her anger and the great cost to her and to Curtis, who must have missed her.

I began to feel angry, too. This family needed support, not challenges from the outside! I could see the connection between Curtis and Rebecca. His eyes followed and searched for her when she moved about or left the room. When she held him, the expression in his eyes and the relaxation in his body showed trust. At this point in our conversation, Curtis reached toward his mother. Rebecca said, "He's just like me. When I don't feel good, I want to be cuddled." She picked him up from the car seat and held him close. She then put him on the floor, where she changed his diaper. He was fussy and resistant, arching as if he were uncomfortable. Rebecca said, "I was like that till I was 8 years old. I always wanted to he held." She picked him up and hugged him again.

Being Still

On our next visit, I was in time for Curtis's bottle. I noticed how nicely Rebecca held him, at just the right angle in her arms as they sat on the sofa. He seemed to be interested in taking the nipple and the formula. Rebecca began to tell me about household needs— food and clothing for Curtis. She then got up, holding Curtis, walked over to the desk, and wrote down the amount of formula that she started with. When she sat down again, Curtis resumed feeding, but soon he began to squirm. Then he disconnected from the nipple. Rebecca stopped to reposition him and help him burp. Then he reattached, sucked briefly, arched, and disconnected again. The phone rang. Rebecca appeared disgusted at the interruption, but she got up, answered the phone, talked briefly, and returned to the sofa. She tried to resume feeding Curtis, who seemed unable to get his comfort back. "He really won't be still for you, will he?" I asked. She turned to face me squarely as I sat next to her on the sofa. She blurted, "That is what I've been trying to tell everyone. But no one will listen!" Her words seemed to hang in the air between us.

"No wonder you feel so helpless," I said. Rebecca seemed to soften and relax a bit. I encouraged her to keep trying by saying, "Even though I can't be still for you, Mommy, I need you to be there for me. Keep trying." At this point I was using the strategy of "speaking for the baby"—trying to put into words the things the baby might say if he could talk. This technique works best when the parent experiences the infant's comments as positive, showing the connection between them.

The feeding continued, but with many interruptions. Curtis attached and sucked, then arched and squirmed. Rebecca grimaced, turning red in the face. I was not sure if she was angry or embarrassed. She appeared very uncomfortable. I continued to offer supportive comments, noting that she was doing her best. I said, "It sure would be a lot easier if he would cooperate." She persisted, in spite of her discomfort, and succeeded in getting Curtis to finish the bottle. Rebecca appeared proud of the accomplishment. I asked her if it would be all right to share my observations with the doctor about how hard she worked at helping Curtis be fed. She seemed to relax. With a smile, she said, "That would really help."

Being Heard

I began to feel relieved. With my supervisor, I wondered what Curtis might be feeling. Could it be that he, like Rebecca, did not feel heard or understood? My supervisor encouraged me once again keep listening. This made so much sense! If I could manage to be a sensitive listener to Rebecca, then she, too, might be still so that Curtis could feel that he was heard and understood.

As I made these visits to Rebecca and Curtis and shared my work in our consultation group, my colleagues also encouraged me. They reminded me to always look for things to like about a family, develop a healthy respect for each of the members, and pay attention to my own feelings and need to feel respected, to be heard, and to help. Their guidance could be summarized as the following: Don't ever forget that it's about feelings, it's about relationships, and it's about family. The feelings you sense inform you about how others feel. They are directly related to the feelings, relationships, and self-understanding models that others display in their relationship with you.

Over the next several months, I kept listening, and Rebecca told me her story. She said that she had always felt as if she didn't matter—not to her parents and not to any adults in her early life, except her grandmother. Her parents, she recalled, were too caught up in their own "sickness" of drinking and self-indulgence. They did have the good sense, though, to leave her with her grandmother when a binge was coming on. This happened often, but, luckily, Grandma was kind and sensitive.

As it turned out, from the time she was 2 until she was 10 years old, Rebecca spent much of her time in her grandmother's home. She remembered love-filled days, laughter, the smell of homemade macaroni and cheese, and silly songs. She recalled many experiences of warmth around the dining room table. Rebecca spoke dreamily about this time in her life: "Grandma always had a dessert after dinner. It wasn't always fancy, but I felt like I was dining with royalty. But what was most special was at bedtime. Grandma always kissed my hand right in the middle. She'd say, 'If you get lonely or scared in the night, you just touch your hand to your cheek and I'll be right there with a kiss.'" Rebecca touched her cheek with her hand. There were tears in her eyes.

In Rebecca's tenth year, her grandmother died. Her life took a downward spiral after this. She grew into a "lost" teen. She began to drink and party. At 18, she became pregnant for the first time by a boy she did not care for. When Nicky was born, she was living alone, depressed and overwhelmed. She realized that she was living the kind of life her parents led—and that she hated them for. "I was a real mess. I didn't know what I was doing," she said.

Warm memories of what it was like to be cared for, combined with feelings of depression and loneliness, prompted Rebecca to accept assistance from a local parenting program. Expecting to be treasured by her home visitor as her grandmother had treasured her, Rebecca soon began to feel betrayed, as if the program staff was "all against [her]." Everyone seemed to know the right thing to do except her. She said, "My worker would say, 'You need to keep all your dishes and baby bottles squeaky clean; you can't let stains soak into the carpeting; you must wash your hands several times each day.' My worker was even better at getting Nicky to stop crying than I was. I hated what was happening, and I hated myself." Rebecca began to feel inept. She withdrew into herself. Her desire to care for herself, her home, and her baby declined, leading to allegations of neglect.

Six months after Nicky's removal and placement in foster care, Rebecca gave up. She never fully understood the charges, feeling she really hadn't done anything wrong. She voluntarily relinquished her parental rights to avoid the anguish of having them terminated in front of everyone in a court hearing. She told me that her child welfare worker had encouraged her in this, saying, "It would be easier on everyone." Rebecca was left with mixed feelings. She thought she had done the right thing for Nicky, but felt demoralized. She said that after relinquishing Nicky, "something [in her] got hot and angry."

Rebecca felt hopeful again when she began a relationship with Steve. He was 20 and had a steady job delivering pizzas. He didn't make much money, but he was a steady worker, and he won Rebecca's heart by singing love songs. He was the one who wanted to move into the house where Rebecca and Curtis now lived, instead of into an apartment. The house was old, but they would fix it up and decorate it. They imagined the dining room with a big table and chairs, filled with people. They talked about marriage.

Rebecca was 19 when she became pregnant for the second time. Feeling supported by Steve, she stopped drinking and began to care for herself. But by the eighth month of her pregnancy, Steve began staying out later and later. One night he didn't come home. When he didn't show up for a childbirth class, Rebecca felt humiliated. They fought and then separated. Steve moved out, taking much of the furniture with him.

Steve was not present when Curtis was born. Rebecca gave birth to her second son with no support from family or friends. From the hospital, she and Curtis returned to an empty—and emptied—house. Rebecca felt lonely, depressed, and betrayed once again. As I listened to Rebecca, I wondered how Curtis had experienced his first days with his mother. I wondered how long the shades had been drawn in the living room and when junk had begun to pile up in the dining room.

A Therapist Listens and Reflects

Rebecca told me her story over many weeks. I listened. As I had promised, I called the hospital social worker, described the feeding I had observed, and noted that Rebecca seemed engaged in our work together, although she was very worried about what she perceived as the doctor's threat of a Children's Protective Services referral. The social worker asked me to submit a written report to include in Curtis's chart and said she would bring this to the attention of the neonatologist and the dietitian. Fortunately, at this point Curtis began to gain weight. (My supervisor told me about Selma Fraiberg's observation that the push toward healthy development in babies is so strong that "it's a little like having God on your side.")

I listened, tried to be still, and kept wondering how to respond to Rebecca and Curtis. Although I am a developmental psychologist, I was new to the field of IMH. I wondered how, as a therapist, I would know *when* to say something, much less *what* to say. I came to realize early that, since every family is unique, there is no recipe for treatment that will work in all situations. In this work, each new family is unfamiliar territory. As I approached the home of Rebecca and Curtis for the first time, I was filled with the doubts I often experience when meeting new families. After meeting the family and hearing Rebecca's story of betrayal and distrust, I wondered if I would be able to do anything helpful at all.

Fortunately, I began working as an IMH specialist in a well-established program in which reflective supervision and group consultation form the foundation for all clinical work. It was within this setting that I first experienced the safety net of sensitivity; responsiveness; and concern for families, in general, and for fellow clinicians, in particular. How it feels to be in the presence of the family is of central importance. One's affective experience, I learned, provides a primary pathway to understanding the internal working models of the family—how it is that they come to think of themselves and their relationships, and why they trust or distrust the world and people. A consistent system of individual reflective supervision and group case consulting provides the secure base from which competent clinicians are able to go out and explore their own skills, and to which they can return to discuss behaviors and feelings that may seem incomprehensible.

I needed this kind of support and opportunities for reflection in order to figure out the relationship between my feelings and those of Rebecca and Curtis. It was within the reflective environment that I was able to understand and develop a respectful way of being while in their presence. Without this type of supervision, I likely would have failed to understand that Rebecca had been trying to tell anyone who would listen just what the trouble really was in her life and in her relationship with Curtis. I would have perhaps attempted to instruct her regarding the "right way" to feed her baby. I probably would have thought of her as being responsible for Curtis's tenuous situation, further contributing to her sense of inadequacy and failing to serve her real need and the needs of her son.

In sum, the experience within reflective supervision provided the milieu in which the following insights were possible: Rebecca and Curtis were attached. Rebecca knew Curtis and his needs better than anyone. Under stress, Rebecca acted in a way that appeared to be harmful to herself and Curtis, but in fact she was desperately trying to convey her own hopelessness. She was trying to let others know how she felt.

In supervision, I learned to listen—to Rebecca, Curtis, and my own feelings. As my supervisor was patient with me, I was able to practice patience, even in a situation where so much was at stake. In the reflective setting, I was able to develop a working hypothesis and a specific set of responses based on my own affective experience. Rebecca and Curtis reinforced in me those very qualities of patience, holding, and understanding that are fundamental to the practice of IMH.

Seeing Her Son

After several months of supportive listening and encouragement, it became clear that Curtis would thrive. I continued to provide IMH services until Curtis was 18 months old. At that time, the family moved out of our service area. Three months later, upon Rebecca's invitation, I visited her and Curtis. Rebecca had moved to a small apartment that was bright, tidy, colorful, comfortably furnished, and filled with stimulating toys. There was a dining room table!

When I arrived, Rebecca and Curtis were listening to a playful children's song. Rebecca said, "I got the music back!" She seemed to have discovered her loving grandmother within herself. Using the gesture she had described to me months earlier, she touched her hand to her cheek and said, "I began to see, as if for the first time, my son right there before me—needing me, loving me, relying on me—reminding me about something within me that went away a long time ago: I'm lovable."

Reference

Pawl, J. H. (1995). On supervision. In R. S. Shanok, L. Gilkerson, L. Eggbeer, & E. Fenichel (Eds.), *Reflective supervision: A relationship for learning discussion guide* (pp. 21-29). Washington, DC: ZERO TO THREE.

Discussion Questions

1. The author identifies intervention strategies as assessment, supportive counseling, meeting concrete family needs, life-coping skills, social support, developmental guidance, infant-parent psychotherapy, advocacy, and crisis intervention. Which strategies were most helpful to this young mother and baby?

2. As described in this article, the true heart and soul of intervention relies on the clinician's sensitivity to what is happening around him and understanding his own reactions to it. Give examples of the author's sensitivity to Rebecca.

3. The author reminds us of the importance of listening rather than speaking. Discuss examples from this case of times when it might have been easier to speak than to listen.

4. The author quotes Jeree Pawl, "It is the 'how' and 'who' we are that ultimately determines the effectiveness of our interactions." What does this quote mean? How does it influence the author's clinical intervention?

5. A therapist's affective, or feeling, response is described as providing a pathway to understanding how the family thinks about themselves, their relationships, and why they trust or distrust the world and people. Describe some of the author's feelings and how they helped him understand Rebecca.

6. The author describes the secure base provided to a therapist by a consistent system of reflective supervision and case consultation. Describe how this secure base enables a therapist, through a parallel process, to provide a secure base for a family.

The Healing Potential and Power of Relationship

Jan Ulrich

Summary

In the context of a home-based Early Head Start program, an infant mental health (IMH) therapist works for more than $2^{1}/_{2}$ years with a single mother and her young son, beginning when the child is 5 months old. This bright, insightful mother has many strengths but struggles to cope with childhood experiences of loss that have led to ongoing relationship difficulties and substance abuse. The therapist describes her use of emotional support and infant-parent psychotherapy as effective strategies. She also explores the issue of appropriate boundaries and transitions for families and therapists in the course of developing long-term working relationships. Also considered are programmatic factors that can support or undermine families' ability to fully engage in and benefit from IMH services.

A Personal View

Throughout my experience in providing IMH services, families have given me the privilege of witnessing some of their processes of growth, change, and discovery. The arrival of a new baby offers incredible opportunity and motivation for change. Parents await their babies with hopes that are integrally related to their own life experiences. Some babies are expected to work miracles, some are seen as bringing joy and satisfaction, and others are experienced as bringing pain and disappointment.

While it is an honor to participate in the beginning of a new relationship, I have come to recognize the responsibility this involvement represents. Every family asks for different help, offers different challenges, and evokes a different response. In offering myself as a support to their process, I must be clear in my intent, stay aware of my own judgments, and consistently use case consultation and reflective supervision to maintain safe boundaries between their lives and mine.

We may be discussing the use of a single model of practice in IMH, but there are many ways to apply that model. Some families may need help in accessing resources to meet their daily living needs, while others may need an advocate to help them navigate the child welfare system. Each application must be tailored to the unique requirements of the situation and relationship. Since families are coming with their babies at a time of great possibilities and varying needs, each relationship must also be given great care.

The following recounts part of the story of my experiences with a family, as well as some of what I have come to understand about this work. I have learned much about the power of the IMH model of practice, about how a baby's development can challenge a parent to complete her own developmental tasks, and also about the healing potential and power of relationship.

Creating a Safe Place

I was given the opportunity to share for more than 2¹/₂ years in the lives of Grace and Sam, as they discovered each other and themselves and developed a new way to be in relationship. As is true with any life story, there is too much to tell to give all the details; some parts of the story are left out and some are altered. What is left is my perspective on how a relationship built with patience, trust, and acceptance can create a safe place to challenge old patterns, feel intense emotions, practice new skills, and fall in love.

This family had been participating in a home-based Early Head Start program for a year when their home visitor left the agency. I was the replacement therapist. Grace accepted this change as something almost inevitable. When later asked about this, she cynically commented that she "was used to it," meaning she was used to having people leave.

Before I met her, I read the background information that said that Grace, a white woman, entered the program at age 30. She was 3 months pregnant at that time and had mixed feelings about having a baby. She had a history of relationship difficulties, including a conflicted relationship with the father of the baby and a previous relationship with an emotionally and physically abusive partner. She reported fairly difficult relationships with her parents. Her mother had left the family when Grace was in the seventh grade, and Grace described her father as a "workaholic." Grace also reported a history of alcohol and marijuana abuse starting in her teen years. She had reportedly stopped drinking several years before and had been in treatment for marijuana addiction during her pregnancy with Sam. She denied current use.

Grace had expressed a desire to learn about parenting and child development. The departing therapist described her as bright and insightful. Grace had demonstrated great resourcefulness and determination as she proceeded with college and accessed supports that could help her along her way. "I think you'll like working with her," the therapist said as she briefed me on the work they had been doing.

Sam was 5 months old when I met the family, and we began meeting for weekly home visits. Grace was always prepared, and we spent time on the floor watching and playing with Sam and talking about her challenges of deciphering his cues. She also used the visits to talk about the stress she was experiencing as she fought her way through legal battles with her former partner, struggled financially, and learned to balance multiple responsibilities. With time, she slowly started to share some of her life stories and steps she had taken toward healing. She would occasionally sigh and comment that she had talked about this with the other therapist, before retelling some experience she had struggled with.

Two months into our relationship, Sam contracted meningitis. Grace fought hard for him, correctly identifying that something was seriously wrong despite the doctors' dismissal of early symptoms. She stayed right with him at the hospital and discovered that she was special to him. She later recounted, "The only time he would stop crying was when I held him. He cried with everyone else." No one else gave him the comfort and sense of safety he experienced with her. She refused to let her fears of losing him interfere with her commitment to stay by him as he fought through the fever and the pain.

A Shift in the Focus

Sam pulled through, but there were worries about setbacks in his development. We made a video for case consultation with other Early Head Start and IMH specialists and a group facilitator with extensive experience in working with infants, toddlers, and their families. Grace, however, did not want to see it at first. After weeks, she finally agreed. We watched the video together and discussed what she saw. Grace interpreted Sam's hand gestures as rejection of her attempts to comfort him with touch. She reported feeling unsure of what he was trying to communicate in his vocalizations. We also discussed concerns that Sam seemed to be struggling to control the muscles on one side of his body.

Noting her reluctance to watch the video, I wondered what

might have been hard for her to see. Grace's response was not what I expected. She reported that she had been high when the video was made, and she had not wanted to acknowledge it. This revelation shifted our focus. Instead of addiction being something off to the side, it was hot on a front burner. We contracted that Grace would not be high for visits and that it would be up to her to reschedule the visit if she were high. I would not play police.

There were numerous reasons for making that choice. Since I was trying to build a relationship based on trust and respect, I thought that starting each visit with questions or doubts about her state could undermine that. I also wanted her to assume responsibility for her choices about using, believing that changes needed to come from internal motivations, not external pressures.

It is not constructive to work with someone who is in an altered state, and I thought that Grace would be able to do some important work when she was not high. I believed that if we stopped working together because of her use, she would perceive that as a rejection of her, not of her behavior. I was concerned that additional feelings of judgment, rejection, and abandonment would only result in increased substance abuse and, thus, increased risk of harm to or rejection of Sam.

Although her use was hurtful to her and emotionally damaging to Sam, I did not perceive him as being physically endangered by her use at that time. I expressed my concerns that her use affected her interactions with Sam. She maintained that she did not smoke around him and that, like me, "nobody can tell" because she functioned so well when high. We talked about generational cycles of addiction, looking at patterns in both her family and Sam's father's family.

Although it was clear she was struggling with an addiction, I believed Grace's use was a coping strategy and that helping her learn new skills and working through some of the underlying motivations for escape would benefit her and Sam. Grace seemed surprised by my concern that her use indicated she was hurting and that there were things she was trying to avoid. We explored the emotions she felt protected from when getting high. We talked about what she had learned from her family about managing emotions and what it was that Sam might experience when she anesthetized herself. Of great significance throughout this process was that I did not go away—I did not reject her. Not only did I care about Sam, I also cared about her, and I kept coming back. Our relationship provided a crucial message for her: I would not abandon her as she opened herself to vulnerable areas.

Grace Risks Trust

Grace began to trust me enough to talk in greater detail about her painful past. She had experienced the sudden death of two boyfriends, two school peers, and several relatives within a year when she was in high school. She experienced little support from others to help her find her way through the grief and shock those traumatic losses provoked. Instead, Grace discovered alcohol and marijuana and used them for years to avoid feeling the rage, sadness, and fear she experienced. Before she became pregnant, Grace had successfully given up alcohol because she recognized it had come to endanger her life. However, despite repeated treatment, she continued to struggle with her addiction to marijuana. Grace was progressively working through the layers of defenses and was now facing the most difficult one to overcome.

Grace showed significant insight into her relationship patterns. She watched Sam and wondered what it must have been like for her at his age. When Grace was 14 months old, a new baby had been born into the family. Grace believed that this child was the prized child. She remembered her sibling as the popular one in school. Her parents talked as if her brother did everything right and wondered why she couldn't be more like him. She reported feeling that she had always been alone in life. She believed she took care of others with no one taking care of her. Her mother had left her with her father before Grace reached puberty. She longed for the guidance and comfort of having someone help her manage life's changes and challenges. She discovered that her fight against addiction was actually a fight against loneliness and the fear of abandonment.

This lifelong loneliness developed from her first primary relationships with her parents. The subsequent losses of other people she had allowed herself to care about confirmed her belief that to experience closeness was to risk pain. Parenting Sam and understanding the origins of her addiction offered her a chance to heal this old wound.

Her mother offered an opportunity to recreate their relationship when she invited Grace to live with her just before Sam was born. As Grace reported to me, "I needed a safe place, and my mother offered help with the baby, some financial support, and a nice house." It seemed that both Grace and her mother understood the possibilities presented by the birth of a child for having a new experience of parenting. Both carried hopes of creating a nurturing relationship that they had never experienced together.

Although Grace was initially appreciative of her mother's help, conflict began to increase between them because of the "mothering." Grace had come into her mother's home with the wounds of an abusive relationship and the fears of becoming a mother herself. She used her mother's nest to recover and build her strength. But soon, Grace became strong enough to assume her new role and began to resent her mother's attempts to be Sam's mother.

Sam was then a year old and was social and eager to play. Since he had mastered crawling, he was mobile and ready to explore his environment. Grace and her mother had very different beliefs about what should be expected of a child this age. Grace believed it was important for Sam to be encouraged to move freely, with toys easily accessible in the living area and the pots and pans available in the cupboard for discovery. Grace's mother, however, resisted the idea of adapting the house, saying, "He's got to learn there are some things he can't touch."

Grace wavered in what she wanted to have happen. She found it convenient to allow her mother to play mom so she could do the other things she wanted to do, including get high. In alternate moments, she would be angry that her mother was robbing her of her right to be Sam's mother. She became determined to move out. She found a place and threw herself into creating a home. Over the course of several months, as she worked on the house and went to school, Sam stayed with his maternal grandmother. Grace often stayed alone at the new place.

The Pull to Stay and the Pull to Be Free

Grace faced many questions: What would have to change if she were really alone with Sam and responsible for all of his care? What would it be like to leave her mother and make a home in which she would need to fulfill all of the adult responsibilities? Could she keep Sam safe and herself safe at the same time? Grace entered treatment and came face to face with her rage. So many years of rage and hurt had been stuffed away inside, she had not learned how to be safe with her emotions. Grace had to find her own way through death, abandonment, and betrayal, because she had lacked someone to be a witness to her pain. If she could not even manage her own feelings, how could she now care for a child?

I sat with her in her discomfort, knowing the decisions had to be hers. I knew she felt stuck, pulled between caring for Sam to give him something different from what she had and placing him in her mother's care to go off on her own. Although it was difficult, I also knew that I could not resolve the dilemma for her. I imagine some part of her wanted someone else to make the decision for her. It would have protected her from losing. If she gave Sam up to her mother, she could blame someone else. If she tried to care for Sam and failed, she could blame someone else. By making the choice herself, she had to make a commitment.

One day, she showed up at my office, furious and needing to talk. We had spent much time discussing alternatives to getting high when she was angry. We talked regularly about her choices and the consequences of them. Her dope was in her car that afternoon, but she was trying something new. She was holding so much inside that she could not stay still. Talking would not be enough—she needed to move—so we went outside to the playground. I listened as she kicked a ball against a fence to release some of her anger.

She said she felt stuck. Grace now recognized she had choices in her life. She could no longer tolerate the tension between the pull to take off and be free and the pull to care for Sam. It was time for her to decide if she or her mother would parent Sam. We explored the possible consequences of each choice. She showed considerable insight into which choices would lead to a continuation of old patterns and which could create new options. She was able to think beyond herself to identify the ramifications for Sam. Something shifted as she vented; she became centered and calm. She went to her car and threw the marijuana in the dumpster.

"I'm Starting to Feel Like a Mom"

Soon after this, she and Sam officially moved into their new home. We watched and celebrated as Sam learned to walk. He challenged her to be present and engage with him. She challenged herself to not run away. I watched and listened and commented and questioned. What were some of the worries she could let go of as Sam met new developmental milestones? Had she noticed how much more she smiled since she wasn't getting high? One day as we played, she turned to me and said, "I'm starting to feel like a mom."

The visits continued. However, they were one of the few things that did not change. Grace left treatment and started using again. She quit college and started another training program, therefore losing her individual therapist at college. She got a full-time job, and Sam went to a new child care provider.

At about this time, near to the anniversary of her first therapist's departure, there were changes within my program. I was to assume some new responsibilities. As a part of this change, it was decided that some of my families would be transferred to one of my colleagues.

When I talked with Grace about this, she clearly expressed her disapproval. I listened empathically, voicing an understanding of how difficult this might be. We discussed choices she had for ways to respond to the decision. Within a day, she had called the Program

Coordinator and the Director of Services to object. She was aware of the program's evaluation plan and participation in research, so she used what she had learned in her college psychology classes. "They are confounding the study because they are forgetting a very important variable. And that is attachment!" she exclaimed. She made it clear that she was going to fight for what she wanted.

Her behavior showed that, along with seeing herself as a mother, she was seeing herself as an adult. Grace's former adolescent behavior would have been to "not say anything, then pout about the outcome," she told me. She saw herself as an adult who could "say something" and appropriately use her emotions to advocate for what she felt was in her best interest. Grace later said she also fought because she was "tired of being overlooked." Needless to say, her request to continue working with me was accepted.

In terms of their relationship, there were times when Grace and Sam were clearly in love and happy to be together, and others when they felt their needs and wishes were incompatible. They had fun trying new activities and discovering new skills, and they got confused about what they were supposed to do. They wondered if they were lovable enough to not be abandoned.

Our visits continued. We played and talked about development. We examined interactions and challenged abilities. As Sam caught up in his motor skills, new concerns developed about his communication skills. He was frustrated by his inability to express the many things he was thinking. He was angry, and his behavior showed it. Sam's aggressive behavior triggered many of Grace's memories of being hurt by a man's uncontrolled rage. She responded in anger because it gave her a sense of power that helped mask the fear.

Grace continued to avoid her anger by getting high. She would try to quit but would then discover an intensity in her rage that frightened her. We made safety plans—she used a parent hotline when she felt she was reaching her limits of tolerance and identified safe people to care for Sam if she needed a break. I tried to guide Grace and Sam in expressing anger in safe activities. We smashed play dough. We pounded pillows. We played with puppets. They got scared. I got scared. But we stayed at it. We built on the little changes, encouraged the feelings of closeness that came when the rage was contained, and identified other feelings like sadness, compassion, frustration, fear, excitement, loneliness, and joy.

We held on to the belief that change was possible. Grace was strengthened by her commitment to offer Sam a different experience than she had growing up. She recognized she could only be responsible for her choices. She could not control the role Sam's father would play in his life and grieved her father's absence in her life and Sam's father's absence in his. We talked about how different things might have been for her if someone had helped her learn to identify and appropriately express her feelings as a 2½-year-old. We talked about how different it might have been if she had had someone she trusted enough to freely express herself as Sam did with her. We talked about the fact that the anger would not drive me away.

Sam Shares His Insights

Then one day I arrived for our visit, and Grace was very agitated. She reported that another woman she knew from treatment had died. Grace expressed intense rage that this woman had been an addict and had not appropriately cared for her 7-year-old son throughout his life. Knowing that this was provoking many issues for Grace, I listened to her judgments of the other mother. I explored how the death was impacting her interactions with Sam, who had been moving in and out of the room, waiting to be included in the conversation. He was not used to being excluded during our visits.

I asked about how Grace was coping with her anger and the other emotions being provoked by the sudden death. Then, Sam came back into the kitchen to the table where his mother and I were seated. With outstretched arms, he offered Grace a plastic box. In it were her marijuana, papers, and a lighter. His mother was suddenly silent. She got up to take it from him and, as she walked out of the room to hide it away, said, "Okay, we'll talk about this."

Although we had talked for over 2 years about how her use of marijuana to escape her feelings had to affect her emotional availability to Sam, his actions that day connected with her in a way that nothing I could have ever said would. I know that some may see the actions of a child this age as purely coincidental. However, neither Grace nor I believe in coincidence. The fact that he was at a point in his development where he could connect his mother's rage with that box hidden in her room forced her to reexamine her beliefs about what he was aware of.

In her various treatments, she had heard many theories of the origins of addiction. Sam had been exposed to marijuana prenatally. Sam had two parents with addiction problems. Sam had grown up in a home where his mother actively abused marijuana. Sam now showed that he understood how emotions and behavior could go together. Sam was learning. Grace knew that she did not want him to take the same road she had taken and that she needed to make changes in her behavior to teach him a different route.

No magic happened overnight. However, over the course of the next few months, Grace put pieces in place that led her back into treatment. As she began to confront the intensity of the emotions she had so long denied and build new skills to cope with her rage, Sam began to move ahead in his ability to use words to identify and express his emotions. Not surprisingly, he frequently met me at the door exclaiming, "I'm angry. I'm very angry." There were many challenging visits as both parent and child tested the safety of their new direct expression of rage and safety plans were reviewed. Grace's substance abuse counselor and I attempted to keep each other informed of what we observed and learned from Grace and Sam.

What both Grace and Sam were discovering was that they could use a safe person to help them manage the emotions that felt so overwhelming. They began to trust that they would not be rejected or hurt for what they felt or who they were. They began to understand that they could control the rage rather than be controlled by it. They began to know that they could have feelings and be safe at the same time. They also began to discover that other feelings were waiting for them when they moved through the rage.

Grace became increasingly able to recognize little triggers for her anger and let go more quickly. She laughed as she told of a situation when she and Sam had locked into a power struggle. He ran off to his room. Grace took a moment to calm herself and disengage from the conflict. When Sam came storming back in to lash out again, he realized his angry partner was not there. "He couldn't dance by himself," his mother said with pride.

Ready for School and Ready to Learn

By that time, Sam was 3 years old, and we were preparing for his entry into Head Start and the family's transition out of the home-based program—we would soon be saying good-bye. It was a hard transition to make, for all of us. Grace had come to wholly embrace her role as Sam's mother. She had come to understand and enjoy being his safe base, the one he came to for help and guidance. Sam had come to trust that his mother would be there for him. She had become much more consistent and emotionally available, since she was no longer getting high. Sam and Grace had also come to trust that they had a safe place in our relationship to work on their relationship with each other. Sam showed an interest in moving into a new world, secure in his relationship with his mother and able to use that as his safe base.

It was Grace who found the transition difficult. When he was in child care, she had left him. Now he was leaving her. When talking about the upcoming change, Grace could speak of her sense of loss and, at the same time, express feelings of excitement and pride. Sam had also established a vocabulary to help him with the transition. On his first visit to his classroom, his teacher asked him how he was. "I'm feeling a little nervous," was his response. He used his mother to help him explore the room and become acquainted with the teacher. By the end of the visit, he was conversing freely with the teacher and was eager to start some of the activities she had shown him.

As Sam moved into preschool, his mother and I both trusted that he would be able to recall and reference the relationship model he had created with his mother. Their relationship had allowed him to see himself as worthy, competent, and special. He had a good foundation in the skills he needed to build other relationships, communicate his needs in a way that would elicit help, use the help offered to him, and tolerate the emotions he would feel as he was challenged by myriad new experiences. He was ready for school and ready to learn in a larger world.

Grace had also built a new relationship model that she could use to allow him to separate and become his own person. She had established other therapeutic relationships that she was using to manage and explore her feelings related to the end of our relationship. As we said good-bye, I knew that she would be able to reference and use our relationship to help her confront the challenges that would lie ahead.

A Parallel Experience

As for me, I, too, said good-bye knowing that I had gained a model for relationships that I would take with me into my work with other families. I had had the opportunity to see great changes in a family. I had seen a mother re-parent herself in a way that allowed her to offer her child a different experience from her own. I was obliged to recognize the healing power of the relationship Grace had experienced with me. At the same time, I had a parallel experience, in that I felt sadness, excitement, and pride as Grace and Sam left me to move on with their lives.

The first therapist who had worked with this family had predicted that I would like them, and I did—I liked them a lot. I had struggled many times to maintain professional boundaries. At one of our last home visits, we discussed the approach of Sam's first day of school. He asked me if I would come visit him there. I asked why he would want me to do that. "Because you are very special," he answered.

Reflective Work

Sam and Grace had become very special to me, too. I had consistently used supervision to understand the many issues that had confronted me as I worked with them. In supervision and case consultation, I had others sit with me and my anxiety. I used them to help me see the areas where I was blind. They guided me through my fears, hopes, disappointments, and joys in a way that helped me do the same for Grace and Sam. It was clear that using reflective supervision was essential to being effective in this work.

However, even supervision and case consultation could not provide clear answers for the questions I had about what should happen next. Grace, Sam, and I had done intensive attachment work, and we had succeeded. I could not help them to attach without becoming attached myself. Traditional therapeutic boundaries designed for a weekly office visit are inadequate for confronting the complexities of intensive in-home work as is done in long-term IMH practice. I had been in Sam's life from the time he was 5 months old until he was 38 months old. Now, according to the rules, we were to end our attachment. Grace, Sam, and I have said good-bye, but we have separated in a way that does not feel congruent with the relationship we had created. I have no easy answers for this challenge. It is an ambiguity that needs to be addressed within the profession.

In sharing this family's story, I have illustrated some of the key aspects of IMH practice. It is my hope that, with it, I can acknowledge the incredible courage of this family and the many others like them. I believe this story also illustrates the healing power that babies offer. As this mother opened herself to face her vulnerabilities, she allowed herself to fall in love, not only with her son but also with herself. As IMH practitioners, we are obliged to nurture this love and build on strengths while guiding families into sometimes new and foreign territory. Together we will then be able to celebrate relationships that foster health, growth, and respect.

Discussion Questions

1. What are risk factors that indicate the appropriateness of an IMH referral for this family?

2. Identify components of the intervention with this family that are indicated in the best practice standards for IMH practice. What are other strategies would have been appropriate but are not identified?

3. What are some of the subtle indicators of increasing attachment between Grace and Sam throughout their relationship?

4. There were many times during the work with this family when there were important safety concerns. What might have been some of the potential advantages or disadvantages of involving Children's Protective Services?

5. What are some of the essential skills that Sam took with him into preschool that indicate school readiness?

6. Given the length and nature of the family-therapist relationship, what guidelines would you suggest for an appropriate transition to the ending of the relationship?

Risk and Resiliency: Failure to Thrive in the First Year of Life

Carol Oleksiak

Summary

A single mother caring for four children under the age of 7, including a 6-month-old with serious feeding difficulties, is referred to an infant mental health (IMH) specialist working in a community family service agency. Visiting the family regularly in their home, the IMH specialist works hard to engage the mother and develop a trusting relationship. The specialist's active support includes comprehensive case management and assistance with concrete needs, as well as emotional support and developmental guidance. Gradually, trusting that the therapist will meet her needs, the mother begins to trust her own ability to meet the needs of her children. Over a 4-year period, the children make steady developmental progress. Today, the child who was the original focus of intervention is in second grade and doing well.

Worries About Terry

Born at 38 weeks gestational age, Terry weighed 6 pounds, 7 ounces. Now, at 6 months, weighing only 11 pounds, 7 ounces, Terry came to the attention of a children's hospital social worker. The hospital social worker noted that the family had missed many of their Women, Infants and Children (WIC) appointments. Jane, Terry's mother, had no formula and had been giving him solid food. She told the sympathetic social worker that she had brought Terry to the emergency room on two other occasions because he was throwing up after each feeding. She became even more worried when Terry stopped eating several weeks ago. Jane's third attempt to get help for her baby was at her local medical clinic. The clinic staff responded promptly and admitted Terry to the hospital.

During his hospital stay, Terry began to eat and gain weight. The hospital social worker referred Terry and Jane to our IMH program. The social worker asked Jane if she would like someone to come visit her and Terry in their home. The next day the social worker called the IMH specialist to let her know Jane was interested and that Terry would be discharged in 2 days; the specialist then called Jane. She listened as Jane quietly told her about Terry's previous hernia operation and her frustration with trying to feed him. The IMH specialist spoke of how hard it must be to feed Terry when he just threw it back up and asked if Jane would like her to come see them both in their home. Jane agreed, and a day and time was chosen.

First Visits

The first home visit occurred when Terry was 6½ months old, a few days after he was discharged from the hospital. As an IMH specialist, I made sure I arrived on time for our appointment. I wanted Jane to know that she could trust that I would come and that I would arrive at the time I said I would—important strategies to help build trust and model consistency. As I was about to enter this family's home, I reminded myself of the mother's many attempts to get help for her baby. It helped me to remember the IMH assumption that parents want what is best for their babies, including a wish for them to be healthy and strong.

The family, which was composed of a single mother and her four children under the age of 7, lived in an upper flat near a busy airport. When I arrived, a timid young woman opened the door, and three curious faces greeted me. The rooms were sparsely furnished, with few books or toys for the children and only two beds for the family. Jane explained that she and Terry slept on the couch.

Terry's next sibling, a 2-year-old boy with big, wide-open eyes, was not wearing diapers but was not potty trained. Jane's other two children, a 5-year-old boy and a 7-year-old girl, went to sit very quietly on the worn couch. They seemed to show their concern about this visitor by the way they stayed close to their mother.

Observing, Listening, and Guiding

Terry's arms and legs appeared very thin and fragile, and his belly looked distended. He was dressed in a thin sleeper that seemed a bit too small. He had a thin patch of curly brown hair on the top of his head and big brown eyes that watched me vigilantly as I spoke with his mother. He did not sit independently and often slid to one side when propped in a sitting position on the couch. However, he seemed curious about a small toy rattle that I had brought with me and had given to his mother. When his mother offered it to him, he reached for it with his thin hand, transferring it from one hand to the other. I was happy to see Terry do this, as it let me know that he was developing fine motor skills. Jane was initially quiet when she offered him the rattle, but after I commented on his ability to move the rattle from hand to hand, she smiled and said, "I didn't know he could do that." After this brief discussion, Jane remained quiet on the couch.

As I watched them sitting near each other but not interacting, I wondered how I could begin to help them. Jane seemed so shut down, and Terry seemed so frail. Jane finally spoke, saying, "I think he has a fever." She was worried about her baby since he had just been released from the hospital; I was worried, too. We called the health clinic she used for the children and spoke with the nurse about our concerns for Terry. The nurse instructed Jane to take Terry's temperature and, if it was below 101 degrees, to give him infant Tylenol®. If his temperature was 101 or higher, she should bring him to the clinic that afternoon. Since Jane did not have any transportation and could not leave home with four little children, I offered to go to the store and purchase a thermometer and Tylenol® for her. When I returned, Jane was giving Terry a bottle of water to keep him from dehydrating. It appeared that when Jane was attended to, she was better able to attend to her baby. We took Terry's temperature, which was 100 degrees. Following the nurse's directions, we gave him some Tylenol®. When it was time for me to go, I said, "I'll be back tomorrow at noon to see how you and the baby are doing." Jane smiled weakly and nodded, "okay."

When I arrived the next day, Jane was waiting for me at the window. I understood her wish to have things be better for her baby and her other children. However, it soon became clear to me that she would need a great deal of support in the coming months. Jane was unable to accomplish the most basic caregiving tasks. I talked with her about how we could become a team. Together we would try to understand why her baby was having trouble gaining weight. We would also need to understand what was making Jane's care of this baby so difficult. She was able to manage a slight smile and nodded her head in agreement. Terry's fever was down, and he seemed a little better.

Active Support

Many families enrolled in our IMH program have very few resources and little or no family support, so comprehensive case management is very much a part of our program. Since Jane seemed to need so much support and Terry's health and weight gain seemed so precarious, we were able to get an emergency appointment the next day with the WIC office, to ensure that Terry had formula.

The whole family came with us to the WIC office. It was a difficult visit. The appointment took a very long time, and the children had not eaten breakfast and were hungry. Since our program also had money to spend for food emergencies, I went to the grocery store and bought a bag of apples for the children. When Jane was called to fill out some paper work, she asked if I would hold Terry. I had brought a few rattles and offered them to him. I noticed that he seemed to avert his gaze when I tried to talk to him and offer him a rattle to hold. I thought it was important to ask Jane if she had also noticed this. She nodded her head in agreement. As a team, we would try to understand Terry's cues and behaviors. She smiled but said very little. I felt worried about Terry's health and scared about being able to really help this family. I wondered what scared Jane. Was she worried about losing her baby? Did Terry wonder about his mother's silence?

I watched Jane tease Terry with his bottle—offering it and then pulling it away. Terry seemed hungry and ready to drink his bottle, but then he would give up and turn away from his mother. He soon began to cry. Terry's cry is difficult to describe in words. It appeared to come in frantic, squawking bursts. I observed how difficult it was for his mother to give him what he needed at that moment. I acknowledged her struggle, saying, "This must be so hard for you." I knew an important part of our work would be to understand what made it difficult for Jane to consistently care for Terry. Over time, I began to understand just how difficult it was for her.

Terry's Story

Jane described her pregnancy with Terry as uneventful. She was alone in the hospital when she delivered after 24 hours of difficult labor. She had no support from Terry's father because he was incarcerated for criminal activity soon after she became pregnant. Following his birth, Terry's Apgar scores (Apgar, 1953; Apgar & James, 1962) were 9 at 1 minute and 9 at 5 minutes. Initially, Terry was breast-fed, but his mother soon gave it up after being advised to give him formula because of his poor weight gain within the first few weeks. Terry seemed fine at birth but soon after began to have difficulty keeping his formula down. His mother described him as different from her other children. She reported no difficulties with them when they were babies. "He is not a happy baby," she said. Terry did not give her clear cues. He often cried and was difficult to soothe.

My observations during these early home visits suggested that Jane was clearly overwhelmed by the care of Terry in addition to the care of her other three young children. Her oldest child was frequently out of school because of asthma; the two other boys were rambunctious and often in need of close supervision. Jane had few supports and fewer resources. There was not enough food to feed the family. The landlord was negligent in fixing the heat, broken windows, and exterior doors that didn't shut tight. The house was plagued with roaches.

Jane's Story

Jane, at 25 years of age, was a quiet and very thin young woman. She told me she is not close to her family and has few friends. The youngest of 10 children, Jane was very close to her father and was devastated at his death when she was only 8 years old. The family had little means of support and relied on government assistance.

During our early home visits, Jane seemed lonely and overwhelmed. The children clamored for her attention. I wondered how much she had left to give them; she was often unresponsive to them. Observing Jane and her children was often painful—they all seemed to need so much.

Gradually we began to form a relationship on behalf of Terry. This was not an easy task: Jane was very quiet and I struggled not to fill the silence by talking. I used Terry's behaviors and development to engage her in conversation. I helped her think about how to support his development. I used anticipatory guidance, encouraging her to consider what might come next for him developmentally. Whenever I observed positive interactions between them, I put it into words. On one visit, Terry had been very fussy and Jane was initially frustrated and terse with him. "He is really having a hard time," I commented. "What do you think he is trying to tell us?" It was often very hard to understand what it was that Terry needed. However, with supportive coaxing, Jane figured out that Terry had not eaten in several hours. With support and recognition of her struggles, Jane began to respond more consistently to her baby—not an easy task for a mother whose baby was fretful and unresponsive.

The IMH Specialist's Response

Holding. After those early visits, I was very worried and had many questions. What made it difficult for Jane to feed her baby? What made this baby unable to keep his formula down? Why did he vomit after almost every feeding? Jane teased the baby with his bottle. When Terry and his mother were together, he often seemed more interested in other things. It was hard for Jane to get her baby to play with her, and, at times, she would withhold his toys. As an IMH specialist, I began to understand that both Terry and Jane needed support and "holding." Jane spoke little during our home visits, and at times she looked depressed. It seemed important to provide a "holding environment" for Jane so that she could feed her baby.

Speaking for the baby. After observing Jane and Terry, I carefully tried to put my observations of their needs into words. I spoke for Terry and also for Jane and her other children. During a particularly difficult feeding, Terry seemed to spit up every other spoonful. Jane was pacing the feeding too fast, so I said for Terry, "I'm trying so hard to keep up with you, Mama. Could you go a little slower?" Jane often had difficulty noticing hunger in her other children. Noticing them licking Terry's empty baby food jars, I said, "Hey, Mom, is it time for a snack yet?"

Jane began to listen and understand as we talked about Terry's development, his cues, and his behavior. Together, we discussed what she thought her baby might be thinking or needing when we observed him. As Jane felt my support and came to trust me, she could begin to look and respond to her baby's needs. During one home visit, she responded, "Look he wants me to sing 'patty cake' with him again."

Assisting with concrete needs. An important role of an IMH specialist is to assist with concrete needs. This was a huge part of our early work together. It seemed as if Jane had no idea how to follow through with things. By gently supporting her in making and keeping appointments, the children got caught up on their immunizations and received routine medical care.

Jane was often out of diapers and formula and let me know in subtle ways. I provided support for the family's needs through funds from our agency, purchasing diapers and formula for the baby, clothes for the children, and food for all of them. Jane never acted as though she expected these things, and she was able to say thank you, but she couldn't provide them herself.

It was important to help this family with life's basic needs so that Jane could then attend to parenting in a more positive way. Together, we worked on a household budget, planned healthy meals, and found resources she could turn to at the end of the month when her money ran out. I made home visits at least twice a week and visited more often if Jane needed to go to the clinic, WIC, or the grocery store. As I cared for Jane, she was better able to care for her children. As I provided for her basic needs, she provided for her children's basic needs. And Terry began to gain weight.

Understanding Failure to Thrive

Through the insights that Thomas M. Horner, Ph.D., has shared in seminars and discussions, I have come to understand that poor weight gain in infants can be caused by many factors. I was working to understand which factors were involved in Terry's poor weight gain. Jane exhibited some appropriate feeding behaviors, yet she was unable to make eating a pleasurable experience, staying silent through most feedings. Just as when I was first getting to know the family, I again invited Jane to join me so that, together, we could try to understand the issues surrounding Terry's eating behaviors and his difficulty gaining weight.

To help us understand Terry's needs and behaviors, with Jane's permission, I regularly videotaped her and Terry. Jane agreed that videotapes might help us understand the problem, so together we watched feeding and eating interactions. We could see that Terry liked to watch his siblings while he was eating, feel and sometimes play with the food, or "talk" to his mother during the feedings. Jane learned how to pace feedings as she learned to read Terry's signals.

We made charts of his food intake, and Jane tried to judge how much he was throwing up. Parents often feel, or are made to feel, that they are to blame for their infant's poor weight gain. As an IMH specialist, it was important to help Jane understand that Terry was an equal partner in mealtimes. He contributed to the difficult feedings—and understanding how he did could help us help him.

It was important to take Terry's point of view and help Jane allow him to take the lead. This challenges the IMH specialist to be aware of the baby's, as well as the mother's, experience in the feeding relationship. "He isn't very interested today, is he?" I might sometimes say. Or on a day when the feeding was going more smoothly, "He really seems to like those crackers."

Another critical factor in reaching our goals was having Dr. G., Terry's pediatrician, as a member of our team. In the clinic setting, we were *always* able to see Dr. G., which meant there would be only one person following Terry's medical and developmental progress over time. A valuable member of our team, he took great pleasure in Terry's weight and developmental gains. Dr. G. also treated Terry's mother with respect and was sensitive to her understanding of her baby.

Supporting Jane

Two months after beginning regular visits with Jane and her family, we began to notice some positive changes. Terry, now 8 months old, weighed 14 pounds, 6 ounces—a gain of 3 pounds! As Jane began to trust that Terry would grow, she also came to trust the IMH specialist. It was then that Jane began to tell her own story.

Moving to a new city following the death of her husband, Jane's mother fell into deep depression. There were many children to care for and Jane, as the youngest, was often left alone. "We were not allowed to go outside. I used to lean over the couch and watch the neighborhood kids play. The quieter we were for my mother, the better it was." Jane described her mother as a fierce disciplinarian, who would cut a piece of branch from a backyard tree and threaten to hit Jane and her siblings with it when they were disobedient. Jane said her brothers often got hit with the branch while she withdrew so as not to be noticed and possibly punished. Jane liked school and had wished to be a teacher. She told me she got good grades and graduated from high school. Her quiet nature allowed her to delve into her studies, but she was lonely and too shy to make many friends. Consequently, when her brothers' male friends paid her any attention, she was very flattered. Jane's children all had different fathers, and Jane had no lasting relationship or support from any of them.

Jane met Terry's father through her brother. He made her laugh. She knew that he often got into trouble, but he made her feel cared for. They had fun together, and he paid attention to Jane's other children.

Alone, Jane acutely felt the loss of support from Terry's father. In fact, none of her children's fathers were involved with their children. Alone, Jane had little energy to raise three rambunctious children and a baby who was failing. I advocated for Jane and her children wherever we went. I began to put feelings into words for the older three children. Jane listened closely and watched closely the video-tapes of herself playing with Terry and the other children. When she interacted positively, I would point out to her the children's positive responses back. She would smile quietly. As Terry gained some weight, she said, "He looks a lot better. Before, his ribs showed."

Developmental Guidance

At 10 months, after 4 months of home visiting, Terry was a stronger baby. He now crawled and was pulling himself up on furniture. Terry was beginning to feed himself and now weighed 16 pounds! Having gained weight, Terry's development was also catching up. He showed interest in playing baby games like "patty cake" and "peek-a-boo." He could find hidden objects and liked dropping toys as a game. He became less fretful and easier to soothe.

In encouraging Jane to look at Terry's growing competencies, she began to take pleasure in interactions with him. She reported that she was holding him more. Jane began to sing to Terry and the other children. There was more laughter, and I wondered if this was a pleasure that she had once shared with Terry's father. Jane, who was initially very quiet, began to talk more to Terry and her other children. She helped expand his beginning language and encouraged his imitative play. I explained which developmental tasks would emerge next and suggested ways she could support Terry. Together, at each home visit, we watched Terry's development and thought about ways to encourage him.

I gathered a large box filled with books, blocks, balls, Legos®, and other toys to leave in the home for the family. Jane said she was playing more and more with the children. Terry's growing responsiveness toward her had encouraged her to play with him, and his play grew more organized.

"He Is Going to Be Okay"

By Terry's first birthday, there were still some concerns but also some celebrations and pleasures. Although he continued to be plagued with fevers, ear infections, frequent spitting up, and asthma, Terry was a much happier baby. He began to communicate using gestures and simple words. He was getting ready to walk, a much sturdier baby who now weighed 17 pounds, 8 ounces!

One hot summer day, as we sat on the porch watching the children play and eating Popsicles®, Jane revealed that she had once thought Terry was going to be "slow" or, even more worrisome, that maybe he wouldn't survive. Only recently did she feel hopeful about his being "okay." She went on to say that she felt better because he was beginning to do more things and he was more responsive to her. Her baby continued to gain weight, and he now seemed to enjoy eating. As Terry grew more healthy and competent, Jane knew now that he would indeed survive, and she was able to be more affectionate and attentive toward him.

This work, slow but steady, paralleled Terry's slow but steady weight gain. As Jane was able to form a relationship with me, she also began to form a better bond with her baby. Jane and I worked together on behalf of Terry and her other children for 4 years. She continues to keep in contact with me by calling when she has questions. Today, Terry is in the second grade and doing well in school. There are no significant developmental delays. After a very difficult beginning, Jane and Terry have an enduring relationship with each other.

References

Apgar, V. A. (1953). Proposal for a new method of evaluation of the newborn infant. *Anesthesia and Analgesia, Current Researches, 22,* 260.

Apgar, V. A., & James, L. S. (1962). Further observations on the newborn scoring system. *American Journal of Diseases of Children, 104,* 418-428.

Discussion Questions

1. Jane is quiet, withdrawn, and overwhelmed. How does the specialist engage her in treatment?

2. Early in the treatment relationship the specialist provides for many concrete needs of the family, including arrangements for medical care, food, and transportation. This is not a traditional strategy for most therapies. Why is it important in infant mental health work? How did it affect the development of the relationship between Jane and the specialist?

3. Each family member had multiple needs. How does the therapist balance the needs of each child and the mother?

4. Tom Horner, Ph.D., suggests that poor weight gain in infants can be caused by many factors and that there is a distinction between feeding and eating. He explains that it is the parent's responsibility to feed and the child's responsibility to eat. How do you understand this? How does this case illustrate Dr. Horner's ideas?

5. A guiding principle in IMH work is attention to the relationship between the therapist and the parent(s). How does this case study illustrate this fundamental tenet?

6. How does Jane use her growing understanding about her own early life to improve her ability to care for her children?

In a Galaxy Far, Far Away: Combining Infant Mental Health and Play Therapy

Nichole Paradis

Summary

Translating the infant mental health (IMH) approach from home visiting to a traditional outpatient mental health clinic, a therapist combines IMH theories and strategies with play therapy in time-limited treatment with two preschool-age boys and their mother. Intervention is initially focused on the 3-year-old, who was expelled from his first child care center and is likely to be expelled from a second because of aggressive behavior. Gradually, the focus shifts to the family's feelings about the father's abrupt departure from the home after a conflict-filled marriage and the mother's return to more-than-full-time work. The combination of both therapies allows family members to express their concerns and begin to find resolution, although it seems likely that the family could have benefited significantly from treatment beyond the 10 sessions for which funding was available.

Introduction

Eager to use training I had recently received in providing clinical services for children from 3 to 6 years of age, I sought contractual work at a traditional outpatient mental health clinic. All of my previous training and experience had come from home visiting models, and I wanted an opportunity to adapt my skills. At the center of my thinking were IMH principles and practices.

The referral came from a colleague who was worried about Jack's expulsion from his first day care center and his likely expulsion from another. Jack, at age 3 years 4 months, was a cheerful, likable boy in one-on-one situations but was accused of hitting, biting, spitting on, and fighting with the other children at both child care centers. When my colleague, a consultant for the second center, encouraged me to see Jack to help his family avoid another expulsion, I agreed to see Jack and his family for 10 weeks. Although the referral was specifically for Jack, my background in IMH had taught me that the primary caregiving relationship (i.e., between parent and child) was often the most effective target for intervention. For young children especially, it is a consistent, responsive, and trusting attachment relationship with a caregiver that allows them to establish appropriate relationships with others. Therefore, in my outpatient practice, I tried to include at least the primary caregiver in as many sessions as possible.

Eager to Tell Her Story

When I spoke with Jack's mother, Lisa, over the phone, she said she was single and worked one full-time and one part-time job to make ends meet. She mentioned that she had another son, David, who was 5 years old, but she was clearly most concerned about Jack. Lisa relayed the same concerns as my colleague and stated that she understood that there would only be enough funding for 10 sessions. We would meet weekly in my office, but she wanted to see me without the children for the first session.

Lisa was well-groomed, thin, and petite. She was charming, but she seemed somewhat anxious during that first visit. Although eager to tell her story, she worried about how it might be perceived. Lisa was concerned about Jack. The reported aggressive behaviors had started shortly after Lisa and her husband divorced and she returned to work full-time. "It just that I had to go back to work. We weren't getting any support from their father," she said with guilt in her voice. I responded, "It sounds like it's been a very difficult time for all of you." She responded to my remark with a weak smile and continued.

Lisa understood that Jack's problems were likely related to Daddy's leaving the house, Mommy's returning to work, and Jack's beginning center-based child care for the first time. She added, "I was really in a lot of emotional distress around the time of the divorce. Putting their Daddy's pictures away was probably the wrong thing to do." Lisa became tearful as she described how she might lose her day job if Jack's center did not stop calling and threatening to expel Jack.

As Lisa and I talked during that first session, it was important for her that I understand the kind of man her ex-husband was and why they were no longer married. "He's trouble. I think, well, I know he's an alcoholic." She thought he might have also suffered from depression. She somewhat reluctantly mentioned that they had argued frequently and that he disappeared for weeks, sometimes months at a time, with no word or contact.

Lisa was feeling guilty, but it was not yet clear to me if that guilt was due to divorcing her husband or for staying with him for so long. I also thought she was hinting that her own actions and feelings about the boys' father were contributing to Jack's behavior problems.

We also discussed Jack's developmental history. Jack was born 8 weeks premature. He had hearing problems, and tubes were implanted when he was 13 months old; they were recently removed when Jack turned 3. Lisa thought it was this hearing problem that caused Jack to walk and talk later than expected. She remarked that, despite the hearing problem, Jack seemed to love to sing and play music. "He's my little musician. He's really precious." According to Lisa, Jack was robust and a healthy eater. He was also affectionate and playful around family, and, as Lisa talked about these strengths, she seemed to relax and express real pride in her son's personality.

Therapeutic Considerations

As we talked, my initial impression was that Jack's behaviors were likely due to the recent turmoil and confusion in his family. Without having met and observed Jack, it seemed reasonable to conclude that the child was quite confused and possibly angry about the sudden changes in his life: first, the unexplained departure of his father, followed by the unavailability of his mother, who was self-described as "emotionally distressed." Lisa's reactions (which included grief and guilt, at least) to the separation and divorce had compromised her ability to help Jack adjust to the changes. Then the switch from being at home with Mom to being placed in a child care center meant Jack had to adjust to new caregivers and experience the unavailability of his mother as well as the loss of his father. Perhaps Jack worried that if Daddy could leave entirely, Mommy might, too.

I asked more about what things had been like for all of them when these changes were occurring. Lisa admitted that she had difficulty finding words to explain their father's departure to the children. She wondered if Jack even remembered his father, saying, "Jack never asked questions about his dad or why he was no longer present."

Especially because I hadn't yet met Jack, I wanted to consider other possibilities that might be affecting Jack's behaviors. Lisa had mentioned Jack's hearing problems, which might have contributed to a language delay. Difficulties with communication might be making Jack feel frustrated, and he might respond to this by acting aggressively in his child care setting.

Another consideration to rule out was that Jack might be experiencing a problem with sensory integration. Sensory integration is the process of the nervous system that organizes sensory input (sights, sounds, textures, touch, taste, and smell) from one's environment. Although his mother said that Jack behaved cooperatively in one-on-one situations, the child care providers reported that Jack's aggressive behaviors were seemingly unprovoked and that he seemed to prefer to play by himself, away from other children. Some of these behavioral descriptions were similar to those of children who could not effectively incorporate all the stimuli that are present in a typical child care setting.

Lisa and I agreed that she would bring Jack to the next visit. I explained, "I want you to participate in our sessions. We should allow Jack to play and explore the room; our role will be to follow his lead in play. I'd like for us to try to learn about Jack together and become a team to figure out how to help him." We briefly talked about the possibility that we might sometimes need to split a session. She agreed to bring her mother along occasionally to watch Jack in the waiting room when we needed to talk alone.

The next week, Lisa and Jack were ready in the waiting room at our scheduled time. Jack offered a shy smile and waited for his mother's approval and hand before following me into the office. Jack was immediately drawn to the dollhouse and figures inside. I hoped that Jack would play independently for a few minutes so that I could touch base with his mom.

"I got called again at work this week," she said. " I think they might expel Jack.." Lisa seemed to be fighting back tears. "I'm so confused; Jack is so easy to manage at home and with my folks." I was confused, too. So far, I did not detect obvious difficulties in the relationship between Jack and his mom that would account for Jack's behaviors.

"These Babies Are Pushing!"

Lisa and I joined Jack on the floor, where he engaged the dolls in play inside the dollhouse. I noted that Jack was not yet appropriately assigning gender, at least not to the doll figures. I was having some difficulty understanding Jack's words and relied on Lisa to interpret part of the time. Jack demonstrated a great deal of aggression in his play. There were twin dolls that Jack essentially slammed together over and over, stating, "These babies are pushing!" He would then look to his mother and me for a reaction. Lisa seemed quite uncomfortable with the quality of Jack's play. She encouraged Jack to do more socially appropriate things with the babies. "Honey, why don't you put them to bed or put them in the stroller for a walk?" Jack responded to Lisa's requests a few times, placing the babies lovingly in their beds, only to have them spring out and begin pushing each other again. "Look, they're pushing!" Jack exclaimed. I gently reminded Lisa that our goal was to watch and follow Jack and to try to stop ourselves from directing his play. My primary objective was to allow Jack to play freely so that we could better understand what he might be experiencing and communicating through his play.

Incorporating Play Therapy and Relationship-Focused Intervention

I reviewed my training in play therapy and relationship-focused intervention and worked to incorporate the two. On the one hand, I wanted to encourage Jack to expand on this game. Could he tell me a story with the babies and other figures in the house? Could he incorporate Mommy into his play? I asked more questions about the babies. "Are the babies fighting at school? Did that baby get hurt?" But my questions were seemingly ignored; Jack would pause very briefly when I queried and then bash the dolls together again. He put the babies on the roof of the house and had them repeatedly push one another off the roof. He also had them push one another down the stairs over and over again.

On the other hand, I was curious about how Jack and Mom would play together. Because I had been directing Lisa, I did not think that I was getting an accurate picture of how they were together. I did get the sense that they did not play often. Our time on the floor seemed especially uncomfortable for Lisa.

We switched to plastic animal figures, and the same kind of aggression dominated Jack's play there as well. It appeared to make Lisa just as uncomfortable as the aggression with the dolls. At the end of the session, Jack did not object as I explained clean-up time. Lisa, Jack, and I picked up the toys and made an appointment for the following week.

During that first session with Jack, and for the next two sessions as well, I kept assuming that the aggression between the dolls had something to do with how Jack experienced his world at day care. Was he trying to show us what it is like to be in his classroom? I wondered if he felt constantly attacked by the other children. The possibility of sensory integration difficulties was becoming more and more prominent in my mind. Also, Jack was not as responsive as I had hoped to attempts to bring Lisa or myself into the play. For instance, I would use a stage whisper to ask Jack what he would like me to do. "What should the lady do?" I asked, referring to the adult doll that he would hand me. Sometimes he would direct me to play teacher and "stop the babies from pushing," but more often, he would simply repeat my question back, word for word.

Using Supervision

I was feeling increasingly anxious. Funding only allowed 10 sessions with this family, and we had already used 3. I was growing very fond of Lisa and Jack and wanted to help them. Fortunately, I had an opportunity to present the case to a group of senior clinicians. I was grateful to gain some help and perspective. As is so often the case in reflective supervision, I began to see the family differently, even as I described them to the group. One of the senior clinicians wondered if the aggression that Jack demonstrated in play at the office and in the day care center was related to Lisa's relationship with her ex-husband—it seemed likely that "the arguments" could have been aggressive incidents.

Did Jack's babies represent Mommy and Daddy pushing? Was Jack attempting to communicate or process something confusing and scary he remembered from home? What about the disappearance of his father? Lisa stated in our initial interview that she had simply taken the pictures of Daddy down. She had more recently mentioned that she had not yet explained to Jack and his brother, David, why their father was no longer around. Lisa felt that, because her husband had been around only sporadically, the boys would not really notice or care that he was gone for good. However, Lisa acknowledged that David did still ask about his father. Throughout these discussions, Lisa seemed to need or want approval for the decisions she had made. She doubted herself; part of her knew that ignoring his departure and the divorce was not enough. As I reported these circumstances to the group, we began to conclude that the lack of adequate information about his father was contributing to Jack's behavior problems.

At our next session, I asked Lisa more about what it had been like when her husband was living with them. "He sometimes got out of control. The arguing could be intense. I got hit a couple of times," her eyes were downcast as she spoke. She felt certain, however, that her sons were not aware of the fights. "It always happened after they were in bed. We, well, I guess I never wanted the boys to be exposed to that." Lisa listened carefully as I expressed my worry that Jack's behavior might somehow be linked to his confusion about the changes at home, particularly the disappearance of his father. Lisa was still somewhat skeptical that Jack noticed or cared that Dad was gone. She did, however, see that the confusion might be impacting David, her 5-year-old.

Lisa talked more about David during our fourth session than she had previously. She was becoming increasingly worried about David's behaviors in his kindergarten classroom, and she wondered if David could begin participating in our sessions.

Wondering About Daddy

We talked more about how the boys might be wondering or confused about Daddy. I thought developmental guidance might be helpful, but I used it with caution. I wanted to help Lisa understand that just because her children did not talk or ask about their father, it did not mean that they didn't think about him, worry about him, or have other confusing feelings related to his departure. However, Lisa seemed sensitive about being judged as a mother, and I worried that this information might make her feel guilty rather than supported. So I approached his departure from the third-person perspective. I talked in generalities about what most children at these developmental stages might be experiencing, that is, how preschool children tend to see the world in egocentric terms and might somehow blame themselves for otherwise unexplained events.

I gently encouraged Lisa to find an age-appropriate way to explain to both boys about the divorce. "If it would be helpful, we could work on finding the right words together and practice here first." Lisa seemed a bit frightened but agreed to think more about it.

Paying Attention to the Story

In that fourth session, Jack's behavior had not changed, but I did watch him differently. As he repeatedly pushed the babies together, off the roof, and down the stairs, I talked about how scared the babies must be. I stopped trying to facilitate Jack's "story telling" and started to pay attention to the story he had been telling me all along. I tried to acknowledge and validate that all that pushing was frightening and confusing and it seemed there was no way to stop it. My change in approach seemed to irritate Jack just a bit. It didn't change his play really; he still mostly ignored me and, at times, seemed lost in his own world with the dolls.

The following week, Lisa brought both Jack and David to the session. The boys played next to us as Lisa showed me a picture that David had drawn in school. "I wanted you to see this and hear what you have to say about it. His teacher is pretty worried." The teacher had asked the students to draw their families. David's picture included himself, Jack, and Mommy. Next to Mommy was another figure that was scribbled over firmly with a black crayon. Lisa felt that she could no longer ignore the impact of Dad's departure on David's behavior and feelings. The drawing confirmed for me that Dad's absence was relevant and mattered very much to David.

After discussing the drawing, Lisa and I joined the boys on the floor. Jack drew me over to the dollhouse for the familiar story of babies pushing each other. I kept trying to validate how confused and scared the babies must be, and, after about 25 minutes, Jack's play changed just a bit. For just a few minutes, there was a brief respite in the aggression when Jack allowed the babies to push the stroller and go for a ride in the car. I looked for Lisa's reactions to Jack's change in behavior, but she was engaged with David and hadn't seemed to notice.

I observed the interactions between David and Lisa out of the corner of my eye. David had pulled down a small group of plastic soldier figures and engaged them in conflict. He declared each one of them a "bad guy." Lisa was encouraging David to let the soldiers get along, but David could not be swayed. It felt strange for Lisa and David to play in one part of the room while I interacted with Jack nearby, but I was not sure how else to configure the session.

Empathizing With Lisa

The following week, Lisa asked for some time for us to talk without the boys in the room, so she brought her mother along to watch the children in the waiting room. In the office, Lisa broke down in tears. "Jack's adjusting to his new center, but now David's teacher called me at work about his behavior. I just don't know what to do!" I felt it was important to validate Lisa's feelings. I knew from experience that progress was slow in clinical work and that sometimes situations get worse before they get better. I was worried that Lisa might become discouraged without some support and encouragement. My IMH training had shown me that parents need to feel supported and understood in order to be able to give their children the same. I empathized with how exhausted and hopeless Lisa must feel, and I reminded her that she was doing something important by bringing the boys in for therapy every week. She acknowledged that she valued her mother's support, but the primary responsibilities still fell on her shoulders. Lisa was clearly overwhelmed, but I hoped she felt heard and understood by me.

Lisa seemed desperate to talk more about her feelings and worries about her ex-husband. "Do you know that he has never called? He hasn't checked to see if we're okay. He hasn't sent any money. It's like we never existed. How can he just forget all about us?" She was feeling abandoned and just as abused as when her marriage was intact. Her husband was still very present in her mind and therefore in the boys' minds, too. Again, I offered her empathy; I validated how lonely and scary her job as a parent now was.

We had intended to take only 20 to 30 minutes, but it had been more like 40 minutes. We went together to get the boys and their grandmother and invite them in. For the next 15 minutes, Jack and

David showed all of us how difficult it had been for them to wait. They were rambunctious, loud, and disorganized; they could not settle into meaningful play but instead bounced about the room. Grandma was clearly embarrassed; she and Lisa both tried unsuccessfully to calm the boys down. I felt that setting limits and attempting a session at that point would not have been what the boys needed. After all, if their mother had needed a safe place to express some feelings, why wouldn't they? I repeatedly voiced how difficult it must have been for them to wait all that time when they had expected to come in and play, but they did not respond to me. I wondered if they had been anxious about what Mom and I had discussed. Whatever the reason, we could not use the rest of the time productively. I did feel that the time Lisa and I had spent without the boys was helpful; it had gone a long way in the development of our relationship.

The Room Went Completely Dark

Jack did not come to the seventh session because he was sick. After Lisa and David entered the room, Lisa said almost immediately, "David, why don't you tell Nichole about your Daddy?" Lisa then looked at me. "There's been more trouble this week. I really want him to talk about it." In response to his mom, David shook his head. "I don't want to talk about it. No!" Then he walked over to the light switch and the room went completely dark. While the lights were out, I felt scared, unsure what I should say or do. I experienced tension and fear in the room. Both Lisa and I asked David to turn the lights back on. He giggled, refused, and then eventually turned them back on.

Later, in group supervision, we concluded that David was doing exactly what his mother had asked him to do. When Lisa said, "Let's talk about Daddy," David made it dark—how it would have been for him when his parents fought. According to Lisa, the arguments occurred at night when David was supposed to be sleeping in his bedroom. David must have been very aware of his parents' fights, the yelling, and perhaps even violence, which would have been so frightening for him. The fear I felt in that room when the lights went out reflected the fear that both Lisa and David remembered experiencing in the dark.

In a Galaxy Far, Far Away . . .

After the lights came back on, the three of us played together. I said, "It might be easier for David to talk to us about how he's feeling through play. Let's see what he'd like to play with." David proceeded to lead us in Star Wars–themed play. He cast Lisa as Princess

Leah, but relegated her to a corner and did not ask much of her. David cast himself as Luke Skywalker and used a plastic wand as his light saber (or "life saver," as he called it). I was cast as Darth Vader. Interestingly, Darth Vader means dark father.

My assigned role was always the same: I attacked Luke, and he would battle me with his light saber. I was also given a light saber but could only use it when David deemed it appropriate. Time and again, Luke was victorious in temporarily defeating my evil embodiment. "I cut off your hand! It's gone!" I would obligingly pull my hand below my sleeve to appear as though it were missing. "OK! Now your hand is back! Ooh! Zap! Your hand is gone again!" Luke would shout. And so it went for the rest of the session.

Jack returned for the eighth session, but David was clearly in charge. Lisa wanted some time to talk, but there was no one to watch the boys in another room, and once everyone was in my office, David insisted we begin the Star Wars story immediately. I encouraged Lisa to join in—I felt certain that the boys would show me how the family was coping through the play. I also reminded Lisa that it might be easier for us to discuss her concerns over the phone between sessions. I did not like putting one family member's needs off in order to address another's, but I had little choice with only a 60-minute session.

David cast Jack as Han Solo, and the story picked up right where we had left off. Using feedback I received in group supervision, I voiced over and over again how scared and powerless I felt whenever my hand was "cut off" in the light saber battle. "Oh, I'm so scared. I wish I had my hand back. Without my hand, I can't protect myself; it's so scary." I wanted to give words to the feelings they all must have experienced when Daddy was attacking Mommy.

Princess Leah Becomes More Powerful

I also encouraged Lisa, as Princess Leah, to take a more active role in our story. David was quite willing for this to happen. Sometimes David would announce that my [Darth's] light saber would immobilize Luke. He would quite dramatically fall to the floor and whisper, "I . . . need the . . . special . . . potion." I quickly tried to decide how to use this opportunity that David was providing to give Lisa some "power" in their relationship. So in a stage whisper, I asked Princess Leah to bestow a special potion that would heal Luke Skywalker. Lisa playfully obliged, crouching down and making a gentle stroke over David's face she would say, "There, the potion has made you well. You can get up. You're not frozen anymore." David quickly picked up on this new twist. For the rest of the session, he alternated between freezing and then healing me and being frozen and then healed by his mother. I was pleased to see David both using his own "powers" and relying on his mother's powers.

Jack eagerly joined the play but with energy that was less focused. Jack seemed to get caught up in the excitement of the "battles" and had a harder time following the story. He enthusiastically included Mom in the play by shouting, "Use some potion on him, Mommy! Get him! Make him frozen!" every time I would "come after" the boys in play. I encouraged this theme by asking Princess Leah to help protect Luke and Han Solo from Darth Vader.

At the end of the eighth meeting, I reminded Lisa that we would be off the next week. I also reminded her that we only had two sessions remaining. She was clearly disappointed and said, "I wish there was a way we could keep meeting. The boys like coming here so much." I responded, "It will be hard for me to say good-bye to all of you; it feels like we've just gotten started. Maybe we could discuss some ways for you to continue to get support for yourself when we aren't meeting anymore." Lisa nodded and finished helping the boys with their coats, and they left.

Until then, we had been meeting every week for 8 weeks. However, I was going out of town, so we planned to skip a week. When I arrived at the clinic for our ninth session, the support staff informed me that the family had arrived the previous week at our regularly scheduled time and had seemed quite confused by my absence. The secretary noted that the boys had been very upset and cried as they left the clinic. I felt terrible, but I was also confused. I was certain Lisa was aware of the change. I wondered if they would come this time and what their reactions might be like.

They did arrive for their scheduled appointment. Lisa maintained that she had not remembered about the schedule change. I thought I sensed a distance from her. I reflected to myself later that it must have felt terrible for her and the boys to come to the clinic to find me unexpectedly missing, especially in the context of her feelings of abandonment toward her ex-husband. For Lisa, the experience validated her own feeling of powerlessness and unworthiness. Once again, she had been unable to protect her sons—this time, from my absence.

Star Wars Play Continues

In the office, it quickly became clear that the boys were upset about not meeting the previous week. The Star Wars play continued but with less enthusiasm and with multiple interruptions. David could not seem to stay with it—he was frequently testing limits by trying to leave the room, turning out the lights, picking fights with Jack, and playing with items in the room he knew to be "off limits." I repeatedly reminded the boys about the rules in the room and about items that were and were not okay for play. Jack cooperated, but David continued to test the limits for most of the session. Lisa was noticeably tense and expressed her frustration. "See, this is how they are at home most of the time. No one knows how difficult they can be!"

I realized again that Lisa was just as much in need of feeling understood as were Jack and David. "I'll bet it is hard at home. It must feel like no one ever sees what they are really like when you're alone with them; especially since they are pretty well behaved here," I said. Lisa nodded vigorously. I added, "It's like when you take your car to the mechanic and just then your car stops making the noise it made before. It sometimes feels like the mechanic thinks you're crazy." Lisa began to laugh, but there was still a visible tension. I decided to move forward and discuss the schedule change from the week before. "Again, I'm so sorry that there was confusion about last week's schedule. I know it must have been hard for you to get here only to find out I wasn't here." Lisa replied, "We were disappointed. The boys really look forward to coming to see you." I wondered how much Lisa had been anticipating sessions for herself, as well.

Eventually, we carried on with the Star Wars story, again using light sabers and special potions to freeze and unfreeze Luke and Han Solo. My anxiety kicked in again; there would be only one more session after this, and it did not seem as though much had been resolved. I was tempted to direct the play a bit more, but neither Jack nor David was able to even stick with the play for more than a minute before becoming distracted or disruptive. I was not sure that simply allowing them a place to play was enough. At the end of the session, I reminded them all again that the next session would be our last and that we would be saying good-bye next week.

At the tenth and final session, I was deeply disappointed to learn that the office and its toys that I typically used were unavailable. I worried about how the boys might react in an environment different from the one they had come to know. Would they be able to carry out their play with different toys?

There was some initial confusion when the boys arrived, but I was amazed at how well they adapted. We explored the room together and found some connector blocks that we used to create light sabers. Soon the Star Wars story was being told but with some remarkable changes. I was struck by the role that light played again in this session. When David first went to the light switch, my initial reaction was to stop him. Then I recalled my discussions in group supervision about how David might be using the darkness to demonstrate how things were when Mommy and Daddy fought.

However, I doubted that Lisa or Jack could tolerate being in total darkness. Fortunately, there was a small lamp in the corner. I turned it on and said, "David, you can turn the big light on and off, but we'll need to keep this little one on the whole time." He readily complied and began explaining the new rules for our game.

David stated, "When it's dark, that's when Luke has the special powers, and that's when you [pointing at me, Darth Vader] can't move." I played along, pretending to come after him when the lights were on and then "freezing" when he turned the lights off. I continued my monologue of feeling scared and lonely while the lights were off. After carefully watching me as I spoke, David would eventually turn the lights on and become still. During one of his moments of stillness, he remarked, "I'm blind. I need help! I can't see!" At that point, I directed Lisa, in her role as Princess Leah, to use the light saber to restore David's sight so he could turn the lights off and render me powerless again.

As I look back, I am still confused about what all the references to light, sight, and power meant. I wonder if David was trying to find some power or control for himself in the darkness, hence his pronouncement that I (as the bad guy) was powerless in the dark. But when the lights were on, he repeatedly declared himself blind and therefore in the dark again, needing assistance from his mother. Was he giving his mother another opportunity to protect him in a way that Lisa had been unable to do when being beaten by her husband? I hope this was the case.

Meanwhile, I was feeling torn as I watched Jack move around the room. In previous sessions, he played Star Wars with us, but from time to time, would move over to the dollhouse to engage the babies in pushing and would rejoin our play when he was ready. Today, there were no babies and no dollhouse, so he seemed a bit lost. However, when he did join the Star Wars play, he seemed better able to play along with the story; he seemed to be more a part of the game instead of an outsider with his own agenda. Additionally, I was encouraged by some obvious progress in his communication skills; his language was more spontaneous than imitative, and his enunciation of words was much clearer.

Saying Good-Bye

With only about 15 minutes left, I knew it was time to start saying our good-byes. I tried to address them together, "I know you realize that this will be our last meeting. I want to say how much I will miss you all. It's hard for me to think about saying good-bye so soon." Lisa started to get teary. "David has been saying that he doesn't want to stop coming. I really wish there were some way to continue. It's been so helpful." Her tears increased. "You just don't realize how good it's been to have a place to talk to somebody. We're going to miss this so much."

At this point, I suggested we make good-bye cards for each other so that we could have something to remember each other by. David thought this was a wonderful idea and helped me find the crayons and paper. Somehow, it was determined that David's card would be from all of them and my card would be to all of them. As he and I drew, Lisa added, "You know, they play differently at home now from before. They make up games and stories; they fight less. I really think they learned that here." I said, "Does that mean that things are a little easier at home?" Lisa nodded and I told her, "I'm glad. I hope that means that this time together has been helpful." I shared with her the improvements I had observed in Jack's speech. Lisa agreed and added, "He's doing well in day care now. He really seems to have adjusted."

Lisa's comments were very helpful. Although I would have wished for many more sessions to work with them, she assured me that the brief interventions had been beneficial.

After David and I exchanged cards, Lisa and I helped the boys put the toys away, and she began putting their jackets on. David insisted on getting the connector blocks back out again to make a new light saber. Lisa and I both reminded him that it was time to go. I said, "It's so hard to say good-bye. And that makes it hard to leave." But David persisted. He handed the light saber to me and explained that it was a special device. "It makes it so that the bad guys can be good." I thanked him and accepted the wand. I walked them to the door and said good-bye for the last time.

The case is over, so there have been no further opportunities for group supervision, no chance to reflect with other seasoned professionals about what David's last gesture meant. Did it indicate that David was recognizing or struggling with the idea of his father being both a "good guy" and a "bad guy?" Or was it David developing a tool that would enable him to change his own behaviors and feelings about himself from that of "bad" to "good"?

I am grateful for the experience with this family. I learned so much. I feel privileged to have worked with them. I am indebted to the group supervision participants who guided and supported my work. I am also thankful for the training I have received in the fields of IMH and family therapy, and from the training sessions held at The Guidance Center, "Understanding and Treating Children 3–6 Years Old and Their Families."

Discussion Questions

1. In what ways do you think IMH strategies enhanced the play therapy?

2. What are other examples of nontraditional settings where IMH strategies might be helpful?

3. In session four, the therapist changes her approach. Rather than trying directly to structure sessions the way she thought they should go, she paid better attention to the story being told. Describe a session when you have had a similar experience.

4. In the seventh session, the therapist describes feeling scared when David turned the lights out. How did the therapist use her feelings to understand what David was feeling?

5. What do you think it was like for the family to come to the clinic and find that the therapist was not there? How was the therapist's response consistent with IMH beliefs?

6. How did the author pay attention to each family member's needs as she developed a relationship with this mother and each child?

Love and Loss: Infant Mental Health Intervention With a Mother With Multiple Challenges

Aldene "Scruffie" Crockett and Maureen Nelson

Summary

A 21-year-old woman with Fetal Alcohol Syndrome, a hearing impairment, and a history of severe sexual abuse is referred early in her pregnancy to a Doula Home-Based Program by her community mental health case manager. A highly skilled infant mental health (IMH) specialist is assigned to work intensively with the young woman and to work as a team with the case manager with whom the young mom has a trusting relationship of several years, collaborating with other service providers in the community as needed. Concern about this mother's ability to care for her baby is an ongoing theme, particularly in the context of state legislation mandating automatic referrals to Children's Protective Services of infants born to families with a history of previous removal of children due to abuse or neglect. The importance of the supervisory relationship is also emphasized, as the therapist describes how she shares her feelings and concerns with her supervisor and planfully considers her responses to this young woman as well as her relationships with community agencies.

Referral and Decision to Enroll

Dawn was referred to the Doula Program by her community mental health (CMH) case manager. She was 21 years old at the time and in the first trimester of pregnancy. Dawn had been a CMH client for several years and was described as having multiple issues, including hearing impairment, developmental delay, Fetal Alcohol Syndrome, and a history of severe child sexual abuse by her biological parents. She had been treated for a dissociative disorder. Dawn was adopted at age 13, and her parents' rights were terminated when she had been living with her foster/adoptive parents for 10 years.

"Doula" describes a woman who helps and supports another woman during pregnancy, birth, and the first years of her child's life. The major goal of the program is the healthy adjustment of the parent and child. All services are need-based.

Services

A Doula volunteer may provide labor and delivery support and is a mentor to a first-time parent until the child is 3 years old. An IMH specialist/social worker provides visits in the home or office. Parents as Teachers is a one-on-one child development education program for parents and their child. IMH consultation is available to professionals who work with parents and young children. Play Group provides monthly educational and fun activities for infants and parents. Doula newsletters offer information on program activities, child development, and other helpful tips. Referrals are made to community agencies. Baby baskets are composed of new, donated items for a new baby and his parents. The Giving Tree ensures new, donated items that the family needs or wants, to be given as holiday gifts. The recycled clothing bank is available to families to receive or donate needed infant care items, as well as to visit informally with staff. Emergency Needs are new supplies for families, including diapers, baby food and formula, feminine hygiene products, birth to 3 new clothes, blankets, and a benevolence fund for emergency cash.

Levels of Care

Level 1. Labor and delivery support with referrals to community agencies as appropriate. Any woman delivering at the local hospital who needs a Doula is eligible.

Level 2. All services listed, with IMH specialist visits as needed. Pregnant and/or first-time parents with a young infant are eligible.

Level 3. All services listed, with an IMH specialist in the role of the Doula instead of a volunteer. As the family stabilizes, they may move to Level 2. Pregnant and/or first-time parents with a young infant are eligible when the family is having significant issues of violence, substance abuse, transience, and/or has significant protective service involvement.

Level 4. An IMH Specialist provides home-based, 24-hour intensive intervention and all appropriate services. A parent or infant who has a diagnosable psychiatric condition is eligible if the parent agrees to a 6-month commitment to the program. Preference is given to first-time parents.

At the time of referral to the Doula Program, Dawn was living with the baby's father and had no contact with her adoptive or birth families. The case manager expressed great concern about Dawn's safety, as there had been several episodes of domestic violence. Concern was also expressed about Dawn's capacity to parent, given her multiple losses and disabilities. Furthermore, the case manager hoped that the Doula Program would support Dawn through her pregnancy and as she decided her baby's care. The Doula Clinical Supervisor believed that, given the complex dynamics of the case, Dawn would best be served by working intensely with a highly skilled IMH specialist.

The IMH specialist and CMH case manager met to further discuss the referral. It was decided that the case manager would introduce Dawn to the specialist, to explain their roles and develop an initial plan. The two workers felt it was critical that Dawn understand that she would not lose her relationship with the CMH case manager by becoming involved with the IMH specialist. The two workers would be a team and collaborate with other service providers as needed.

Beginning the Relationship

During the initial meeting, the specialist observed Dawn's positive, trusting relationship with her CMH case manager. She thought that this relationship must be preserved and any new services and relationships must augment, not supplant, the existing services. The specialist provided information about services offered through Doula. Dawn was open to involvement, stating, "I want all the help I can get to be a good mother." It was apparent that she had not yet considered releasing her baby for adoption. She wanted additional services during her pregnancy, labor and delivery, and parenting of her infant so that she could be a good mother. Her plan was to continue living with the baby's father and co-parent their child.

The specialist scheduled a home visit to begin the assessment/enrollment process. She began by asking, "How can I help you?" and listened intently as Dawn shared her worry that her family wanted to take her baby from her. She stated, "I want to keep my baby!" The specialist responded, "I know you want to keep the baby." From there, the two began to lay the groundwork for their working relationship. In that visit, Dawn appeared overwhelmed and easily confused. She had difficulty communicating, due to her hearing impairment and cognitive delay.

From the beginning, the IMH specialist was very involved in scheduling and transporting Dawn to appointments, immediately sensing that Dawn needed nurturance, protection, and advocacy before she could begin to bond with and meet the needs of her infant. The specialist was thankful to have several months to build a trusting, positive relationship with Dawn before the baby's birth. Many questions arose as the IMH specialist and supervisor assessed family dynamics and the complexity of the case and began to strategize clinical interventions.

Early Wondering

Answers to the following questions would enable the IMH specialist and her supervisor to assess Dawn's strengths, her capacity for parenting, and the degree of risk surrounding the infant:

- Does Dawn have the capacity to enter into and maintain a helping relationship with an IMH specialist and CMH case manager?
- Can she create a safe and nurturing environment for herself and her baby?
- Will she be able to develop a strong attachment relationship with her baby?
- To what degree will Dawn's developmental delays and impair-

ments impede her ability to parent?

- Will IMH services be able to provide for all of Dawn's needs so that she can be a "good enough" mother?
- Will Dawn have and be able to use a positive support system to sustain her beyond the intervention?
- What about the father of the baby? Can he be a "good enough" support for the mother and child?

Relationship Intensifies

As the pregnancy progressed, the IMH specialist made herself readily available to Dawn by keeping weekly appointments and being available to her by phone. The specialist encouraged Dawn to discuss her own infancy, childhood, and relationships within her family. Dawn discussed the abuse by her biological parents and her mother's alcoholism. The specialist asked, "Do you remember your biological mother?" Dawn answered, "Yes, but I can't live with her because she drinks a lot, and Dad hurts me." The statements were made without emotion. Dawn was unable to express how she had felt as a child, so the specialist helped her by providing the words to express her feelings of sadness and disappointment. The specialist said, "That must have been hurtful to you." Comments such as these were made to Dawn to help her recognize that the therapist understood how the experience might have felt. It was also an attempt to learn if Dawn was capable of insight therapy.

As Dawn began to explore early experiences of parental abuse, contacts with the IMH specialist increased to two to three times per week, with almost daily phone contact. The specialist was very attentive to the young woman's emotional state. She spent a lot of time coordinating services with other providers and made a referral for services at the health department. The nurse from the health department became an integral team player with the specialist and CMH case manager.

The specialist found herself in the role of "interpreter" of information from other service providers, so that Dawn, who is hearing impaired, could hear and understand the instructions. The specialist became quite adept at learning how to communicate important information by getting eye contact, speaking clearly, giving only essential information, and reinforcing what Dawn most needed to hear. Dawn soon learned to use this help and would often ask the IMH specialist, "What's he talking about?" For example, when Dawn was preregistering at the hospital before the delivery of her first child, the nurse asked if she wanted an epidural for pain. Dawn turned to the specialist and asked, "What does that mean?" The specialist always waited until Dawn cued her that she needed help.

Whenever Dawn was able to negotiate on her own, the specialist did not interfere. The IMH specialist became a very good observer of her cues—the furrowed brow, the turning of her head toward the specialist, or a questioning look on her face each was a sign that Dawn was asking for help.

Dawn was also able to use the specialist as a resource for concrete assistance. The specialist took her grocery shopping and helped develop a budget within her limited income. With the presence of the specialist, Dawn was able to organize plans for the baby. Together, they gathered maternity and baby items and shared Dawn's excitement about planning for her baby. Dawn showed, in many ways, that she trusted the specialist, and the specialist showed, in many ways, how important Dawn was to her. Dawn asked the specialist to be her labor and delivery coach, and she agreed!

Building a Support System

During the summer, when Dawn was in her second trimester, it became increasingly apparent that she was unable to manage her life independently. The relationship with the baby's father became more violent. He was verbally and physically abusive and, eventually, incarcerated due to his abuse of her and his destruction of government property. Dawn was virtually alone, having abandoned her friends and family for her boyfriend. She was desperate to establish a support system but did not know how. She continued to suffer from nausea and was hospitalized several times for dehydration. Because her environment was so unstable, Dawn could not monitor her diet or prescribed medication. She found it difficult to take her medication in a routine manner and was becoming more emotionally needy. For example, Dawn repeatedly missed the first daily dose of antinausea medication by sleeping too late. She was then nauseated and unable to keep anything down the rest of the day.

It was a worrisome time for Dawn and all of the professionals working with her. After several runs to the hospital and doctor's office for illness and noncompliance-related problems, Dawn, together with her support team, made the decision to move into an adult foster care facility. The CMH case manager described the foster home as a temporary placement. "The foster care mother will help you remember to take your medication. They will have meals prepared for you. There are other people around so you won't be alone at night." The IMH specialist added, "I'll continue to come to the residence and see you and take you to your appointments." Dawn agreed, and the move to a more structured, nurturing environment helped to quickly stabilize the pregnancy-related issues.

Dawn requested that the specialist arrange and supervise a visit with her adoptive parents. Her parents were mobilized to act as supports during this chaotic time in their daughter's life. They were eager to be a part of the expected grandchild's life. When Dawn became helpless, many people rallied around her. Her parents and the foster care director assumed the roles of protector and rescuer. At times, they made conflicting demands on this already overloaded young woman. For example, the adult foster care worker took Dawn shopping to buy baby clothes. The adoptive mother was disappointed because she wanted to be the one to take Dawn shopping. Dawn discovered that, despite the conflicts, her needs were often met when these caregivers were concerned with her infant's well-being. There continued to be a shared concern about the baby's safety and well-being.

Toward the end of her pregnancy, Dawn began to demonstrate the classic "repetition of past in the present." She had repeated "accidents" and falls down the stairs. The specialist wondered what Dawn was trying to tell her about herself and her baby. Interesting enough, these were the same sort of incidents that reportedly happened when her biological mother was in the last trimester of her pregnancy with Dawn. (This family history was shared by the adoptive mother, who explained that these falls were the result of severe alcoholism and, eventually, caused her biological mother to deliver Dawn prematurely).

As the pregnancy progressed, Dawn became hypersensitive to pain and repeatedly curled into a fetal position when she experienced physical discomfort. Her entire body began closing down and tightening up at the time most women open up and get ready for the birth of the baby. Again, the specialist wondered about Dawn's growing ambivalence about the birth.

To address growing concerns about Dawn's emotional readiness and the increasing risk of premature delivery, the IMH specialist arranged a case conference for the service providers and Dawn. Dawn was encouraged to express her concerns, feelings, and needs. She was asked, "What can each of us do to help you prepare for the birth of your baby?" This allowed her to see that the providers were working together as a team to support her. Dawn received positive feedback about her ability to grow a healthy, strong baby by taking care of herself and keeping the baby safe. Thus, she felt more in control as she and the providers defined their roles for the expected birth.

The Baby's Story

In December, Dawn delivered a full-term, 6 pound, 5 ounce baby boy. She had a difficult labor and was unable to tolerate the pain and "touching" by hospital staff and her adoptive mother. The baby was delivered by emergency cesarean section due to a significant drop in the baby's heart rate. It was later discovered that his umbilical cord was wrapped around his neck. The specialist was present and helped Dawn focus and maintain control during delivery. As Dawn became increasingly anxious, the specialist leaned over so that Dawn could see and hear her and spoke in a calm voice, "Dawn, look into my face. Do not look into the faces of the others. They need to get the baby out quickly. Concentrate on my face and breathe." The specialist did not use technical, medical language but worded the physician's instructions in simple, short phrases that Dawn could understand. The young woman understood and became calmer and more compliant. She obviously trusted the specialist, who was the only person in the room who explained what was going to happen so that Dawn could understand.

The Relationship Begins

Dawn seemed proud of her son, Seth, and quickly focused her attention on him. She snuggled and nuzzled him to her breast as she looked at him adoringly. The baby nursed eagerly while Dawn appeared unconcerned about her own pain and discomfort.

At the hospital, the specialist observed Dawn comforting and stimulating Seth and reading his cues. In those early weeks, the specialist observed Dawn talking to the baby and explaining what she was going to do, without coaching from the specialist. "It's okay. Mama's coming—I'll be right there. I know you're hungry." This made the specialist surmise that Dawn, herself, had received loving care or had a positive role model early in her life. The bonding and attachment between mother and baby appeared healthy and positive. Dawn continued to view her personal and professional supports as helpful and nonthreatening. She was comfortable asking questions and followed through when feedback was given.

Following delivery, Dawn and Seth lived in their own apartment at the adult foster care home. Then, when Seth was 2 months old, Dawn began to resent the foster mother's control and monitoring. Dawn appeared to feel secure in her parenting and believed that independent living would give her freedom and control over her life. After much consideration, the IMH specialist, CMH case manager, and her adoptive parents helped Dawn and Seth move from the adult foster care home into a one-bedroom apartment. All of them would continue to maintain an active role in their lives, supporting and monitoring this new family.

The Relationship Intensifies

As Seth turned 4 months, Dawn began to perceive him differently. He became more assertive in making his needs known with louder crying, and Dawn felt she had less control of their relationship. She felt violated. The specialist attempted to offer developmental guidance and explain that changes in Seth's behavior were developmentally appropriate, but Dawn was unable to change her perception of her baby's behavior as "controlling." This triggered multiple issues for Dawn, and she began to talk with the specialist about how difficult breastfeeding was becoming. Seth grew to be more demanding, grabbing for her breasts and strongly latching on and sucking. Dawn stated, "He sees me!" She could not tolerate his gazes or his sucking. The specialist supported Dawn by letting her lactation nurse know how difficult breastfeeding had become. The nurse explained how Dawn could wean Seth from breast to bottle.

As the months went by and Seth became more independent, mobile, and curious, his care became more complicated. As Dawn struggled to parent him, her disabilities made it increasingly difficult to care for her young son. She was easily distracted by friends and visitors and had a difficult time keeping the cluttered apartment safe for Seth. Service providers and adoptive family members became increasingly concerned about Seth's safety and well-being in his mother's care. Dawn invited perceived "friends" to live with her to help with her son's care in exchange for room and board. Dawn found comfort in helping others by providing food and shelter. However, these friends took advantage of Dawn, and Seth's care deteriorated. His feeding schedule was sporadic, his environment was unsafe, and his maleness became threatening. The specialist observed that Dawn was again helpless, overwhelmed by Seth's neediness for her. Her friends assumed more and more responsibility, as Dawn became more neglectful and less protective and loving of Seth. She spent more time away from her baby and encouraged her friends to feed him. She was rarely the person who put Seth to bed. Although a troublesome routine, the multiple caregivers kept Seth safe from his mother, who now viewed him as a threat.

Dawn struggled for acceptance as a competent parent. She wanted to please her parents and agreed to a tubal ligation. Her parents continued to be attentive to Seth, but they started to withdraw emotionally from Dawn. During this time, Dawn also began to emotionally withdraw from the IMH specialist. For the first time in their relationship, there were many "no shows" for scheduled appointments. The specialist worried about the well-being of this vulnerable young woman as well as her ability to provide adequate infant care.

A Fight for Custody

When Seth was 6 months old, CPS received an allegation that his health and safety were in jeopardy. A CPS worker made a home visit. Abuse and neglect were not substantiated, so a referral was made to Prevention Services at the Family Independence Agency. Dawn, however, believed that this was the beginning of a plan to take Seth from her. Within 2 weeks, she moved to Seth's paternal grandmother's home in Texas for rescue and support. Dawn believed that she would receive much positive support and wealth. Instead, she found hardship in an environment she did not understand. Dawn was unable to find supportive services to assist her in caring for herself and her son. At about 16 months, Seth was reported to CPS, removed from his mother's care, and placed in foster care. Both sets of grandparents fought for custody, and eventually Seth's adoptive maternal grandparents were appointed temporary conservators. They were given custodial care and allowed to bring Seth back to Michigan. Dawn's parental rights were not terminated; she was assured visitation.

Ten months had passed since Dawn left Michigan. When she returned and contacted both her IMH specialist and CMH case manager, she was very confused. In the first phone conversation with the specialist following her return from Texas, Dawn explained that her son had been taken away and she was pregnant for a second time! She was very confused about all that was happening and questioned, "How can I be pregnant? I was fixed, remember?" She also stated that she had no idea who the baby's father was. The specialist assured Dawn that she did remember the surgery, as they were working together at that time.

The specialist, in shock herself, quickly sought out her supervisor. Dawn contacted the other service providers, including the CMH case manager and the health department nurse, who had offered positive support during her first pregnancy. She and her original team reassembled.

Wondering as Dawn Returns

Together, they wondered what Dawn and Seth had experienced in Texas, and many concerns came to mind:

- What about the baby? How long has it been since she has seen him?

- What happened to them both in Texas?
- What is the nature of her current relationship with her parents?
- Who and where are Dawn's supports now?
- Will Dawn be able to parent a new baby?
- If this is a little girl, will it make a difference?
- Will visitation with Seth continue?
- Will CPS allow Dawn to parent this new child?
- How will the team develop a plan to answer these questions and will they work again with Dawn?

Resuming the Relationship

Dawn had not seen her son or adoptive parents in the 4 months since she returned to Michigan. She attempted to contact her parents but they did not return her phone calls. Dawn asked the specialist to help her understand the allegations against her and gave permission for the specialist to contact her lawyer. The specialist explained the charges to Dawn, who responded, "I did not neglect my son!" The specialist asked Dawn to help her understand what had happened to her in Texas. She asked, "Who did you live with? Where did you live? How did you support yourself and Seth? Were the baby's paternal grandparents a support?" The story that unfolded was very sad. Seth's grandmother was alcoholic, mentally abusive, and controlling. Dawn stayed with her only a short time and then moved from place to place and was on assistance. She left Seth with multiple caregivers and it was during this time that CPS got involved. Seth was placed in temporary foster care and then returned to his mother for a brief time, but soon returned to foster care. Dawn's life greatly disintegrated after losing Seth. She began abusing alcohol, was raped, and found herself pregnant—again, without knowing the father.

Dawn connected with old friends when she returned to Michigan and selected a partner who she believed would help with the expected baby. Ken, the new partner, had learning disabilities, a history of child abuse, and had lost custody of his own son due to neglect. Ken told the IMH specialist, "I don't trust agency people." Dawn assured him that the Doula Program was different, that the staff was helpful and could be trusted.

Immediately, the specialist was concerned about Ken's capacity to positively support Dawn and worried about his history and lack of ambition. She knew that without a strong support system, this young woman would be unable to provide a safe and nurturing environment for her infant. Although Ken stated that he was committed to an ongoing partnership with Dawn and wanted to help raise the baby, his behavior did not demonstrate this. He did not work and seemed very comfortable being supported by Dawn's meager social security benefits. The couple moved from the home of one friend to another and utilized food pantries and clothing banks.

The specialist discussed with Dawn and Ken the preparations needed for this baby. They needed stable housing, a steady income, and a positive peer support system. She was very clear that, since they had both lost custody of other children, CPS would watch them closely. Unless they could make significant changes, they were at risk for losing custody of this baby. They appeared to acknowledge her forewarnings.

Emotional Reunions

Not long after returning to Michigan, Dawn asked the specialist, "Will you call my parents to set up a time for me to see Seth? I really want to see him. I have tried to call them, but they do not return my calls and they have told me not to come to their house." The specialist contacted the adoptive parents to arrange visitation. They reluctantly agreed but requested that visits be supervised. Dawn was excited about the visit but worried that her son might not recognize her. The specialist tried to prepare Dawn for the reunion with her son and adoptive parents. She, too, was unsure whether Seth would remember his mother and wondered what her parents would say about Dawn's pregnancy. Dawn had called them once to tell them, but they had not seen her since she returned from Texas. She wanted the specialist to show them a copy of her recent ultrasound picture.

It was a very emotional visit! Dawn's mother was absolutely shocked to see her daughter pregnant and to see the ultrasound. She knew that her daughter had had a tubal ligation and had believed that this pregnancy was fabricated. At the visit, it was apparent that Seth did, in fact, remember his mother. He was cautious, at first, but eventually warmed up. Dawn asked many questions about how to interact with her son, and the specialist made suggestions. Toward the end of the visit, they were playing together, and Seth even snuggled up in his mother's lap. When his grandmother came to pick him up, Seth did not want to leave his mother.

After a tearful good-bye, the specialist helped Dawn discuss her feelings. Dawn was able to describe how much she missed her son, yet she acknowledged that she made the right decision by asking her parents to obtain custody of Seth. The specialist talked to Dawn about her right to have ongoing visitation and offered to provide supervision for the visits. Dawn replied, "Thank you!"

During the third trimester of pregnancy, the specialist repeatedly attempted to discuss with Dawn and Ken how their homelessness would increase the risk of losing custody of the new baby. She referred them to programs and services to assist with subsidized housing, but they consistently failed to follow through with the necessary paperwork. The specialist stated, "I know how much you want to parent this baby, but there won't even be a chance for you to try unless you have stable housing." Ken began to offer a defensive retort, but Dawn replied, "Listen to her!"

Dawn expressed concern that the state might remove her baby at the hospital. When she had gone to the women's shelter on two occasions, other residents had warned her about the "new law" (legislation that mandates automatic referrals to Children's Protective Services of infants born to families with a previous history of removal of children because of abuse or neglect). They told her that two former residents had infants removed while they were still in the hospital. Both mothers also had children previously removed. Dawn repeatedly asked the specialist, "Are they going to take my baby?"

When Dawn was about 7 months pregnant, the specialist asked Dawn, "Would you like me to call the Family Independence Agency to see if I can get information about whether they intend to take your baby?" Dawn replied, "I'm afraid to know, but I guess it is better to know than to worry for nothing. Yes, go ahead and contact them, but you have to tell me exactly what they tell you!" The specialist contacted the Family Independence Agency (FIA) to find out the status of Dawn's situation. She wanted to prepare herself, so that she could prepare the couple for the outcome. (The Doula Program and FIA have a long history of a positive, supportive relationship. Workers from the two agencies have together served and supported numerous families during the past 23 years). During this conversation, the specialist shared her concerns about the couple's ability to provide the stability and nurturance the baby would need. The FIA foster care worker (on call to screen CPS referrals) explained that the family would most likely be referred to Prevention Services for monitoring. He stated that he did not feel that the baby would be removed at birth since so many services were in place, and he agreed to pass the information on to the CPS staff.

The specialist shared this information with Dawn, who was relieved to learn that the state did not intend to remove her baby from the hospital. Dawn was delighted that she was having a girl and continued to bond with her unborn daughter. She prepared for her arrival by collecting baby items and clothing.

Dawn and Ken continued to rely on the specialist to advocate for them and to explain information. Although the specialist was very specific about what needed to be done, Ken stated that he trusted and liked this worker. Dawn appeared pleased that she did not have to choose between her supports.

The Second Baby's Story

Dawn was preparing for natural childbirth, but the baby was in a breech position. It was determined that, for the safety of mother and infant, Dawn would have to deliver again by cesarean section. Dawn's disappointment was evident by her continued question, "Why can't I deliver again?" The specialist repeated the information the doctor had given, empathizing with Dawn's loss.

Katie was born 2 weeks early. Dawn had gone into the hospital in labor, excited to be having her daughter. The medical team decided to proceed with the cesarean section. In many ways, it was a repeat of her previous birth experience. Things happened so quickly that Dawn became overwhelmed and frightened. She could not process all the confusion or make sense out of what was happening. Her hearing impairment greatly increased her confusion and anxiety. The staff was patient and explained what was happening to her, but Dawn still needed explanations from the specialist. Dawn began to slip into a helpless role as the operation came closer. She was crying and closing down just as the attendant needed her cooperation to insert the IV. The specialist held Dawn's hand, bent down, and whispered in her ear, "You can do this!"

Dawn changed; she appeared stronger. Able to converse in a normal tone with the attendant, she showed him the best place to put the IV. Dawn held the specialist's hand during the procedure, appearing in better control as she was wheeled into the delivery room.

Katie was born at 2:00 a.m. She weighed 6 pounds, 1 ounce, and was 19 inches long. When the specialist greeted Dawn after delivery and recovery, she observed Dawn snuggling her daughter to her breast, proudly showing her off, "Look at all this hair." Dawn showed much pride in her accomplishment. Katie was perfect!

Her Joy Is Short-Lived

The morning after Katie's birth, the IMH specialist received a phone call from the CPS worker who had been informed by the hospital social worker that the baby had been born. The specialist told her about Dawn's involvement with CMH and the Health Department. She provided her with names and numbers of the other service providers and encouraged her to call them as well. The

CPS worker seemed reassured that Dawn was involved in many supportive services, and indicated that one of the CPS workers would, most likely, make a visit to the hospital but again stated that she thought a referral to Prevention Services would follow. The specialist asked to be informed of the visit, so that she could accompany the CPS worker. The CPS worker agreed.

Later that day, the specialist received an emergency call from Dawn whose sobs had alerted office staff that something was wrong. She would not talk with another available worker, so the specialist was paged and called the hospital room as Dawn had requested. Dawn cried, "They're taking my baby!" She was so hysterical that the specialist could not understand what was going on. There were other voices in the background interrupting and adding to the confusion. The specialist told her that she would come to the hospital right away. When she arrived, she found a room full of distraught people. Dawn, Ken, their friends, and a nurse were discussing what had happened. A CPS worker had given Dawn a court order and would take Katie into custody the next morning. The baby would be removed from Dawn's care and transferred to the neonatal unit until the court hearing the following morning when she would be placed in foster care. Ken was furious and had reportedly intimidated the CPS worker.

This was extremely difficult for the specialist. Like the CPS worker, she shared their very serious concerns about Dawn's ability to parent a new baby, yet she had wanted to prepare Dawn should removal occur. The information the IMH specialist provided to the FIA foster care worker had not been passed on to the CPS workers before Katie's birth. Although in shock herself, the specialist found the strength to control her own emotions and offer support to Dawn and her friends. She encouraged all of them to tell their story. They repeated it several times until they felt a little more in control. Dawn clung to Katie as she nursed her and sobbed throughout the visit. The specialist gently reminded her that they had talked about the possibility of removal but, at this moment, she was as shocked as they were. She briefly explained the Binsfeld legislation and how it might apply to Dawn's situation. The specialist told Dawn that she would meet her in court the following day.

The nurse followed the specialist out of the room and tearfully stated, "It is easy for Toni and Jane (the hospital social workers) to make the decision to take the baby. But I am left with the family and friends. It is hard to see the pain. Sometimes babies don't fuss when they leave their moms. This baby does." The specialist offered support to yet another distraught person and empathized that her job was very hard. She explained, "The decision is difficult for

everyone. Dawn is doing well now with the baby and there is promise of a relationship between this mother and her baby girl. But
Dawn has many issues to work on."

A Parallel Process

The specialist was stunned and felt a range of emotions, including
anger, sadness, loss, helplessness, and betrayal by the CPS workers.
She was not ready for Katie's removal and, therefore, had been
unable to prepare Dawn. It was very difficult to feel so unprepared
to support a client she had come to be so fond of. She needed to
share her feelings with someone she trusted, so she immediately
called her supervisor. The IMH specialist repeatedly processed the
anger and frustration she felt for being unable to prepare Dawn. For
more than 2 hours, the supervisor listened to the story and offered
support, understanding, and permission to say whatever she wanted. The supervisor did for the specialist exactly the same thing that
the specialist had done for Dawn. She "held" the specialist's feelings
while she put her own feelings on hold, even though she too felt the
same range of emotions as the specialist. Together, they were able to
work through and process the current crisis. It was important for
the specialist to have the emotional energy to assist Dawn during
this most stressful time. Dawn would need her support at the court-
house the next day, and the specialist would need her supervisor as
a support to them both; the supervisor would attend the hearing
with the specialist.

The Court Hearing

Before the hearing, the specialist went to Dawn's hospital room,
where she found Dawn alone with her baby. The specialist
explained that she was sorry for what had happened and for the
pain Dawn was feeling. To help ready Dawn for the hearing, the
specialist explained the court process and what to expect. Dawn
continued to show much pride in Katie and offered the specialist a
chance to hold her. Dawn was tearful as they talked about how
wonderful "her" Katie was.

Dawn left the hospital despite running a temperature; she would
not miss the court hearing. Ken, her friends, the CMH case manager, the specialist, and the supervisor supported her. The hearing,
very difficult for Dawn, brought back memories of losing her son.
Dawn was cooperative and when asked questions she did not
understand, Dawn turned to the specialist to have them explained.
She was given a court-appointed lawyer and another court date. She
was introduced to the intake worker from the Foster Care Agency
and given a number to call to arrange visitation. Following the hear-

ing, Dawn was tired and emotionally drained from the ordeal. She returned to her home to sleep for the rest of the day.

Later that day, the Doula staff, FIA foster care worker, and the CPS worker met to discuss what had happened. The FIA staff made it very clear that they believed Dawn did not have the capacity to parent and that, eventually, parental rights would be terminated. They also stated that the baby would not be returned as long as Dawn and Ken remained together as a couple. Although each professional felt sad about Dawn's loss, they all felt great relief in knowing that this worrisome issue would be resolved; Katie would be taken care of.

Resolution Between Doula and FIA

During a conversation with the specialist prior to the hearing, the FIA supervisor apologized for not advising her about what would happen once a decision was made. He explained that the CPS worker heard that Dawn had talked about moving to another state, and they were afraid she would run with this baby as she had run previously. Additionally, FIA had information about Ken and the circumstances surrounding the termination of his rights with his son, as well as a recent charge of fourth-degree criminal sexual conduct.

The specialist responded, "I understand the reasons that you decided to remove the baby. I, also, have great concerns about whether Dawn can parent once the baby becomes mobile. However, I am very upset that I was not told about the decision to remove the baby when I inquired several times during the pregnancy and after delivery. Because I was not prepared for the removal, I was unable to provide emotional support to Dawn when she needed me to do so. I know you have a difficult job, but I can be helpful to you. I can help prepare and support parents if I know what is going on, just as I have done on many other occasions."

Later that day, the two supervisors openly and thoroughly discussed the situation. They discussed strategies so that staff from both agencies could work more effectively to support families during very difficult times.

The Work Continues

The specialist, as well as the other service providers, continued to work with this young mother. Dawn visited the baby for 1 hour, twice a week, with the specialist participating to support their visits. Positive interactions were observed as Dawn cuddled Katie and made positive comments while holding and changing her. Dawn showed concern when Katie came to a visit dressed inappropriately for the weather. She also met one-on-one during visitation with a Parent Educator from the Parents as Teachers program.

Although Dawn broke up with Ken after the baby was removed, it soon appeared that they were seeing each other again. Dawn continued to move from place to place. The foster care worker stated that the goal was reunification, and that if Dawn met the conditions of the Parent/Agency Agreement, Katie would be returned to her. However, the specialist also remembered the conversation with the FIA worker when he stated that termination of parental rights was the goal.

Final Thoughts About This Family

It was apparent to the IMH specialist, from the beginning, that she would probably not be able to help Dawn solve all of her problems. Although she felt a great deal of respect and admiration for this young woman for her kindness, courage, and survival skills, she doubted whether Dawn would be able to regain custody of her daughter once she had been removed. She did not think that Dawn had the capacity to negotiate the complicated legal system and to comply with the conditions of the Parent/Agency Agreement. Dawn and the specialist discussed this as Dawn began emotionally to withdraw from Katie. Dawn was tearful but recognized the probable outcome. She asked the specialist, "Will I still be able to see you if I release my baby?" The specialist replied, "I will be able to work with you for a while longer to help you through this time. And even when you do not have an open case, you can still call when you are in town, or you can write me and I will write back. I will always care about you."

Final Thoughts About Termination

The practice at Doula may be somewhat different from other agencies in regard to termination. The clinical staff learned (and continue to learn) much from the dedicated Volunteer Doula Parent-Aides. Doulas found that after young mothers were officially "discharged" from the program, they still needed to continue the relationship on a much less intense basis. As the years went by and the children grew up, Doulas received calls about the good and bad things that happened. Often it was to report the accomplishment of a long-term goal that a young woman and her Doula had identified many years before. Sometimes it was to discuss a problem and ask for suggestions about available resources. The same kind of "after-care" has proven to be effective with the clinical staff and their clients. No one has ever abused this open-door policy. It provides the staff with the rest of the story and provides the parent the opportunity to see that their specialist really does not forget about them.

Discussion Questions

1. There were extensive risk factors for this mom and her unborn child. What were these risks? Why do you think the Doula Program accepted this referral? Where does the hopefulness lie?

2. Describe the capacities of both the IMH specialist and Dawn that helped them develop their very strong therapeutic alliance.

3. What do you think the role of the IMH specialist should be when there are very serious concerns about a parent's capacity to care for and nurture her young child?

4. At what point do you decide that a parent can no longer provide adequately for her child?

5. As you worked your way through this case, what were your emotions? How do your emotions help you understand this case?

6. How do you balance the right of a child for permanent family relationships with the parent's right to rear a child? How long can a baby wait?

7. What are important therapeutic considerations for termination? Discuss ways to help clients with this phase of treatment.

Becoming Whole: Combining Infant Mental Health and Occupational Therapy on Behalf of a Toddler With Sensory Integration Difficulties and His Family

Julie Ribaudo and Sandra Glovak

Summary

After coping alone for almost 2 years with their second child's severe sleeping problems, feeding difficulties, and emerging behavioral problems, a couple contacts the state early intervention program, on the advice of their pediatrician. An infant mental health (IMH) specialist and an occupational therapist begin to work collaboratively with the toddler and his family, identifying and addressing the child's sensory integration challenges and the effects of those difficulties on his family. The case study describes in detail an integrated assessment, planning, and intervention process that focuses on the family's concerns and offers information, specific treatment for the child's hypersensitivity and other sensory integration difficulties, and emotional support to the parents. An understanding of what the baby brought to this relationship was crucial in developing a treatment plan that effectively alleviated the distress of the toddler and his family.

The Early Months

Jacob, a healthy, handsome, 22-month-old boy, was a much anticipated addition to the Williams family, which included 4-year-old Liam and his parents, Rebecca and Jonathon Williams. Liam had been such an easy baby that making the decision to have a second child was not difficult, but, from the beginning, everything about this baby was different. Jacob demanded to be held constantly, and everyone had to be quiet when he napped. Because Jacob awoke at the slightest sound, Liam could not talk and play with his mother without disturbing his little brother. The considerable amount of time Jacob took from Liam forced the older child to be more independent than a 4-year-old should be, all of which saddened their mother. Jacob could not fall asleep unless rocked, which often took up to an hour. He woke repeatedly during the night and needed his parents' help to fall back to sleep. The pediatrician, Dr. Ledford, had assured Mrs. Williams that the way to help Jacob sleep was to put him in his crib awake and let him fall asleep by himself. Although Jacob might cry at first, she could go to him periodically to reassure him and then leave. The doctor told her that children often settled into a better sleep pattern within a few days, but, since Jacob had been rocked to fall asleep for so long, it might take up to 2 weeks. Mrs. Williams was assured that crying for prolonged periods would not cause Jacob any long-term trauma; by following this method, Jacob would be better able to regulate his sleep patterns and settle himself at night. Greatly relieved, Mrs. Williams decided to follow Dr. Ledford's directions exactly, with the expectation that Jacob would sleep through the night. If she could only get some sleep, she felt hopeful that she would be better able to face the demands of caring for Jacob during the day.

No Easy Answers

For 3 days, Mrs. Williams followed the prescribed method, but Jacob got worse. His sleeping patterns had not changed, and he had begun to cling during the day; he would not let Mrs. Williams out of his sight. In frustration, Mrs. Williams gave up and resumed her old pattern of comforting Jacob three or four times a night. Her husband would relieve her on weekends, but the lack of sleep was wearing on both of them. After a few months, more problems developed. Jacob could not handle textured foods, sometimes gagging at the mere sight of anything with lumps. Worried that Jacob was losing weight, Mrs. Williams made another appointment with the pediatrician, who assured her that Jacob's weight and height were close to the 50th percentile. Dr. Ledford listened carefully to Mrs. Williams' concerns regarding Jacob's temper tantrums, sleep problems, and feeding issues. Although he was not concerned about Jacob's growth and development, he did recognize that Jacob had difficulty with self-regulation. He suggested that Mrs. Williams call Early On, Michigan's early intervention system, to help her deal with Jacob's problems.

The First Call

The next day, as soon as Jacob had fallen asleep for his afternoon nap, Mrs. Williams called Early On. The Early On parent specialist who took the call heard the concern in the mother's voice. Mrs. Williams said that Jacob was not a happy baby. "He cries all the time. He flies into temper tantrums for no apparent reason, and some last for 20 to 30 minutes." As she talked, the parent specialist listened quietly, asking an occasional question but, more importantly, letting Mrs. Williams know that her worries would be heard and addressed. When the parent specialist told Mrs. Williams that she had talked to other parents with similar problems, she could hear relief in Mrs. Williams' voice. The parent specialist offered to have an IMH specialist call Mrs. Williams to schedule an appointment to discuss her child's behavior. Although Mrs. Williams was initially hesitant, the parent specialist assured her that the home visitor would be able to help Mrs. Williams with Jacob.

Beginning the Relationship

When I called Mrs. Williams to set up an appointment, I initially had difficulty hearing her over Jacob's screams and Liam's pleas for attention. She was clearly having a difficult moment, so I offered to call back at another time. She broke into tears saying, "That would be better," but stayed on the telephone. After a moment, when Mrs. Williams calmed down, she said she wanted to set a date for an appointment as soon as possible. Jacob quieted, and I could hear Mrs. Williams gathering her children for an instant to talk to them in a soft voice. She went on to say that it was becoming increasingly hard to find foods that Jacob would eat, and, although her husband understood that Jacob was sensitive, her in-laws accused them of spoiling Jacob. Mrs. Williams choked up again, admitting that all of this made it hard to feel close to Jacob.

Jacob's sleep problems were very frustrating. "I can't get anything done around the house. As soon as I start to cook or clean, Jacob wakes up. He sleeps so lightly I can't check on him because the sound of the clasp clicking in the door wakes him." She felt trapped in the house because Jacob loses control even more easily at restaurants, stores, or social gatherings at church. Mrs. Williams was grateful to have someone to talk to who didn't think that her problems with Jacob were unimportant. We decided on a late afternoon appointment so that Mr. Williams could join us after work. I told Mrs. Williams that I looked forward to our visit.

Preparing for the First Visit

As I drove to the first appointment, I wondered if I would be able to understand the difficulties of this little boy and his family. It would take time to tease out the many strands that had led to this moment. I knew I had to be careful not to make too many suggestions or comments but, instead, to listen and watch carefully. Although I have been making home visits for years, the first meeting always holds a sense of anxiety as well as hope and anticipation.

It helps to remember times when I felt uncertain in meeting a new doctor or "specialist," wondering what they would find, think, or say. This understanding has helped me empathize with a family in a first meeting. I have heard many stories of frantic moments spent cleaning the house, worrying about being judged, and wondering who this stranger would be, stories that have left me in awe of the ability of families to let me in the door and into their lives.

When Strangers Meet

Mrs. Williams answered the door, smiling shyly. Liam came running up and greeted me with an exuberant, "I'm Liam!" I greeted each member of the family, "Hi, I'm Julie Ribaudo," allowing them to choose how they wanted to address me. I asked Mrs. Williams what she would like to be called, and she said, "Rebecca is fine." Jacob hid behind his mother's leg, holding tight to her pants. He looked at me warily and then reached up for his mother, saying "Up." We all settled in the family room, and Rebecca put Jacob down. He immediately fussed, saying, "No! Me up, me up!" and climbed back in her lap. Rebecca sighed, saying, "You're not ready yet, eh?" She explained that it took Jacob a long time to warm up to new people and new situations. "I was shy when I was little. I was hoping my children wouldn't be that way." She got a faraway look and mumbled that it had been hard to be shy, but stopped short, as if to say, "That's not why you are here." Wanting her to know that her thoughts, feelings, and memories would be important to me, I replied, "It's hard when we see our children face some of the same struggles we did. You want to protect him from that." Rebecca agreed, saying how she was relieved that Liam is so outgoing. Liam, playing with a puzzle, looked up at his mother before going back to his work.

Learning About Jacob

Jacob sat in Rebecca's lap, with his hand on her chin, rubbing it gently. I said to Jacob, "You look so comfy on your mommy's lap," and then asked Rebecca, "Is that one of the ways he soothes himself?" Rebecca nodded, looking chagrined. They had tried very hard to find a blanket or other item that he would use, but he never seemed to find them soothing. Rebecca thought that the fact that Jacob was a nursing toddler might have something to do with it, but added that Liam had nursed and also had a favorite blanket that he still slept with now. I replied, "Liam and Jacob have been so different from each other. That isn't quite what you had expected, is it?" Rebecca shook her head, half-laughing, but in a pained way. I asked if there were other things that had been different from expected.

Rebecca teared up and explained how even the pregnancy was different. Liam had been delivered at full term after a happy, healthy pregnancy. With Jacob, she felt fine for the first two trimesters, but she was suddenly confined to bed rest at 28 weeks to keep her from early delivery. I reflected how scary and hard that must have been. Rebecca agreed, stroking Jacob's hair. He looked at her, smiled a little, and climbed off her lap, then pulled a pillow off the floor to lie on. He lay there for a while, twirling his hair, as I wondered when, and if, he would begin to play with some toys. I asked Rebecca what Jacob liked to play with. She replied that he really didn't focus much on toys unless someone was playing with him. He liked games such as peek-a-boo but seemed uninterested in toys, themselves. She had tried various ways to encourage his interest, but it was hard to figure out what he enjoyed. He didn't like having dirty hands; anything that was slimy or sticky upset him. Rebecca felt guilty because she was so tired during the day that she often didn't feel like playing with him. Still, she enjoyed the interest he was taking in the world. He liked listening to stories and having her name things around the house. I acknowledged how enjoyable the "labeling" phase could be, yet also reflected to Rebecca how hard all of this had been, how tired she spoke of being, and how hard they were working to understand Jacob.

As I listened to Rebecca, I instinctively focused on understanding what Jacob brought to the relationship instead of focusing solely on the present difficulties between them. I knew it would take time to understand how his parents' interpretations of his behavior had affected their relationships, but I also thought that Jacob was telling us something about the way the world felt to him.

I decided to pursue questioning that would help me understand how Jacob was taking in and responding to the world. When asked if she had noticed other things that upset Jacob, Rebecca rattled off a long list: loud noises, being in the car, being swung or moved too fast, diaper changes, getting his face washed, the sun in his eyes, big group gatherings, even the breeze of the church fan. "Should I keep going?" she asked; I nodded. She described how certain clothes seemed to bother Jacob. He often tried to take off his socks. He was getting fussier about what she could dress him in, and mornings were becoming a nightmare.

Jacob Shows Us

As she talked, Mr. Williams came in. After greeting the boys, who eagerly called out and went to him, he sat down to join the discussion. His wife told him what we had been talking about. Jacob climbed in his lap and sat contentedly. When asked to add to the list of things that upset Jacob, Mr. Williams (who asked to be called Jonathon) added that one of the things he missed was being able to roughhouse with Jacob, who seemed to hate to be swung in the air or tossed, something Liam had enjoyed. Jonathon quickly added that he didn't think that it meant there was a problem. He just thought that Jacob was a bit sensitive.

"What is that like that for you?" I asked, wondering for a split second if I had asked too much, too soon. I wanted to know a bit about what Jacob's behavior meant to his parents. Did they feel rejected by him? Did they think he was being intentionally oppositional? Jonathon noted that he had not been much of a roughhouse kind of kid either, but that he had enjoyed that type of play with Liam. Trying to figure out what Jacob liked was more of a challenge. At that point, Liam came by his father, bumping up against Jacob, who struck out at Liam yelling, "No!" Rebecca offered to look at what Liam wanted to show his dad, but he wanted to show it to him. As Jonathon tried to look at a Lego tower Liam had built, Jacob quickly escalated. I noticed that he kept trying to push Liam away as if he suddenly felt crowded, in addition to not wanting to share his dad's attention.

I stayed quiet, wanting to see how the parents intervened and how they normally helped Jacob and Liam negotiate. Jonathon gently asked Liam to come to his other side, all the while rubbing Jacob's back. I noticed how carefully Jonathon tried to meet the needs of both children. As the situation calmed down, I asked, "How does Jacob usually react when other children come close to him?" They paused a moment, as if they hadn't ever really thought about it. Then Jonathon said, "When we take Jacob to playgrounds, he often hangs back. By the time he is ready to play, it's time to go." I asked, "What have you said to yourself about that? What do you make of it?" Both parents thought he was just shy and had difficulty warming up. Rebecca noted that she had noticed that there were times when he might get warmed up, but, when other kids came around, he would have a "meltdown." She figured he was just worried about sharing. Jonathon added that Jacob really seemed to have tantrums when it was time to leave places, even if he had been upset by the place initially.

Addressing Presenting Concerns

Our first visit would be ending soon, so I turned the Williams' attention to giving me a better description of the sleep and eating problems described in the first call. I wanted to make sure that I addressed their presenting concerns, not just those I was curious about. Rebecca noted that Jacob was taking longer and longer to fall asleep. "He has to have everything in a particular order: saying goodnight around the house, two stories, rocking, and then nursing. I usually end up rocking with him for up to an hour before he drifts off. If I try to put him in his crib before he is sound asleep, he wakes up almost immediately, and I have to start the whole thing over again." They were especially perplexed because Liam had been such a good sleeper. Jonathon noted sheepishly that they had thought friends who had their children sleep with them in order to get sleep were just "wimps," and that they had created sleep problems somehow. That, however, was before Jacob.

Now they better understood the desperate need for sleep and were less likely to judge parents who were having trouble getting their children to sleep. To help address their underlying worries about their capacities as parents, I asked what they had done with Liam. Rebecca replied he had slept easily—and through the night—by the time he was 6 months old. They had rocked and nursed him as well, but he seemed to stay asleep more easily; when he did wake during the night, he fussed only briefly before settling himself back down. The Williams said that, from the start, Jacob was different, that he needed the house to be absolutely quiet to sleep and that the slightest noises seemed to wake him. He never liked to be in his crib, either, which was also different from Liam. They discussed how doing the same things they did with Liam, such as letting him fuss for a bit, only seemed to make the problem worse with Jacob. Letting Jacob fuss during the night only seemed to work him up, and he was unable to settle himself back down. After a few weeks of trying when he was about 6 months old, they realized that the longer he fussed the more likely he would to go into a full-blown cry. The longer that went on, the harder he was to calm down. While the family's stress level, marital dynamics, or any number of other factors may have been different when Liam was born, leading to different parenting abilities, I began to see that these parents were able to respond to the differing needs of their children. I wondered what Jacob's physiological system brought to the family.

Before the Williams could talk about the eating problems, the boys' behavior told me it was time to end the session. Liam was bringing over every toy to show his parents, and Jacob alternated between crying and nursing, not quite sure of what he wanted. I shared a story of an 18-month-old once taking me by the finger, leading me to the door and saying, "Bye-bye," hoping to highlight and normalize that even young children can tell us their needs and that it is okay to listen to them. I acknowledged to the boys how hard it was to share their parents' attention and how appreciative I was, letting them know, "I'm only going to take your parents' attention a few more minutes." Liam smiled and brought a dinosaur over to me. I said to Jonathon and Rebecca, "I know you have not discussed all of your concerns. Would it be helpful to set a second appointment?" I added that I had heard their concerns and knew how hard they were working to understand Jacob. Saying, "I know how hard it can be to ask for help," I told them I was glad that they had called.

I offered reflections on what I thought I had heard. Jacob seemed to be easily overstimulated and overwhelmed. Sounds, lights, movement, and touch all seemed to cause varying degrees of difficulty for him. Jonathon and Rebecca nodded, and Jonathon added, "I never really thought about all of those things being connected." Rebecca asked, "What causes that and what can we do?" I suggested that we meet again to watch more carefully how Jacob played and how he took in the world. I offered to help them look at several areas of Jacob's development, so that we would be sure we weren't missing other factors that might be making things difficult for him. I explained and showed them a copy of the Infant Toddler Developmental Assessment (IDA) (Provence, Erikson, Vater, & Palmeri, 1995), a tool used to gain an idea of a child's overall development. I assured them that Jacob was developing well and using a lot of language—during this visit I had heard various words, such as "up," "truck," "no," "Mama," "Liam," "me," and "Daddy home." I also explained that sometimes the difficulties of being overwhelmed affect other areas of a child's development in subtle ways, even in things like how he plays with toys. We would want to have a clear idea of what challenged Jacob and where he was doing well, to best know how to help him. The Williams agreed, and I explained what we would look at by using the IDA and how they would be the ones primarily interacting with him throughout the evaluation. I asked that they have their physician fill out a medical form I provided. We set our next appointment, and I left.

Reflecting on the First Visit

As I drove off, I thought about what I had seen and heard. I was hopeful; I didn't have the ache I sometimes feel when I leave a family where no one feels nurtured or cared about. Although some of Jacob's behaviors certainly could come as a result of an insecure or disorganized attachment, I didn't think the relationship between Jacob and his parents was seriously disturbed. They were exhausted, perplexed, and overwhelmed, yet they were responsive to Jacob, not openly hostile to him, and able to talk about him affectionately. I had also noted that Jacob responded positively to the subtle ways his parents had adapted to his needs. His mom's ability to label his feelings when he was anxious and not ready to leave her lap, and his father's ability to reposition Liam and Jacob while they negotiated attention, showed me some of the many capacities they had. I realized that Mr. and Mrs. Williams had confronted a challenge that many families face in welcoming a second child into the family. Ambivalence is not unusual for two young parents as they adapt to the needs of two young children and as they experience the loss of the singular relationship with the first child. Although they had seemingly negotiated the integration of Liam with ease, the unexpected differences that Jacob brought were presenting a challenge. Understanding those differences would be a priority.

Finally, I sorted out my own conflicting thoughts. Early in my career I had been taught that a baby's cries most often reflected the unheard cries of the primary caregiver, usually the mother. "Ghosts in the nursery" had been the most often and well-accepted explanation for difficult babies (Fraiberg, Adelson, & Shapiro, 1975). What soothing did the mother need? Who was there to hear and "hold" her cries? Those were often the first questions considered when seeing fussy babies in the past. Yet I had come to understand, as the field was also coming to understand, that the baby brings something to the relationship as well (Sameroff, 1993).

In this instance, it seemed as if Jacob had come into the world wired in a different way. Although parental anxiety was high at this point, I wondered if that were in response to some of the difficulties Jacob experienced. This baby seemed very different from what Rebecca had expected.

Is There a Medical Reason for Jacob's Cries?

Within a few days, I received a medical and health summary. Rebecca had been healthy, with good prenatal care. As she had noted, Jacob was born following a pregnancy complicated by bed rest due to preterm labor at 28 weeks. Jacob was born full term by caesarian section, due to breech presentation. Birth weight was 7 pounds, 4 ounces; length was 20 inches. Apgar scores were 9 and 10. Jacob and his mother were hospitalized 3 days because of the C-section. Jacob had difficulty beginning to nurse because of a poor latch (the ability to engage the nipple in the right position in the mouth), and a lactation consultant was called in. After a few days, Jacob was nursing better, although he still needed much external support through positioning and containment to organize his latch. His growth was average. Developmental milestones were reached on time. When Jacob was immunized, he had a reaction to the DPT immunization, with high-pitched screaming for 24 hours afterward. Because of that reaction, he received only the DT in subsequent immunizations, which were up-to-date. Jacob had a history of eczema and three ear infections. The current concerns were Jacob's sleep problems and transitioning him to textured foods.

The Assessment Offers Clues

I arrived on the appointed day to take a closer look at Jacob's play and abilities using the IDA. I had asked permission to videotape, so we could look at it afterwards to make sure nothing was missed. The tape would give us another way to look at what Jacob was telling us. Rebecca agreed and talked of feeling more hopeful, even just knowing they were getting help. She felt less tired and overwhelmed in the days following our visit. I was glad to hear that—it was yet another indicator that this family would be able to make use of support and intervention. Some adults come to the therapeutic relationship so hurt by past experiences that the development of a trusting relationship can take months, if not years. Unable to feel the support of the interventionist, they often have great difficulty coming to support their infant or toddler. This did not seem to be true for either parent.

Once again, Liam greeted me, gleefully exclaiming that he was going to play with his grandma. This had been prearranged so that Jacob would have as few distractions as possible during the assessment. Since Jacob was highly sensitive to noise and other distractions, I wanted to limit external stimulation as much as possible. Seeing him in his own home offered him the security and comfort that an unfamiliar office would not. I wanted to see what Jacob could do when he felt comfortable and not under stress.

Rebecca, who had been prepped for her role as the primary examiner, sat Jacob in her lap to begin. She had already tried to put him in his high chair, but the mere presence of a visitor made it too stressful for him to accept it. Jonathon could not leave work to be home for the evaluation, but he was glad to have the videotape to see later. After some initial resistance, Jacob responded well to the test items. Rebecca had been told that, since Jacob was at the lower end of the age range for the items being administered, he was not expected to be able to do all of them. When it looked as if she were becoming anxious about Jacob's abilities, I reminded her of that a few times during the evaluation. Jacob showed strong cognitive, fine motor, and communication skills. He showed problem-solving skills and good spatial-relation skills. He was able to build a tower of seven cubes and showed delight in doing so. He had many words and was already saying "me" and "you," reflecting an awareness of himself as separate from others. He had, at least, basic self-help skills. He used a spoon to get his pureed food to his mouth with little spillage. As had been seen in the first home visit, Jacob was able to defend himself from Liam; he used speech to protest and ask for help, and he was trying to do things for himself. Jacob used his parents as a secure base, used words to make his needs known, and was beginning to imitate the actions of his parents. He loved to help his mother unload the dishwasher and liked to wipe windows with her. The areas that gave Jacob more difficulty were gross motor, emotions and feelings, and coping. Jacob resisted walking upstairs, could not stand on one foot briefly and could not jump off the floor with both feet. Despite the fact that Jacob scored as competent in this area, I knew that the constellation of missed items gave a clue to his difficulties. He seemed challenged to do anything that involved taking his feet off the floor, which led me to wonder about his balance, motor planning, and gravitational security. Could it be that his inability to feel fundamentally secure in his relationship with the earth (i.e., gravity) made him more anxious and less likely to explore? I wondered if this also affected his emotional regulation; could this be part of the reason he appeared easily overwhelmed and frustrated or had prolonged temper tantrums? The IDA also revealed that Jacob demonstrated significant fear and anxiety in new or highly stimulating environments.

I reviewed the IDA patterns with Rebecca. Although more time was needed to fully understand his developmental profile, I felt sufficiently secure in my initial impressions to be able to make some recommendations. First, I wondered if the Williams had ever heard of sensory integration difficulties in young children. I explained that children with difficulties in their ability to take in and respond to stimulation from the world are often described as infants with difficulty in self-regulation. I described, "Some babies are over-reactive to sights, sounds, smells, touch, and movement and that makes them irritable or fussy." Rebecca nodded, seemingly relieved to hear there was a name for all of this. "I always thought he was just extra sensitive; I didn't know there was a name for it," she explained. We talked of some ways sensory integration can affect a child's behavior. As we talked, Rebecca held and nursed Jacob, who fell asleep in her arms. Rebecca cried softly, stroking Jacob's hair, noting how sorry she was that the world seemed so overwhelming to him. I sat quietly for several moments, and then asked, "Has all of this been overwhelming for you, too, Rebecca?" She nodded and said that she wanted to know how to make things better for Jacob.

A Plan for Jacob and a Plan for His Family

At that point, I had to make a decision about whether to stay at the feeling level and address Rebecca's sense of being overwhelmed or to respond to her attempt to make sense of it all by offering information. I was sure that Rebecca was beginning to know that her feelings were important to me and fairly certain that we were developing a relationship that would allow us to address her underlying feelings about all of this later. The most important thing was to get some answers to their questions.

I offered three ideas to Rebecca as a plan of action. First, I offered to meet with the Williams on a regular basis to provide support for them as they grew to understand the particular challenges that Jacob presented and how best to help him be more comfortable in the world. I tried to normalize their experience. "Meeting the needs of a young child like Jacob is exhausting, Rebecca. How could it not be? Having the support of an understanding person has been helpful to some families I've worked with in the past." Rebecca said that she had started to feel hopeful, that she felt better able to understand Jacob and less overwhelmed by him, just in the two times we had met. "I'd really like it if we could keep meeting," Rebecca replied. "Maybe you can give me ideas on how to handle my in-laws!"

Next, I recommended that Rebecca contact an occupational therapist (OT) for a full sensory integration evaluation. I had the name and telephone number of an OT whom I highly recommended. I warned Rebecca that the evaluation might seem costly but that I thought it would be worth it. We talked of getting a prescription from the pediatrician, thus making it easier to get insurance reimbursement for the evaluation and for any recommended treatment.

Finally, I explained that writing an Individualized Family Service Plan together often helps to develop a clear plan of action, and I suggested that we use our next appointment to explore any other issues the family would like to address in their plan. I described how some families want to connect with other parents of children who have similar difficulties and that sometimes looking at the impact on the family can be helpful. Rebecca nodded, "I've been so worried about how all of this has affected Liam. He doesn't have the same mom he used to have."

Getting an OT evaluation to more fully understand Jacob was the Williams' top priority. I offered to give them some reading material and Web site addresses so they could begin to learn more about regulation and sensory integration. I offered to assist in arranging the OT evaluation and to accompany them if they liked.

Our relationship, as well as information, was a powerful part of the treatment. Rebecca seemed relieved by that offer, and the visit ended.

Understanding Jacob's Physiological System: An Occupational Therapist's Perspective

As the OT, I take in information from the moment a child enters my office and at times even watch to see how they leave the car. As I prepared for the evaluation, I listened down the hallway to Jacob's reactions to an unfamiliar place. His mother, father, and the referring IMH specialist, Julie, accompanied him. He was a little apprehensive, and Rebecca reassured him several times that this was not a doctor's office and that he was going to play and have fun. Julie had explained what the evaluation would be like, but, of course, the family was still anxious. I entered the quiet waiting room and crouched to Jacob's eye level, saying, "Hi, my name is Sandy. You're Jacob, right?" Jacob looked at me, nodded, and smiled. I let Jacob know immediately, "We're going to have fun playing today, and guess what? We'll even have your mom and dad come along." I introduced myself to his parents and invited them to follow me. Jacob had difficulty leaving the waiting room; he fussed and refused to go. Rebecca had to playfully interact with him to persuade him to follow us into the therapy room, which was set up for Jacob's visit. On the way to the room, Jacob sometimes walked on his toes; the IMH specialist indicated he occasionally did so at home, too.

The room contained a large carpeted barrel lying on its side, sturdy foam steps, a foam incline, and a wooden platform suspended from one point with an inner tube inside and a large multicolored foam dome. The attractive equipment was placed on vinyl-covered foam mats. As I reviewed the information on the *Infant-Toddler Symptom Checklist* (DeGangi, Poisson, Sickel, & Wiener, 1995) completed by Mr. and Mrs. Williams, I watched Jacob surreptitiously. The responses on the checklist indicated that Jacob wakes more than three times a night; avoids textured foods; becomes excited in busy areas, such a supermarkets and restaurants; and is distracted by sounds that most people do not hear or notice. In the area of self-regulation, Rebecca indicated that Jacob goes easily from whimper to intense cry, demands adult attention constantly, and must be prepared several times in advance before change is introduced. Of the several tools available for the evaluation, I determined which to use on the basis of my observations of Jacob's play skills. These tools included the *Peabody Developmental Motor Scales* (Folio & Fewell, 2001) and *The Pediatric Evaluation of Disability Inventory* (Haley, Coster, Ludlow, Haltiwanger, & Andrellos, 1992).

While I talked to Rebecca about Jacob's sensitivity, I observed Jacob's approach to the environment. Under the fluorescent lights, Jacob had a tendency to squint, suggesting sensitivity to some types of lighting. He left his mother's side very slowly, and, when changing from the carpeted to matted surface, he went to his knees and crawled to avoid walking across changing surfaces. He held his hands in a fisted position when crawling, to avoid tactile input from the mats to the palmar surface of his hands. Jacob did not play on the equipment spontaneously but moved about the room without engaging in any goal-directed play. He appeared to become more excited as he moved about the room, so I attempted to engage him in activity. Jacob played peek-a-boo and appeared curious about the barrel. I persuaded him to get into the barrel with minimal physical assistance, but I held it so it would not shift. As soon as I released the barrel a bit and Jacob's weight shifted while he was on his belly, he looked frightened and ran back to his mother. I had to work hard to regain Jacob's trust and did get him to move tentatively up and down the foam incline on his hands and knees. I attempted to get him to walk up and down the incline while holding his hand, but he did not seem to like my touching his hand and pulled away.

Jacob seemed fearful of unexpected movement, which was apparent both in his response to the barrel's moving and in the way he went to his hands and knees to avoid walking across changing surfaces. I explained the concept of gravitational insecurity. Gravity should be the most consistent input that we receive and if Jacob could not feel stable when moving about, it would certainly affect his emotional security. Rebecca denied seeing much of this behavior at home, but, when asked if Jacob liked to swing, noted, "He sometimes used to throw his hands back, as if startled, each time the baby swing moved backward." Jonathon reminded his wife that Jacob did not like roughhousing or being swung in the air by his father. I explained that a child could have an adequate sense of balance yet have difficulty with modulation of movement. That was why Jacob seemed to score within the normal range on the IDA. The IMH specialist then expanded this information by pointing out how this was affecting Jacob emotionally, that is, not letting Rebecca out of his sight. Since he didn't feel fundamentally safe in the world, he used his mother to gain a sense of safety. Although this was initially adaptive, Jacob needed to explore the world, and this was becoming increasingly difficult for him.

How Jacob Feels in the World Becomes Clearer

Referring back to the Symptom Checklist, I began to explore some of the items Jacob's parents had noted. We talked about how Jacob appeared to be sensitive to touch and sometimes walked on his toes. I explained that the soles of the feet, palms of the hands, and mouth were by far the most plentiful location of touch receptors. This explains why Jacob seemed to avoid bearing weight on his hands, sometimes walked on his toes, and had problems with textures of food. Jacob might even have trouble sleeping because of the tags, seams, or footies in his pajamas. I noted that the Williams had clearly known ways to help Jacob learn to accept some forms of touch since he enjoyed contact with them. "Deep touch pressure, like hugs, are generally much more comforting than light pressure." I also noted that, with others, he might prefer to be the one to touch rather than be touched. He might react by hitting or kicking if someone unexpectedly touched or startled him.

Although I did not observe Jacob's sensitivity to sound in the quiet test environment, I trusted the parents' observations of his sleep being disturbed by the slightest sounds. I also explained how his sensitivity could be connected to the low muscle tone that I had observed in Jacob. That was seen through the fact that his joints bend far back in his fingers and by watching him "W-sit" (i.e., knees forward, buttocks resting on the floor with lower legs and ankles out to the sides and behind the buttocks). I explained that when children have low muscle tone, it takes extra effort to stay upright. The W-sit provides Jacob with a little extra stability while he plays. I asked Rebecca if Jacob felt heavier than expected when she picked him up. She described that, compared with his brother, who assisted when you lifted him up, Jacob felt "like a sack of potatoes." I went on to explain that just as his body had soft muscles, his ear muscles may also have low tone. The muscles of the body stabilize the joints so injury is less likely to occur. The muscles of the inner ear need to have a little tone, too, so they can be prepared to protect the ear from unexpected sounds. I explained that the ear never falls asleep. That is why we use smoke alarms. Jacob was in a state of hyperalertness, protecting himself from any unexpected harm, making it hard for him to stay asleep when he heard the normal sounds of the house. It might be relatively easy for Mr. and Mrs. Williams to learn some techniques to help calm Jacob.

I faced a decision about what to do next with Jacob. I explained to his parents that, while a test called the Peabody Developmental Motor Scales would give discreet information regarding Jacob's fine and gross motor skill development, it would be somewhat challenging to Jacob and probably not worth the violation of trust we have developed during the evaluation. I assured Rebecca that, once Jacob was more trusting of others and the environment, he would perform better.

Another area I addressed was difficulty with motor planning. Because of differences in sensory feedback to his body, Jacob may have difficulty using his body for tasks. Rebecca denied that this was a problem at home and seemed somewhat defensive regarding Jacob's decreased play skills. I referred back to the sensory profile and asked, "In what situations do you see difficulty with adapting to change?"

Rebecca replied, "Well, when I drop him off at the nursery at church, he cries every time, even when his favorite aunt is there. Then, when it is time to go, he cries when we leave." Jonathon added, "He loves to ride in the grocery cart but creates a scene when we try to get him into the cart. After we shop, he screams when we try to take him out." I explained to the parents that this was pretty common in children with motor planning problems. "Jacob cannot figure out how to change his plan himself. He knows what he wants to do but just cannot figure out how to accomplish the task. When others change it for him, he becomes uncomfortable because he takes longer to get ready for a new plan." Although Rebecca had noted that Jacob didn't seem to play well with toys, it seemed somewhat overwhelming for her to consider that this, too, was connected to his overall sensory integration difficulties. Recognizing that all of this information was a lot for a parent to incorporate, I decided not to administer further testing at this point. I changed my focus to demonstrating techniques that I thought would have more immediate results.

During the rest of the evaluation, I demonstrated calming techniques, including deep-touch-pressure skin brushing, joint compression, and hand hugs. I demonstrated them on Mr. and Mrs. Williams, and then had them try the techniques on me to ensure that they were comfortable and knew how to perform them correctly. Next, they used them on Jacob. He had been running around the room and immediately sat down, holding up his leg so his mother would repeat the stimulus. I pointed out that Jacob's face looked less stressed after this firm input, and, instead of crawling up the incline, he walked somewhat hesitantly up and down. I explained that increasing information to the joints of the legs (lower extremities) made him feel a little more secure with movement through space. A final observation was that Jacob did not often interact with the unfamiliar toys, which could be associated with a fearful response to the environment. As the session progressed, he would have likely interacted more with the toys.

As the assessment drew to a close, we discussed a plan of action for OT. The Williams knew they would need time to digest some of the information they received, and I reassured them that, as they had more questions, they could call me. I suggested twice-weekly treatment to start, combined with a "sensory diet" that I would help them plan. Treatment could be done in the course of their daily routines, to help make the treatment hour even more effective for Jacob.

Julie, who did not want to overwhelm the family, wondered how all of this sounded to them. Rebecca laughed, "If it will help us sleep, I'll do anything." We all discussed how it would be intensive at first, but, within a short time, things were likely to improve and be less overwhelming. It was also noted that, because so much of what would be done with Jacob at home would be play based, Liam could also join in, thus reducing the chance that he would feel left out.

Becoming Whole—The Epilogue

Follow-up home visits with Julie, the IMH specialist, were spent in various ways. Some sessions were spent in play activities designed to engage Jacob in ways that he could tolerate. Other sessions were spent talking about what Rebecca was learning about Jacob and the sadness and guilt she felt about those early months. However, she quickly came to see the gifts he brought to their family, even if they had been a bit hard to discover at first. Julie listened carefully, pointing out to Rebecca that she had understood Jacob's problem but didn't have words for it in the early months. Julie was careful not to dismiss Rebecca's feelings of guilt but instead to allow them and then gently remind her of all the ways they had tried to help Jacob. There was a conscious effort to highlight their strengths and how what they had done allowed him to be as secure as he was.

Once Rebecca let go of her guilt feelings, she was ready to respond to Jacob as he was. One day, about 2 months into their work together, Jacob tried to take a toy from Liam, who protested and pulled the toy away. Jacob looked angry. Everyone paused with bated breath, because this would usually lead to a quick meltdown. Rebecca said quietly, "You can have a turn when Liam is done. Do you want this instead?" Jacob hesitated and took the toy that Rebecca offered. Julie and Rebecca looked at each other, and Julie asked, "Do you think he could have done that 2 months ago?" Rebecca laughed and said, "Maybe not even a week ago!"

Julie acknowledged that they'd all been working so hard and asked if it felt good to have some of it pay off. Rebecca talked of feeling much more able to respond quietly and calmly to Jacob, knowing that not every limit set would result in a tantrum. "So you are feeling more relaxed, too," Julie affirmed. "You've really come to know what he needs." Rebecca grinned. By paying attention to

Rebecca's ability to respond to both boys, Julie had tried to support her in her attempts to come to know Jacob as he was. When Julie saw Rebecca respond to subtle cues from Jacob, she often said things like, "Your mommy knew just what you wanted!" Rebecca found herself realizing that, although Jacob was different from Liam, she was just as capable of meeting his needs, once they were clearer, as she had been in meeting Liam's needs. Although Jonathon was not frequently involved in home visits, he enjoyed some of the home program routines that allowed him to rough-house with Jacob in ways different than what he first imagined but equally rewarding.

Between OT appointments and Julie's home visits, the time invested in treatment was initially a struggle for the Williams. However, the results soon helped family life improve. Jacob was sleeping better, with less need for parental support. He was still fussy about foods but was eating a wider range and no longer gagging at the sight of textured foods. As he began to feel more secure in his body, he became more independent and began to explore his world more readily. Liam seemed happier that he could play without worrying that he would be told to be quiet because Jacob was sleeping. Although parent-child treatment alone would have been supportive, without specific treatment for Jacob's hypersensitivities and other sensory integration difficulties, he would not have been able to contribute to the relationship in ways that allowed for more joy and pleasure in the family. An understanding of what the baby brought to the relationship was crucial in developing a treatment plan that effectively alleviated the distress of the child and the family. Just as crucial was a place for these parents, particularly Rebecca, to explore their feelings of sadness and to develop a sense of their own ability to understand and meet their child's needs.

References

DeGangi, G., Poisson, S., Sickel, R. Z., & Wiener, A. S. (1995). *Infant-Toddler Symptom Checklist*. Tucson, AZ: Therapy Skill Builders.

Folio, M. R., & Fewell, R. R. (2001). *Peabody Developmental Motor Scales* (2nd ed.). Los Angeles: Western Psychological Services.

Fraiberg, S., Adelson, E., & Shapiro, V. (1975). Ghosts in the nursery: A psychoanalytic approach to the problem of impaired infant-mother relationships. *Journal of American Academy of Child Psychiatry, 14*, 387-421.

Haley, S. M., Coster, W. J., Ludlow, L. H., Haltiwanger, J. T., & Andrellos, P. J. (1992). *Pediatric Evaluation of Disability Inventory: Development, standardization, and administration manual* (ver. 1.0). Boston: New England Medical Center.

Provence, A., Erikson, J., Vater, S., & Palmeri, S. (1995). *Infant-Toddler Developmental Assessment: IDA*. Chicago: Riverside Publishing Company.

Sameroff, A. J. (1993). Models of development and developmental risk. In C.H. Zeanah, Jr. (Ed.), *Handbook of infant mental health* (pp. 1–13). New York: Guilford Press.

Discussion Questions

1. How did Jacob's sensory integration challenges affect his developing relationship with his parents?

2. The IMH specialist used strategies to begin to develop a relationship even before the initial visit. Describe what strategies were used.

3. Describe Jacob's behaviors that led the IMH specialist to consider sensory integration difficulties.

4. If you were working with a child with sensory integration issues, what resources would be available to support the child/family within your own community?

5. Describe a child you have worked with who may have had sensory integration challenges. Describe behaviors that led you to consider sensory integration difficulties.

6. How did each therapist support and promote the importance of each discipline with the Williams family?

7. Discuss additional ways therapists from different perspectives can develop positive working relationships.

Nurturing A Family When There Is a Nonorganic Failure to Thrive Diagnosis

Carla Barron

Summary

This case study describes the 9-month relationship between an infant mental health (IMH) specialist working in a child welfare intervention program and a family that included a 25-year-old single mother, her three children under age 3, and her male friend, who eventually became her live-together partner. At the time of referral, the 18-month-old middle child, identified as failing to thrive, was at high risk of removal from the home due to substantiated charges of neglect. The IMH specialist describes her process of establishing rapport, gathering information and understanding intervention needs, focusing on the parent-infant relationship, addressing feeding issues and other sources of stress in the family routine (sometimes through humor), and helping the family make the transition to longer-term IMH intervention.

Parents and Children Together (PACT)

The following case description came from PACT, a child welfare intervention services program housed within Wayne State University (WSU). Since 1977, the PACT program has trained post-bachelor level interns to provide child- and family-centered, home-based services to families referred by the Child Protection and Foster Care staff of the Wayne County Family Independence Agency (WCFIA). Home visits, parenting groups, and parent-child interaction groups are offered for a period of 6 to 12 months to parents and their children from birth to 17 years of age. In 1996, PACT received funding from WCFIA to hire an IMH specialist and became the first FIA-funded IMH services program in Michigan. PACT currently employs three Merrill-Palmer Institute/WSU–trained IMH specialists and two additional staff members who will soon complete the graduate certificate training program. The family described below received PACT home-based services from an IMH specialist for 9 months.

Introduction of the Family

The Hughes family came to the attention of PACT following a substantiated child neglect charge. The Children's Protective Services (CPS) worker who referred the Hughes family to PACT stated that an 18-month-old child in the home had a severe developmental delay due to the fact that the mother was negligent in providing appropriate food. The CPS worker stated that she was very concerned about the 18-month-old's appearance, since she appeared to be the same size as her younger brother, who was 7 months old at the time. The family included Ms. Hughes, the 25-year-old single mother of 3-year-old Michael, 18-month-old Stephanie, and 7-month-old Matthew, and her male friend, Mr. Joseph, who eventually became her live-together partner. The family lived in a blighted urban neighborhood in an upper flat.

When I first met Stephanie, her physical appearance was visually concerning. At 18 months, she weighed almost 16 pounds, about the same as her 7-month-old brother. Her face had a decidedly triangular shape, with a broad forehead and a narrow jaw. Her body appeared to have little strength; her muscles appeared floppy and unusable. Stephanie's hands and arms were often extended sideways, and she would wave them up and down when she was excited or upset. She cried when she was upset—when her bottle was taken or when food was visible but she was not being fed. She also became upset when she was placed on the floor in a prone position or when her mother left her on the floor sitting alone. She was able to sit independently but tended to lean back on her hips to keep her balance. She was unable to stand independently or while holding onto furniture.

During the first weeks of observation, I often saw Stephanie smiling at her mother, especially when her mother used an exaggerated "motherese" when talking to her. She appeared to have the capacity to engage others and to be engaged. After getting Ms. Hughes' permission, I successfully involved Stephanie in a game of turn-taking as we passed a small toy back and forth between us. She remained involved in the game for quite a long time, becoming increasingly interested and persistent. She laughed each time she passed the toy to me and held out her hand for me to pass it back to her. Her purposeful communicative behavior did not include the use of words.

On meeting Stephanie's brothers, Michael and Matthew, I

observed their physical development to be age-appropriate. Three-year-old Michael was extroverted in his way of getting attention, often throwing toys or hitting his mother. These behaviors often occurred several times before he was punished. His mother's usual response was to yell at him to "stop" and to isolate him by making him stand in a corner or by sending him to his room.

At 7 months, Matthew was able to make several sounds, roll over, sit independently using his hands for support, and manipulate small toys with his hands. Matthew was often alone, lying on the couch or in a bassinet or swing, sometimes holding his bottle or sucking on a propped bottle. However, he was also very engaging; he often looked intensely around the room and smiled on finding his mother's face.

Ms. Hughes

Ms. Hughes, the children's mother, immediately impressed me as a woman who could really get things done for herself and her family. She was very knowledgeable about the types of assistance she could and did receive from the state and from other community resources. She was an effective advocate for herself and her children when she was in need. She was adamant that the CPS report was made as "revenge" against her by a family member and stressed with fervor that she would protect her children against "the system." Ms. Hughes recognized that Stephanie was not growing, especially when Matthew began to surpass her in growth and developmental skills. She willingly accepted assistance to help her learn more about Stephanie's growth delay and to help Stephanie walk, which Ms. Hughes stated was her main goal for Stephanie.

While Ms. Hughes was affectionate toward all of her children, this affection was often paired with aggressive name-calling. Although she was able to verbalize how she felt about her children and about her role as their mother, she was often seemingly unaware of her children's immediate needs. For example, when Matthew or Stephanie squirmed or cried to be picked up or moved, or when Michael sought attention, Ms. Hughes did not respond until something was broken or thrown at her or until I brought attention to the children's behaviors.

The Children

Michael's aggressive behavior toward others, his lack of response to his mother's directions, and his combative, attention-seeking behaviors often overshadowed his curiosity, his engaging qualities, and his need for one-on-one attention from his mother. I was concerned that Ms. Hughes' need to control Michael's behaviors would get in the way of providing him the care and attention he needed.

Stephanie's developmental delays were of great concern, and her lack of growth was a priority to PACT, CPS, and the family. It seemed, however, that there were many concerns regarding the interpersonal relationships in this family. Clearly, these relationships needed to be addressed and discussed so that Ms. Hughes could begin to understand her role in helping all of her children to thrive.

Establishing Rapport

Because of the many issues raised by Ms. Hughes, CPS, and me, it was often difficult to focus on just one thing. During the first few weeks of service, I would often watch the family interact and ask questions about my observations. These questions were asked to learn more about the kinds of discipline used by Ms. Hughes and Mr. Joseph and to understand what they thought about development and developmental needs. These were often stated as "Tell me more about that," or "Tell me what just happened when Michael started yelling." Other questions were information-gathering questions such as, "What do you think children need to grow?" and "What expectations did you have about being a mom?" I used this technique partially because I was overwhelmed by the interactions I was seeing and also because Ms. Hughes was so adamant about what she wanted for her family. I did not think it was my role to come into her home and tell her what she should do.

During this phase of establishing rapport, I did a lot of listening. I used many of the active listening tools I learned in school, and they really worked. Simple statements that reflected what I was hearing identified feelings and demonstrated empathy, making a tremendous impact on Ms. Hughes. I began to sense that she had never had anyone really listen to her concerns, her thoughts, or even her jokes.

Initial Observations

During the first weeks with the family, I was impressed by how they worked to fix up their home. It was clearly very important for them to fix up the flat to reflect their belief about what a home should be. As the work was being done, I was often greeted at the door with proud looks on the faces of Ms. Hughes and Mr. Joseph, who wanted to show me the latest home improvement project that had been finished since my last visit. It was an amazing transformation from a very cluttered, dirty, and unsafe collection of rooms into a pleasant, bright, freshly painted and carpeted home. I often drew on these changes as evidence that this family wanted to have a real home that was a good, safe place for all of them to grow and develop. I would often simply state, "Wow, you have done so much work! And you did it on your own!" or "I can see how important it is to you that you have a comfortable home."

Statements that emphasized how they provided a safe space for the children to explore and play were also important. I used developmental guidance and identification of strengths to say, "It is so important for Matthew to have a safe place to crawl around, and you have been able to give him that space." I believe that my positive response to their pride in their home, as well as brief comments about their accomplishments, supported their own feelings of achievement. By emphasizing the family's strengths and acknowledging their successes, I believe I encouraged them to continue working on their home and, in turn, to see successes in how they were caring for their children. Identifying and encouraging strengths in one area can allow a family to attempt changes in other areas where success has not been so easy.

Gathering Information and Understanding Intervention Needs

Early in treatment, Ms. Hughes expressed concerns about Stephanie's delayed development and was able to ask me for information, help, and support. Ms. Hughes also identified concerns about the hospital staff and the treatment that Stephanie was receiving. She had heard that another hospital clinic provided better service. Although this hospital was much farther from her home, it was important to support her wish to provide Stephanie with the best possible medical care. Assisting Ms. Hughes in scheduling an appointment at this hospital and offering transportation told her that I was listening carefully and that her concerns were valid and appropriate. She needed to feel that she knew what was best for her child. She also needed to know that I would respect her choices, which were based on her perception of Stephanie's needs. Although the CPS worker worried that I had allowed Ms. Hughes to ignore the broader scope of the neglect issues that had brought her into "the system," my supervisor and I agreed on the importance of this approach. Only later was I able fully to realize how important this first step was in building trust with this mother who had always done things on her own. I was one of the only "professionals" who did not attempt to change her mind about the hospital and, instead, encouraged her to find the name of the hospital clinic and assisted her in obtaining a referral from her primary physician.

Providing Focused Attention

During my visits, Ms. Hughes also shared her concern about Michael's increasingly aggressive attention-seeking behavior. We struggled to find time to focus on Ms. Hughes' identified concerns about Stephanie's development and to explore her relationship with Stephanie, while at the same time attending to Michael. My supervisor and I discussed the need for more support. The severity of Stephanie's failure to thrive (FTT) status needed immediate attention, but so did the emotional well-being of her siblings.

At PACT, I am lucky to have access to Bachelor's of Social Work (BSW) placement students who do field work with us. With permission from the family, a BSW student joined me in the home to provide Michael and Matthew with specialized attention and opportunities for supported play. This allowed Ms. Hughes and me time during each visit to watch Stephanie's interactions and behavior to learn more about her.

During this time we were able to discuss Ms. Hughes' feelings about Stephanie's delays and to reflect together on her pregnancy with Stephanie and what had happened in her life following Stephanie's birth. Having this brief, relatively uninterrupted time to focus on Ms. Hughes and her identified concerns aided in the development of our relationship. I was able to focus my attention on her while feeling confident that Michael and Matthew were appropriately engaged. When I was there on my own, I often felt overwhelmed, watching all that was happening. Having a student with me in the home lessened my feelings of helplessness in trying to identify what each child, Ms. Hughes, and Mr. Joseph needed.

Assessments

Since Stephanie continued to remain at the same weight, without any gain at all, the relationship between her and her mother moved into the spotlight. Stephanie was beginning to demonstrate maturity in developmental skills, such as pulling herself to a stand and cruising, and increased maturity in emotional development, as evidenced by an increased ability to separate from her mother without extreme distress. For example, in the doctor's office, she gradually moved from clinging to her mother and sobbing when she had to let go, to allowing her mother to stand close by while she sat alone on the examination table. These small gains in development, however, were overshadowed by her lack of weight gain.

After five months of working together, Stephanie was admitted to the hospital to be monitored more closely. Ms. Hughes stayed with Stephanie throughout the 3-day hospitalization. Since Stephanie ate well at the hospital with her mother present, specialists suggested that the home environment probably affected her ability to eat food and gain weight. As a result, Stephanie was diagnosed with Nonorganic Failure to Thrive (FTT) (see Table 1).

Table 1 Definition of Failure to Thrive

FTT is a multifaceted problem involving biological, nutritional, and environmental factors. It is generally agreed that FTT is present when there is at least a one-month history of one or more of the following:

1. weight below the fifth percentile for age on standardized growth charts;

2. deceleration in the rate of weight gain from birth to present, or

3. weight for height-age less than 90%.

FTT with contributing medical problems is classified as organic FTT while FTT with no contributing medical problem is considered nonorganic FTT.

Environmental concerns in nonorganic FTT may include poverty, violence, substance abuse, criminality, and dysfunctional relationships (Benoit, 2000).

In nonorganic FTT, communication between a parent and child while the child is eating is of particular interest. In some cases of nonorganic FTT, there is negative communication or a lack of communication while feeding. A parent's own issues regarding food may influence how the child is fed. T. Berry Brazelton writes, "While food is critical to survival, the quality of a baby's future life also depends on the nurturing that parents offer along with a feeding" (Brazelton, 1992, p. 287).

Personal Reflection on the Diagnosis

It was very difficult for me to hear that the diagnosis was nonorganic FTT. As I addressed my own feelings in supervision, I realized that, even though I knew there were signs of relationship stress, I had hoped that the hospital would find biological causes. I had already observed the difficulty that medical staff experienced trying to describe nonorganic FTT to Ms. Hughes. While no one said to her directly, "You are causing Stephanie's lack of weight gain," it was implied at each office visit and hospital consultation. By this time I had learned that, if concerns or problems were not clearly presented and discussed in concrete terms, Ms. Hughes did not seem to understand the implications. It was my job to find ways to talk about this diagnosis with Ms. Hughes, who was looking everywhere except at her own caregiving practices, to find a cause. It was also my job to consider how Ms. Hughes' feelings about the nonorganic FTT diagnosis contributed to her difficulty in understanding her baby's diagnosis.

I knew it was important for me to understand my own feelings, so I discussed them during supervision. I knew that the intensity of my feelings was probably a reflection of the intensity of Ms. Hughes' feelings. By allowing myself to feel these emotions, I understood Ms. Hughes' hurt and anger better and could use my understanding to support her and help her shift her response to Stephanie. After a supervisory session, it was easier to remember that it was my relationship with the family that would offer the possibility of change. Also, Stephanie was depending on my intervention.

Challenging Parenting Strategies

I watched carefully for the best opportunity to discuss, in the context of the relationship I had built with Ms. Hughes, the meaning of nonorganic FTT and its implications. The first opportunity came while we were driving home from an appointment following Stephanie's hospitalization. Ms. Hughes was angry with the doctor who had stated, "If Stephanie doesn't gain weight, I may have to recommend a feeding tube or temporary placement in a home that can focus specifically on Stephanie's eating problems." Ms. Hughes had responded, emphatically and repeatedly, "I will not allow anyone else to take care of Stephanie or any of my children."

She wanted the doctors to find out why Stephanie was not growing. It was then that I had to explain very concretely what the doctor had been saying. My words were carefully chosen and very difficult to say. "The doctors believe that part of the reason Stephanie isn't growing is because so much is happening in your house and because it is hard for you to be consistent." She became visibly angry with me and did not respond to anything that I had said. We were silent the rest of the ride. I wanted to change the subject and start talking, but I knew that my own feelings of discomfort and fear were prompting me. I wanted to make her feel better; it was difficult not to start talking again. I worried about her response to all that I had said. I wondered if I had said too much and overstepped the boundaries of our relationship, and I wondered whether she would open the door to me at our next visit. I didn't really know what it was like for her to hear the words I was saying, and I didn't know whether she understood the severity of Stephanie's situation. I did know that waiting for her to decide when to talk, instead of my trying to take the lead, honored her power of choice and control over further discussion.

She Lets Me Back In

In fact, Ms. Hughes did open the door to our next visit, and, over the next months, she seemed to be more open to trying things that we had been discussing for months. At each visit, we discussed suggestions she heard from the doctor. She tried to set up a meal schedule that involved the whole family. We discussed the importance of making mealtime enjoyable for all family members. Since Ms. Hughes seemed receptive to the doctor's suggestion that the family eat together at one table, I began to focus on that. Each time I was at the home, I asked her about the dining room table that was being used in the kitchen as a shelf to store extra food and other kitchen necessities. We discussed what it would be like for the family to sit and eat together. Ms. Hughes had often talked about being too busy and unable to sit and take care of all of the children's needs at the same time. One day, however, I arrived to find that the dining table had been moved from the kitchen to the front room of the house. Ms. Hughes announced that this was where they now ate every meal together and where all the children ate three snacks between meals.

Ms. Hughes then tried to establish a routine for Stephanie to use a cup instead of a bottle, because Stephanie didn't drink all of the milk in the bottle. Ms. Hughes also insisted that her boyfriend and her sister, who was often at the Hughes' home, stick to the schedule and routine whenever they cared for the children.

Creative Strategies

During supervision, the possibility of my being in the home while the family was eating was considered. At my next visit, I asked Ms. Hughes if she would like me to observe Stephanie during mealtimes and support her while Stephanie ate. She thought this would be helpful, so we arranged a regular time when I could be present during a meal. Ms. Hughes and I agreed that my role would be to sit at the table with them so that I could observe what was happening and be present to support Ms. Hughes when necessary.

By observing mealtimes, I learned that Ms. Hughes had been feeding Stephanie from her own plate. She explained that, because Stephanie did not eat much and ate better when they sat close together, she would rather just feed Stephanie bites of food from her own plate. I initially agreed with Ms. Hughes' observation, but we talked later about allowing both Stephanie and Matthew to have their own plates.

While discussing this visit with my supervisor, I decided to videotape part of a mealtime. As Ms. Hughes and I watched the video together, I commented on how much Stephanie depended on getting her mother's attention to get food. Stephanie needed to wave her arms up and down when she wanted another piece, and Ms. Hughes did not always see this behavior because her two other young children needed her, too. On one particular visit, I asked Ms. Hughes to get another small plate or just put food on the tray of Stephanie's high chair. I discussed how important it was for Stephanie to be able to take the lead in how, when, and how much she ate.

Through support from me, I watched the family move from eating separately in various areas of the house to eating together at a table with Matthew's and Stephanie's high chairs moved next to the table where Michael, Ms. Hughes, and Mr. Joseph sat. Over time, I began to see food placed on separate dishes in front of each child. These were major achievements for this family.

It was also interesting to see how these achievements seemed to increase the family's willingness to address other eating issues. For example, Mr. Joseph had a pattern of cleaning up the children as they were eating—wiping their faces or wiping the trays of their high chairs and vacuuming the carpet while they were still eating.

Using Humor

After observing Mr. Joseph cleaning up a couple of times, I used humor to identify strategies that were developmentally inappropriate for the children and to suggest other ways that would accomplish what he wanted. During one visit, a dialogue went somewhat like this:

Mr. Joseph (cleaning Stephanie's tray while she was still eating spaghetti):

Boy, she really makes a big mess when she eats.

IMH Specialist:

I wonder what Stephanie thinks of your cleaning her up before she is done.

Mr. Joseph:

Oh, she doesn't mind.

IMH Specialist:

Really? I think I would really be upset if someone started cleaning up my plate without even asking if I was done! *(Pause)* What if you were in a restaurant and your waiter took your plates without even asking you if you were done?

Ms. Hughes (laughing):

I would say, "Hey, I paid good money for that food!"

IMH Specialist:

Yeah—I didn't even think of that! And what if the cleaning staff came by and lifted up your plate to wipe off the table while you were still eating?

Mr. Joseph:

But she was really making a mess.

IMH Specialist:

I know it is really important for you to keep your house looking clean and in order, but I wonder how Stephanie understands your behaviors. *(Pause)* Because she is having trouble eating the amount of food she needs to grow, it is so important that you and her mom give her the right messages about eating. She looks to you to know what to do! So, if you sit down by her and eat your plate of food, she sees that and then will know that she can eat everything on her plate, too. If you come behind her and clean up while she is eating, she may think that she is done eating because she is getting cleaned up.

Mr. Joseph:

So, when we are all done eating, then I can clean her up?

IMH Specialist:

Yes!

I knew I was being very direct, but the danger to Stephanie and the threat of removal from the home warranted a strong response. I knew the relationship we had developed could withstand a direct approach.

Other Issues to Explore

I had observed that both playtime and cleanup were sources of stress in the family's day and needed to be addressed. The dinner table had been moved to the living room so that the family could eat together. The children played with toys in the living room and were expected to put their toys away when it was time to eat so that the family could focus on eating. However, each time they were to clean up, Mr. Joseph went over to the children, especially Michael and Matthew, and took toys from their hands without saying a word. Michael would then cry and rage, usually screaming and stomping his feet. Clearly, Michael and his family needed another way of dealing with this necessary part of their daily routine.

It was important for Ms. Hughes and Mr. Joseph to understand how they could help the children learn social skills. I used developmental guidance to increase parental understanding of what Michael needed and why he behaved that way. Once again, I used an adult analogy so they might develop empathy for the children's feelings when their toys were taken from them without any warning. I reminded them of our earlier discussion about restaurant employees taking their plates before they were done and without asking if they were finished.

I coached Mr. Joseph and Ms. Hughes to give the children a warning, such as, "In 5 minutes we have to clean up to eat lunch" or "Remind Michael that it will soon be time to clean up for lunch." When it was time, I coached them to say, "Okay, it's time for lunch; let's all clean up these toys. I'll clean up these blocks with Matthew. Michael, what do you want to clean up? You can clean up the trucks or the puzzles." These words gave Mr. Joseph something to say and allowed Michael to assist in cleanup so that he had some control over what was happening.

The parents and I acknowledged that it was really much easier for them to clean up by themselves. We talked about how it felt to allow the children to assist them, and we acknowledged that it would always take longer and wouldn't be done as neatly as they might wish. It was difficult for Mr. Joseph to discuss this, but he responded positively to my coaching. Over time, the temper tantrums at cleanup time decreased, and Michael showed that he understood this new daily routine. He would often turn to look at his mother and Mr. Joseph, waiting to be praised for doing what they had asked.

During one visit, Mr. Joseph and Ms. Hughes expressed concerns about Matthew's emerging gross motor skills. They worried about his new ability to get into things in the kitchen and to move quickly toward the stairs. When 10-month-old Matthew crawled into the bathroom and pulled himself up onto the toilet, they started putting him into a swing to keep him from getting into places and things that could hurt him. I listened to their fears and agreed that Matthew needed to be kept safe, but I spelled out the dangers of putting a 10-month-old child into a swing built for very young infants.

Helping Us All Feel Safe

Parenting strategies used with Michael were especially important to address since his behaviors were extremely difficult for Ms. Hughes to handle. She and Mr. Joseph used several inappropriate discipline techniques, including strapping the $3^1/2$-year-old into a car seat as time-out and making unrealistic, threatening statements because he refused to stay in the time-out chair. It was important to talk with them about alternatives and to discuss how Michael's behaviors made them feel.

At other times, I had to clearly and directly tell them that strategies they were using to control behaviors, especially Michael's, were inappropriate. For instance, I arrived for one visit and observed Michael strapped into a car seat that had been placed on the couch in front of the television. He was watching a horror movie that I knew he liked to watch. When Michael saw me come in, he looked at me and used an obscene gesture. First, I silently counted to ten. I pointed out to the parents that they were giving Michael extremely mixed messages by punishing him and, at the same time, allowing him to watch a movie he liked. Furthermore, the movie was clearly inappropriate for a $3^1/2$-year-old. I explained that children this age are both fascinated and terrified by displays of cruel and violent behavior, and that they need their parents to protect them from sights and feelings that they can't handle. Their implied approval of violent behavior he saw on television was bound to confuse him when they then punished him for the same behavior. I explained that neither the movie nor their method of punishment could continue because they confused Michael. By setting clear limits, I was demonstrating that they, too, could provide strategies to keep their children safe. As we talked, both Ms. Hughes and Mr. Joseph were able to identify other ways they could have handled the situation. With each issue raised, I empathized with their attempts to implement effective discipline, but I was straightforward in letting them know when their methods were teaching the children what they didn't intend for them to learn. I encouraged them to explore ways to teach the children self-discipline and self-worth. When they agreed that this was important, I pointed out that "strapping-in" methods teach children that they have no control whatsoever over their lives and that they are at the mercy of whatever more powerful person comes along. It was very important to help them learn the benefits of talking to their children; explaining what they may do, not only what they may not do; and praising them when they do something right.

In supervision each week, I talked about the issues being raised during visits. Together we recognized that the parents' letting me see conflict and chaos and then engaging in thoughtful conversations with me about alternatives was an important indication of how much trust had been built into our working relationships. I was pleased to think that they actually believed that I could help them, but I still found myself feeling pretty anxious as I knocked on the door for visits.

In the course of supervision, I discovered that I was modeling the very behavior I was encouraging them to use with their children. As I helped them face the developmental challenges of parenting and encouraged positive parenting behaviors, I praised their successes and helped them conquer their doubts. I realized how important it was to draw their attention to how good they felt about themselves when they were successful. As they experienced and recognized the power of these feelings, they were better able to understand the importance of a positive approach for their children. They needed to feel nurtured, in order to nurture.

Child Welfare Versus Community Mental Health

In reviewing our work together, it was clear that Ms. Hughes, Mr. Joseph, and each of the children had made significant progress as a result of the intervention. Stephanie had gained weight; Ms. Hughes and Mr. Joseph demonstrated positive parenting behaviors, appropriate disciplinary techniques, and realistic expectations; and Ms. Hughes and Mr. Joseph learned to set limits that were clear, firm, and fair. However, since intervention was still needed, the family would be best served by long-term intervention offered in our community only by a preventive community mental health program. Following discussions with my supervisor, Ms. Hughes, and the CPS worker, the family was referred to a local community mental health agency's IMH program.

The relationship that Ms. Hughes and I had built over the previous 10 months, and the responses she made to intervention, were evidence that she would be able to develop a similar relationship with another helping professional—one who could provide the family with the long-term support they needed.

Saying Good-Bye

As we anticipated the upcoming change in service, we talked about the new worker they would meet. To prepare to establish rapport with a new interventionist, Ms. Hughes shared how it felt to begin again. I arranged a meeting between the family and the new IMH program supervisor, to help Ms. Hughes shift her working relationships to a new therapist.

Ms. Hughes talked a lot about how much her children would miss me. I knew that I would really miss her family, too. She talked about how they felt comfortable with me, how it seemed like I was a part of their family. She said the children would like to have my picture to help them remember me.

Looking back on our work together provided an opportunity to reinforce the many positive changes that occurred. I talked with Ms. Hughes about how she had allowed a stranger into her home and accepted help when she was feeling so vulnerable. I was amazed at how many changes they had implemented. I reminded her of these changes and how their family had improved as result of their hard work. I felt privileged to have contributed to their process of becoming happier and healthier.

Saying good-bye was very difficult. I worried about the support I had provided, and I worried that it hadn't been enough. I worried that I hadn't seen the right things and that I hadn't carried the right observations to my supervisor so that she could help me understand what was really happening.

I have come to understand that we learn things from every family we work with. The Hughes family taught me the importance of drawing on my own feelings to understand the family's experience. They taught me how it feels to be invisible and how much work it then takes to be seen. I allowed myself to try to feel the loneliness of each family member. It was a strange feeling to be alone in the midst of chaos. It was an incredible learning experience to describe in supervision the way I felt in this home and then to realize that what I described was probably the way the children felt, too.

I continuously draw on my own feelings, and, even if I can't identify them initially, I am intensely aware that I am sensing or feeling something important for me to understand. I remember this family while thinking about other families I am working with or when I supervise other staff members. One question I have learned to ask is, "What did it feel like for you to be with this family?" Using our own feelings and reactions when we are with families is one assessment tool that is often overlooked, but it is incredibly important and immensely useful.

I have great respect for each member of this family. They allowed me, a stranger, to come into their home and identify very difficult feelings, and then they had the courage to change. I will always remember them, and I know that I will continue to learn as I reflect on our experience together.

References

Benoit, D. (2000). Feeding disorders, failure to thrive, and obesity. In C. H. Zeanah, Jr. (Ed.), *Handbook of infant nental health* (2nd ed.; pp. 399–352). New York: The Guilford Press.

Brazelton, T. B. (1992). *Touchpoints: Your child's emotional and behavioral development*. Reading, MA: Addison-Wesley/Lawrence.

Discussion Questions

1. The IMH specialist states that she felt invisible when she was with the family and that she shared this feeling during supervision. This feeling was difficult for her to recognize and understand. Discuss how it was useful for the IMH specialist to understand her own feelings and how she used this insight to better understand the family.

2. Another challenge for the specialist was the mother's need to believe that she was providing adequately for her children, while, in reality, there were serious concerns about the care of the children. How did the IMH specialist handle this? What other strategies might be used?

3. Despite Stephanie's delayed development, she was able to engage others and to be engaged. She was attentive, persistent, and laughed easily. How did her easy temperament affect her relationship with her mother?

4. How did Stephanie motivate her mother to become involved in IMH intervention?

5. The IMH specialist provides examples of purposefully using humor to make a point with the family. Discuss how humor was used successfully in this case. Consider when it could be therapeutically appropriate to use humor and times when it could be detrimental.

6. The IMH specialist encountered discipline techniques that she considered inappropriate. Do you agree or disagree with her responses? What alternative strategies might you consider?

Courageous Decisions: Using Relationships to Support Growth and Change

Sheryl Goldberg

Summary

A 31-year-old divorced mother is referred by a public health nurse to a home-based infant mental health (IMH) program. She has a 16-month-old son, is 4 months pregnant, and is on medical leave because of postpartum depression and agoraphobia following the birth of her first child. The case study exemplifies the centrality of the therapeutic relationship in addressing issues of early and ongoing abandonment, potential family violence, substance abuse, mental illness, and poverty, which interact in this family to threaten the optimal care of the toddler and his mother's preparation for the birth of her second child. As part of the work, the IMH specialist offers to coach the mother through her delivery and remains emotionally available through a series of unanticipated medical crises.

Using the Fraiberg Model

This story outlines the treatment relationship between the Alden family and an infant mental health (IMH) specialist working in a home-based IMH program in Michigan. The program is strongly influenced by Selma Fraiberg's model (Fraiberg, 1980); families who are expecting a baby or parenting children under the age of 3 are seen in their homes, multiple times each week if necessary. Program goals include supporting parents in the early care of their young children; strengthening developing attachment relationships; and reducing risks of emotional impairment, developmental failure, and parental abuse or neglect.

Four central themes required attention while I was working with the Aldens. Very early in the treatment relationship, issues related to isolation, mental illness, conflicted relationships, and compromised attachment surfaced. Then a traumatic birth and special needs of both the infant and young toddler required immediate attention. Next, increasing stress related to worsened financial status added to the complexity of the case. Last, disturbing memories from childhood interfered with the parent's optimal functioning and well-being. Significant effort was required on the part of the IMH specialist to initially engage and to sustain the parent. The therapeutic relationship became an anchor for Carol, the mother. After many months of work, she was able to enter into more positive relationships with her young children and with other adults as well.

Referral

Carol, a 31-year-old divorced mother, was referred to our program by her public health nurse due to postpartum depression and agoraphobia following the birth of Kyle, then 16 months old. Four months pregnant with her second child, Carol was described as a very conscientious mom whose worries about the many things requiring her attention could not be assuaged. In particular, Carol was concerned about her relationship with Allen, the father of her son and unborn child. Allen was no longer in the home, but their contacts were increasingly distressing. Carol was also concerned about Kyle, who was eating poorly, and about how she would handle things after the second baby's birth. Carol's mental health status had prevented a return to work after Kyle was born; she was on medical leave, but benefits would expire by the time the new baby was a few weeks old, leaving the family with no income.

First Visits

I called Carol to inquire about when we could meet to discuss the possibilities of working together. A few days later, I went to the home, a two-bedroom apartment in an old house in the center of our small town. It was clean and sparsely, but comfortably, furnished. The curtains were open, and the TV was on "for company." Carol invited me to sit down on the couch while she sat across the room, at the edge of the seat of her rocker. Her son, Kyle, did not leave her side; he remained in physical contact with her leg or on her lap the entire visit and refused to engage in anything other than brief eye contact with me.

A 16-month-old blond boy with large, watchful eyes, Kyle did not make a sound during the first visit. He was small for his age but coordinated in his movements. His mother described him as "such a good baby; we've always been very close." She reported that he said few words and primarily used gestures to make his desires known. When I commented on "having a new and strange person coming to see him and his mommy," Carol picked up on his insecurity and allowed him to stay as close to her as he needed. Although there were toys in the room, neither he nor Carol reached out to play with them, despite my comments that my interest in learning about Kyle's toys was a method to more comfortably engage them. I wondered then if Carol was clinging to Kyle as much as Kyle was to her.

During the first visit, I discussed how difficult it must be for Carol to let me into her home to talk about her worries. I explained that I would listen carefully to what she felt was important for me to know about herself and her family and that I would ask questions if I needed to better understand something. After a few visits, we would have an understanding of the issues we would work on together, if she decided to work with me. This clear acknowledgment of her control in the process was extremely important to her.

By the end of that first visit, I knew that she was most concerned about how she would emotionally handle parenting two children and eventually face the working world. She shared some of her mental health and family history: panic attacks since elementary school; depression and self-seclusion; a "possible" eating disorder; compulsive behaviors, such as alphabetizing her canned goods; and a mind that "would never stop going a hundred miles a minute." Carol left home at 14; her mother had problems with alcohol and mental illness, and Carol, on occasion, had been abused. When she was 21, she married a man who became abusive. She once took an overdose of pills in his presence and eventually left that relationship. In an effort to allow Carol to limit the information she shared and to assess her ability to reflect on important experiences, I asked if she thought any of these things impacted her now as she parents Kyle and anticipates her second baby.

Carol shared information in a manner indicative of having experienced unprocessed trauma, suggesting an attachment history that was anxious/ambivalent or, perhaps, disorganized. Indicators included a lack of coherent presentation, huge gaps in memory, and preoccupation with her parents' favoring of Carol's younger sibling. With the continuous theme in her stories of being judged as "bad," I grew concerned that, after sharing her stories with me, Carol would feel afraid that I, too, would judge and reject her like almost everyone else in her life.

Carol had limited childhood memories and felt disadvantaged because the little she did remember was bad. "I never know if what I'm doing with Kyle is right because I don't remember anyone doing anything like this with me. I can't tell if what he is doing is normal or not." "What is he doing that you wonder about?" I asked. " It seems lately that he is rejecting me," she said, as he clung to her leg.

"So, even though he seems to want to keep you very close to him, sometimes—like now—he acts differently with you than he has before," I responded. "Yes," Carol said. "Sometimes he doesn't want me to read or play cars with him. He wants to do it himself. He even goes in his bedroom and says 'No, Mommy!' if I come in after him. Am I doing something wrong?" "I'll be better able to understand after we spend more time together, but my guess is that Kyle may be telling you he is ready to do some things by himself. Many healthy toddlers do that at Kyle's age. What do you think about that?"

My intent during the first visit was to provide a safe experience so that Carol could continue to work with me. We discussed what it felt like to share her thoughts and feelings with me. Since Kyle didn't seem convinced that it was safe to be with me, I wondered if Carol was feeling cautious, too. Given Carol's significant history of depression, anxiety, and abuse, I hypothesized that she felt relatively helpless to affect what others did. I knew it was important to offer her control and choice, especially since she had been victimized and was uncertain if relationships would bring hope or hurt. "Do you want to take the next step and talk more?" I asked Carol. She did. We agreed that next time I would position myself on the floor. I hoped she would join me so that Kyle could begin to feel more comfortable in my presence, too.

The Next Visits

During the next few visits, Carol discussed conflicted and hurtful, yet intense, relationships with her parents, a sibling, and the baby's father. Other family relationships were virtually cut off to her. She could describe only one or two friendships ever. Her wish for a more satisfying relationship was sometimes expressed in expectations that were never met. She described the role of alcohol in her life—drinking at age 14 to numb her pain and to "give everybody what they expected of me."

She stopped drinking during her pregnancy with Kyle, but resumed when she stopped nursing him to help her cope and to "be with" her partner. Again, she stopped when she found out she was pregnant with this baby. She denied being addicted or fearing that she would resume drinking. It was clear that she did not want to associate herself with the type of parenting she had received.

"How do you know this about yourself, that you will not resume drinking after the baby is born?" I asked. "Being a good mother is everything to me. It wasn't that way with my mother," she said. "What do you remember about that time in your life?" "Not much," she explained, "but the few images I have are bad; I was hurt. I don't have good memories like normal people." "Normal people?" I asked. "People whose parents took care of them, cared about them. My parents screwed me up and now I don't know things I should know," Carol said. "You sound angry when you say that," I responded. "I am. It's not fair to me or to my kids—I feel like such a failure. When will it stop?" "Carol, by taking steps to really think about how your past influences you now in your relationships with your children, you are doing the work that will help it stop. This will be part of our work together, okay?"

By working with Kyle and Carol together, I hoped to help Carol better understand Kyle and increase the pleasure in their relationship. Kyle, less trusting of me, had to be cautiously wooed. Once we sat on the floor, he was intrigued with me. While casually talking with Carol, I handed Kyle a toy and he took it briefly before folding back into his mommy's lap. She described him as shy around strangers but very smart. I encouraged her to play with him while I was there so I could learn what he liked to do. Playing was awkward for Carol; she needed reassurance from me. For example, if Kyle got frustrated while playing, she needed help to learn that his frustration might not be the result of anything she did. Self-criticism and need for support of good parenting was evident. When Carol was anxious, Kyle became less self-assured and clingier.

The Baby She Was Carrying

Carol did not readily talk about the baby she was carrying; she had only a vague labor and delivery plan. She described feeling that something wasn't right, and worried that she would not be able to love this baby or handle having two children. It was as if she were afraid to invest too much hope in this baby. Indeed, her relationship with Allen had seriously undermined her shaky self-esteem, and she was struggling to feel competent and confident as a parent. After discovering she was pregnant, Carol had initially hoped that her relationship would improve with the baby's father. Now, the baby was so strongly associated with her rage at the father and her disgust with herself for being in this situation that I, too, wondered if she would be able to make room emotionally to love this baby. She shared many memories of how awful the first labor, delivery, and postpartum period were because of Allen's unpredictable behavior. Carol was beginning to accept that he would probably not be there for this delivery unless, somehow, she did everything according to his wishes.

A Glimpse of What It Is Really Like

I learned that Allen, 8 years Carol's junior, used drugs and alcohol and was verbally and emotionally abusive toward her and possibly

Kyle. I witnessed an example of Allen and Carol's difficult relationship early in my work with the family. Allen walked into the house and threw himself on the sofa. Carol wandered in and out of the room anxiously. He roughhoused with Kyle to the point that Kyle fell and hit his head on the table. Then, Allen called Carol to take care of Kyle. Next, he proceeded to criticize Carol because she had not potty-trained Kyle and because she was "hormonal," among many other criticisms. She quickly became enraged and tearful, and he continued to try to make her feel foolish. Things deteriorated quickly between them.

I knew that I was being shown what it was really like in this family, so I waited a few moments. I watched and wondered. Could Carol set limits to protect herself? If so, what would Allen do? I wondered if I would have an opportunity to work with Allen, too. I didn't want to miss an opportunity by running out too quickly, but I didn't want to be in danger, either. As I realized that Allen would remain cool and that he was invested in appearing rational while provoking her rage, I decided it was safe for me to stay in the house. As I attempted to talk with them together, Allen tried to change the subject and invited me to "figure out what the h— was wrong with her, 'cause she's a head case." He avoided any attempts I made to engage him in meaningful discussion about himself or Kyle. When Carol finally insisted that he leave, he slammed out of the house. Kyle witnessed all of this, silent and watchful. After Allen left, he cried. That introduction, and my responses that validated Carol's and Kyle's perceptions and distress, were important demonstrations that I would not judge Carol as defective, that I could be trusted with difficult issues, and that I could tolerate her grief and pain as she tried to face yet another hurt.

Our Plan

Given multiple issues that needed to be addressed simultaneously, we agreed to meet twice a week with Kyle present for at least part of those sessions. This frequency would allow us to talk about Carol's present concerns and connections with the past as much as she could tolerate. She had shown a tendency to become easily overwhelmed once she let her guard down. I knew that I needed to work slowly and allow enough time for Carol to process her feelings during each session. To invite a parent to observe her child with you and, additionally, to reflect on her own thoughts and feelings, enough time must be allowed.

This schedule provided ample time to focus attention on interactions between Kyle and Carol to support their strengths, offer developmental guidance, and reflect on their experiences together. I also hoped that I could help them both be more secure in their relationship before the baby arrived and added new demands for all.

Initially, Carol needed to address her disappointment in her relationship with Allen. She had hoped that this relationship would somehow be different than the others but, again, she was deeply disappointed. As Allen became more threatening and unpredictable, she needed a safety plan for herself and Kyle that would include contacting the police, if necessary. Understanding that Kyle suffered from witnessing his parents' conflicts gave Carol the motivation to set parameters to reduce the stress resulting from Allen's visits. Carol needed help to observe and put into words how Kyle's increasingly clingy and whiny behavior after visits or threats from his dad were signs of distress. She also needed encouragement to acknowledge fears for her own safety. We explored her options, and Carol decided to consult the local domestic violence shelter's legal advocate for help in obtaining a personal protection order.

Carol needed much support to work toward her own improved emotional health. She agreed to learn about depression and anxiety; how to recognize connections between events, thoughts, and feelings; and ways to more effectively cope with her feelings. Already having identified some connections between her childhood experiences and her current emotional well-being and parenting, Carol saw the need to continue talking about this over time. She became reconnected with a psychiatrist to prepare for quick postpartum treatment, if needed. We also continued to work on skill building, insight-oriented therapy, and problem-solving strategies.

Skill building focused on things Carol wanted to do better and things she had never done before. Her primary wish was to "get myself together so I can be a better parent." She was horrified that her depression and anxiety were so severe that she was on medical leave. She truly could not imagine being able to go back to work, yet she would have to. We began working on managing symptoms of depression and anxiety without medication until after the pregnancy, when she might consider their use.

Learning From Kyle

Carol learned how to become a supportive play partner to her toddler. This required a shift from being the primary choreographer of the play to following Kyle's lead while she responded and sometimes offered suggestions. The idea of play as a child's emotional work was intriguing to Carol, and she became better able to look for ideas that Kyle might be trying to express or worries he might be trying to play out. She began to encourage him to play out themes such as mommies feeding babies, controlling aggression, getting hurt, and getting "fixed."

Strengthening her relationships with Kyle and the baby-to-be was a central goal. Carol wanted very much for her children to be able to count on her. Strategies related to accomplishing this involved guided interaction in play, helping her wonder how Kyle experienced all kinds of events, good and bad, and giving voice to her feelings through parent-infant psychotherapy. Carol would say, "I think he feels I'm being mean to him when I say no." Then I would respond, "What is it that makes you think that?" "He cries and throws himself on the ground." "Yes, he is doing that. Do you remember feeling that way when you were young?" "Sort of; what I remember is the mean voices and probably being scared. I must have been scared. I can't remember letting myself go like that, though. I'd get beat." "Could that have something to do with why you think that Kyle feels you are being mean and why that scares you so much?" "But, I would never hurt him," she reminded me.

"Carol, I think he knows that. That has not been part of your history with him," I responded. "He doesn't expect that of you. He just wishes that everything would go exactly the way he wants. Like all toddlers, he is learning that sometimes it doesn't. Sometimes, it is Mommy who frustrates his wishes. That is different from being hit or mean voices telling you that you are bad. I think that might get confusing for you, though. Am I right?"

Often, the play and subsequent discussions led to memories surfacing from Carol's own childhood or earlier in her adult life. Carol was beginning to direct the anger, blame, and disgust she felt for herself to her parents. As Kyle did things she would have been beaten or rejected for, she began to empathize with her childhood self.

Considering Relationships

Carol's own lack of a consistent relationship in her past and present was an important focus of our conversations. She began to explore why the two significant men she had chosen in her life were abusive to her. She continued to perceive herself as defective for attracting this kind of man and at fault for relationships gone wrong.

During these discussions we began to talk about our own relationship. Carol greatly valued my input that supported her good mothering, her responsiveness to Kyle's expressed needs, her willingness to be brave enough to try new approaches with him when she needed to, and her attempts to reflect about why she experiences parenting the way she does. She also needed to think realistically about a birth plan and was encouraged to continue to voice feelings about this baby and the father.

Carol needed to increase her use of appropriate and available supports in the community. At the early stages, this meant helping her become aware of resources, considering the possible benefit to her family, and supporting her through anxieties about early contacts. Through this emotional support and coordination of services, Carol established connections with the Women's Case Manager at our substance abuse treatment center and with our Parents as Teachers parent-child play groups, the latter of which we visited together the first three times.

Carol learned to identify what triggered her most negative thoughts and feelings about herself and began to challenge some of those by recognizing when her behavior contrasted with her historical experience with her parents. She began to allow herself to hear Kyle's distress, frustration, or anger and, as my accepting presence and validating words emotionally held her, she could respond to him with sensitive nurturing and appropriate limits. She began to enjoy going to play groups and watching Kyle enjoy them as well. She was offered help with rides to the group by one of the other mothers after Allen wrecked her car shortly before the birth of the baby.

Protecting Her Family

As increasingly frightening incidents with Allen continued, Carol pursued court action to restrain him from contact with her. She continued to express a great deal of anger toward him and herself for the destructiveness of this relationship and the consequent loss of ever having a normal family with the father of her children. Through these discussions, she decided that Allen could not be present at the birth of this child, nor could he be trusted with Kyle's care. Her parents agreed to watch Kyle while she went through labor and delivery. She did not want to go to the hospital alone, and there was no one in her support system to coach her. I had done this for two other mothers in the past and suggested this as an option for her to consider.

A Therapist's Offer

The offer to coach Carol through her delivery was made after careful deliberation. Our discussions began with how different her reality would be from her wished-for experience. She knew that even if her mother agreed to be with her during delivery, there was an extremely good chance that something would come up and her mother would avoid the delivery because it would be emotionally too much for her. There was no one else to even remotely consider. I contemplated the possible pitfalls of offering myself in this role. I might not be reachable when the time came; Carol might experience an intense increase in transference with me, or it might become difficult to maintain professional boundaries after this experience. I might also be less of a support than she hoped I'd be. It seemed that all of these possibilities were either unlikely, based on our working relationship to date, or that they could be avoided or dealt with by careful exploration as time passed. Eventually, Carol requested that I be with her at the birth, and putting the plan in place helped reduce her anxiety.

The closer the anticipated due date came, the more Carol voiced worries that she was burdening me too much, that I would not be able to be there, that I would think badly of her. She grieved because she did not have the family support and care that "normal" people do. Where were her sisters, her aunts? How could she have gotten to this time in her life with no close women friends? How could she have been so foolish as to drag on a relationship with someone who so obviously couldn't care for her or share this event with her? Along with an increasing excitement for meeting the baby she carried, there was a great deal of pain associated with these questions she asked herself. I encouraged her to do this important work, as processing these issues would help her become emotionally more available to develop a relationship with her new baby.

The Therapist's Response

Once Carol decided that I would share her birth experience, I began to feel as if I'd taken on an enormous responsibility. Not one too large to handle, but a symbolic distillation of how much we can be counted on to hold families through trauma and growth. This responsibility forced me to consider my own limitations. I began to study everything I could about labor and delivery. I talked with colleagues about my fears that I might somehow let Carol down or that something might go wrong. I remembered the sad circumstances of the other labors I had attended. Although somewhat different, I wondered if this one would also be sad. I began to think about my own deliveries and the support I received from my husband. I remembered feeling a need to protect my own parents from seeing me in pain that neither they nor I could contain. I remembered the excitement and fear as each labor began. I also remembered the beautiful babies my husband and I brought into the world together. I could not have done that alone. I would not let Carol experience that alone, either. So I prepared.

Carol and I spoke at least once each day as labor drew near. My intent was to reassure her that I was thinking of her and could handle this responsibility. Her intent was to reassure herself that there would be no last minute change that would pull me away. Although that had not been her experience with me, it was her most common experience in the past.

When the day came, her parents arrived to care for Kyle, and we went to the hospital. Carol hoped the baby, approximately a week premature, would be all right. She practiced focused breathing while labor progressed very slowly. Induction was agreed upon because she was concerned about leaving Kyle with her parents for too long. As planned, she got an epidural when the pain became too intense and then relaxed and began looking forward to the baby's birth. Labor progressed quickly, and Carol asked me to call her father so he could cut the cord. He sped over.

Feeling Fear . . . and an Opportunity

When Mari was born, our joy was immediately disrupted. She had a large mass on her shoulder and neck, half the size of her head. Totally unexpected, we were frozen with fear, myself included. As professionals with responsibilities, the nurses, doctor, and I had to put our feelings aside to care for this mother and baby. We needed to talk about the mass and deal with it without panicking Carol or ourselves. How could I emotionally hold Carol now? What if her baby were to die?

When the doctor determined that the condition was not immediately life threatening, the nurse wrapped the baby and gave her to Carol while we waited for further medical consultation. The nurse and I praised Mari's wonderful ability to latch on as Carol nursed her; Carol was able to chuckle at the voracity of the baby's appetite. Overwhelmed with emotion, Carol's father left quickly. Carol began to wonder if she were being punished somehow. That is when I began to feel fear. How could I possibly convince Carol, so sure that most of what was difficult in her life was her own fault, that this was a random and unfair occurrence not brought on as punishment to her?

As Carol was being attended to, Mari was warming, being cleaned, and checked in the isolette. Carol asked me to watch the baby and tell her what the staff was doing. That offered an opportunity I am now grateful for, a situation of forced careful observation. Mari was calm, pink, bright, and alert. She sucked on her hand, looked at me, and tried to find our voices. She was a competent newborn, which was a great comfort to me and something I could latch on to. However, a huge mass nestled between her shoulder and neck, and we didn't know what it was.

I remember feeling as a husband or parent must feel in a similar situation. I held my own fears: primarily, that the baby would be seriously handicapped, that we would not be up to the task at hand to nurture her, or, most frightening, that she would die. I tried to hold Carol's fears by helping her articulate her fears and asking the doctors questions. At the same time, I tried to help her be receptive to her new baby. I wondered if she would suffer another terrible loss and worried if her family could be counted on to help.

The pediatrician gave a preliminary diagnosis of lymphangioma and recommended transfer to the nearest neonatal intensive care unit the next morning for evaluation by specialists. When Carol called her son, her parents reassured her that he would be fine and that her dad would take them to the next hospital when Mari was transferred. That night we stayed up late, quietly watching Mari, taking turns holding her and wondering about what she was feeling now and what she might face in the future. Carol tried to prepare herself to say good-bye to her new baby.

The next morning was a blur of activity. Carol's eyes were red from crying when I arrived at the hospital. I tried to help cut through necessary hospital paperwork. The baby's father found out that Carol was in the hospital and came in blustering and blaming Carol and the hospital staff. He reinforced all the self-blame Carol had convinced herself of through the night. When it came time to sign the birth certificate, he questioned paternity, creating a public outburst of pain and rage from Carol. I had to encourage him to leave, calling on hospital staff to assist. I saw Carol and her baby off to the new hospital with her father and awaited a call.

I Went to Wait With Her

Carol called later that day to tell me that the baby would undergo surgery to remove the growth, which was encroaching internally on her airway. Mari might not survive the surgery. Carol was concerned about how Kyle was doing with her mother and had sent her dad back to be with them. I could not fathom going through something like this alone, so I went to sit with her.

My own family had been waiting for this baby, too, I realized. Of course, I had to prepare them for possible calls beckoning me to the hospital at odd or inconvenient times, and I had asked for their understanding, which they gave. At that time, I had second thoughts about opening my family up to that knowledge. Perhaps I shouldn't have done this after all? However, I knew I could help my children deal with any fears that arose from the minimal information I had to share with them. Their father would take charge while I was briefly preoccupied with this new baby. I could see no other course of action with as positive a therapeutic outcome as the one I had begun.

The surgery went very well; the baby came through with an

excellent prognosis. Carol would have to stay with Mari for about a week while she recovered. Then Carol's family fell apart. Carol was blamed for demanding too much from her parents when her sister needed them to watch her children for the weekend, so her father drove Kyle down to her at the hospital and dropped him off. Carol and I problem-solved over the phone, and I contacted her aunt, who could get some of Kyle's diapers and clothes and tend to Carol's dog. I helped arrange care for Kyle and supported Carol while she learned to care for and feed Mari. Those few days of crisis and response will, as Carol said, "keep you always with me."

The Next Months

After Mari's birth and surgery, we often talked about the painful contrast between my real and emotional availability to her and the abandonment she repeatedly experienced by her family. "Once again," she said, "they've let me down. What is it about me that makes them not love me? Why are they always there for my sister, even though she dumps her children on them and goes out to the bars?" "What do you tell yourself is the reason for this, Carol? That is an important thing to understand," I often said. These discussions were painful for Carol. In her experience, relationships were all or nothing. She wanted to cut off all ties with her family, to hurt them back, to protect herself. I, too, wanted to protect her. I had to deal with those feelings, knowing that in reality cutting off ties with family would be a decision of momentous proportions. Helping Carol process the limitations of her family, her own self-blame for the abuse and abandonment she received through the years, and the meaning and limits of our relationship truly began at that point and has continued to evolve over the last year.

The Story Continues

There have been many other successes and crises for Carol and her children during the last year. She has found excellent day care that the children enjoy, and she has held a few temporary jobs and is gaining good work experience. She has periods of emotional growth and stability, and often feels that she is a good mother. Yet there are still periods when Carol is emotionally and physically overwhelmed with strong temptations to turn to alcohol. Kyle and Carol continue to use play as an avenue for expression. They play monsters and rescue and all kinds of things. Kyle has suffered from multiple infections; Carol is working closely with doctors to meet his needs. An engaging and sensitive little boy, he is still a barometer of his mother's feelings, yet he has an emotional life of his own that Carol enjoys.

As Mari approaches her first birthday, she is beginning to take a few steps. She is delightful and engaging. Her first 6 months were very difficult, because she developed a severe reflux problem that required surgery. She receives occupational and physical therapy for muscles and nerves in the scapular area that were affected by the original growth and scarring. She will need surgery again, most likely before her second birthday.

Carol still asks herself if she's a good mother, but now it is in response to the never-ending financial crises she is in, despite her own consistent efforts and the many resources we have identified. She believes that I have faith in her and has found strength in that knowledge. She watches her children play together and with her and is amazed at what they've brought to her life and taught her about herself. She describes being afraid of losing a daughter she has grown to love; a daughter she calls "my gust of wind" and who is clearly attached to her. I continue to support her efforts to cope with extreme demands from within herself and in the world, to watch her grow, share in the joy of her children, and be there when she struggles as their story unfolds.

As my work with this family continues, I am renewed and reinforced by Carol, Kyle, and Mari's growth and development and by the knowledge that our work together has helped facilitate this growth. It is, however, a challenge to remain emotionally on call, in what are sometimes very demanding situations. Reinforcing boundaries and the reality that our relationship is therapeutic rather than a friendship has also been a significant issue, as I had anticipated. I believe that, at this time, Carol understands that our relationship is unique and that, while there are important things to learn from it and experience within it, it will not be the same with other people. She knows that when our work is over, we will carry a piece of each other within us, and that she and her children will always remain important to me.

References

Fraiberg, S. (Ed.). (1980). *Clinical studies in infant mental health*. New York: Basic Books.

Discussion Questions

1. Safety dominated the work in this case. When confronted with a scene in which Allen's and Carol's relationship deteriorated in front of her, the IMH therapist decided it would be safe to stay in the home. What does an IMH therapist need to think about when considering issues of safety? Would you have made the same decision? What else might you have chosen to do? What might the outcome have been if you had handled the situation differently?

2. In what ways does the IMH therapist help the mother to understand her toddler's developmental struggle to be independent while still closely connected to her? How might this developmental struggle relate to the mother's need to be separate, yet dependent, too?

3. The decision to accompany a woman in labor and delivery is very complex. In this instance, what factors did the IMH therapist consider before making her decision? If this were your case, what alternatives might you have considered? What were the benefits of the therapist's decision to work so intimately with Carol? What were some of the risks?

4. How did the work with this family change when the infant was born with special medical needs? What other issues needed to be considered and addressed?

5. If this were your case, where would you have started with the family?

6. When living in a small town, an IMH therapist might see clients outside of their homes, e.g., in the grocery store. How does one protect a client's confidentiality and prepare a client for this possibility?

7. Carol was reconnected with a psychiatrist before the birth of her baby. Discuss when it is important to have psychiatry involved in IMH intervention and how the two disciplines can collaborate.

8. The development and use of the therapeutic relationship with the IMH therapist profoundly altered the way that Carol explored and made use of other relationships. Discuss the importance of the therapeutic relationship to IMH work.

Margrete and Her Babies: Creating a Holding Environment for a Cognitively Impaired Parent and Her Children

Bonnie Daligga

Summary

In the context of a Healthy Families home visiting program, an infant mental health (IMH) specialist works with a Healthy Families Family Support Worker to provide relationship-based home visiting to a pregnant 25-year-old woman with significant cognitive impairments who uses her relationships with program staff as a replacement for the supportive relationships that her family has never been able to offer. The Program staff is challenged to stretch —as well as to establish and maintain—appropriate boundaries while providing steady, caring support over a period of years to this woman and her two children. Work includes efforts to help the mother build an alternative support system with new friends and informal social supports, such as a weekly group for parents with learning difficulties and their children from birth to 5.

Introduction

My initial meeting with Margrete confirmed the emotions that had first awakened when her Family Support Worker (FSW) told the Healthy Start team about her early home visits. A tall African-American woman, now 28, Margrete is sometimes striking, even regal, in her appearance. More often, though, she carries a quiet sorrow on her face and in her body. She is a woman who was placed in special education classes when she was a child. Margrete tearfully recalled her mother's common refrain: "You are nothing, you stupid piece of shit." As an adult with learning difficulties, barely able to read, she has managed to negotiate her world by becoming accustomed to asking people for help. When we began to work with Margrete, she felt competent about very little and suffered recurrent depression. Still, her demeanor did not convey the shame we so often see in other cognitively impaired adults with whom we work. When Margrete flashes her smile and directs her gentle gaze at us, she quickly captures our hearts and our interest with a genuine connection.

Over time, Margrete has helped us to better understand the dilemmas and complexities of life as an adult and a parent with special needs. She has used her relationships with our program staff as a replacement, inadequate though it is, for the supportive relationships that her family has never been able to offer. This was a fairly frightening realization for our program staff, and it has challenged us to stretch as well as to establish and maintain appropriate boundaries with Margrete, while providing her and her children with steady, caring support in our home-visiting program. We have witnessed many examples of the undermining efforts of her mother, aunts, and cousins, and the results of her periodic attempts to reach out to them. The stories of her toxic beginnings had shocked us, and they were confirmed when she tried to introduce her new daughter to her family members and was rebuffed with more cruel words. Our work with Margrete necessarily focused on being more independent of her family, protecting herself from their heartlessness, and trying to build an alternative support system with new friends and informal social supports, as well as the formal services to which she was accustomed, if not resigned.

We have learned how enormously difficult living in almost any community can be for a person with cognitive limitations. We have come to believe that there are many community and system changes necessary to truly be able to "hold" families such as Margrete's in the manner Winnicott (1965) described with regard to a mother's task, ensuring children protected and nurturing beginnings. When an infant experiences the warmth and safety of being regularly held in a loving, dependable caregiver's arms, she is generally able to settle down, quelling fears or other disturbing emotional states. Thus calmed and assured that her world is responding to her needs, the baby becomes able over time to self-regulate and to turn her energies to mastering new skills, leading her to maturation and relative independence. Applying D. W. Winnicott's (1965, 1972) eloquent holding metaphor in a therapeutic relationship, and even wider to the community and family relationship, we have come to know that families such as Margrete's need more enduring, comprehensive, flexible assistance. Perhaps even more, they need and deserve compassionate, nurturing communities and sensitive individuals to provide supportive services and positive relationships that can be sustained over time (Kirshbaum, 2000). However, let me return to Margrete's story of the last 4 years, when our Healthy Families program provided support to her and her family.

Early Services

As an IMH specialist and supervisor of FSWs, I have had two distinct roles related to Healthy Families' service to Margrete and her growing family. When first assessed at the hospital prenatal clinic, Margrete was pregnant with Brigette. At 25, she was older than many mothers in our program, although she had previously given birth to a child who was removed from her care. The special medical needs of her son, born when Margrete was 18 and still in school, were more than she was able to handle, and her living arrangements were, at that time, quite unstable. Children's Protective Services stepped in and moved quickly to terminate Margrete's rights. We only heard bits and pieces of the story, since Margrete seemed to have buried much of that time of her life deep inside.

We assigned a FSW, but decided that I might be helpful in offering IMH support as well. Because the Healthy Families assessment revealed a host of losses in Margrete's history, including a baby for whom she seemed not to have fully grieved, we knew that the attachment to a new baby could easily be compromised. The FSW and I communicated often and planned ahead to keep our roles distinct; there was certainly enough to be done that we were both grateful to share the load. Primarily, I expected to focus on Margrete's unresolved grief over the loss of her son, but over time, other relationship issues also shaped our work together. Sometimes I have reinforced or supplemented the concrete supports offered by the FSW. Sometimes I have not been connected directly to her at all but simply a background supervisor, trying to keep in mind what we know about Margrete's needs and her ways of negotiating the world.

In our Healthy Families program, the tasks of the FSW in partnership with the parents are considerable. Primary among those tasks are the following:

1. share the program's curriculum on child development, health, and safety as well as activities to promote positive parent-child interaction;
2. help the family link to appropriate community services and to coordinate those services as appropriate;
3. assist in developing goals and working to meet those goals;
4. provide emotional support to the parent(s); and
5. assist with tangibles such as transportation, when necessary and possible.

For example, during her pregnancy, the FSW made sure that Margrete got to her prenatal appointments and helped her with such things as writing down questions for the doctor. They worked together to find a more appropriate house or apartment in which to begin to raise her baby. Fortunately, the FSW and Margrete were able to enlist the help of the agency that monitored and assisted the living circumstances of many recipients of Supplemental Security Income (SSI), and an apartment became available fairly quickly through their help. This cleared the way for me to focus my work on the clinical issues that threatened Margrete's beginnings with her next baby. Recognizing that our roles would overlap at times, the FSW and I were vigilant in our efforts to be clear with Margrete about what she could expect from each of us.

Prenatal Clinical Work

During the days before the birth, I helped Margrete to remember her prior pregnancy at age 18 and the events that led to her son Sedrick's removal. I hoped we would be able to remove some of her emotional burdens and leave her free to connect with her new baby. At first, Margrete would stare out the window and have little to say. When she could begin to tell me about her son, she would sometimes light up and speak of her dream that he would grow up strong and smart and would help the world. At other times, she would begin to sob as she recalled how fragile he was in his first days. "I was so scared he might die, but no one would help me. They would laugh and tell me I was being silly and stupid; Sedrick was fine, maybe he had a little cold. They would not even make sure I took his temperature right. I was afraid to ask them to drive us to the emergency room." Finally, after she had recounted the same events again and again, she began to feel her anger about her family's sabotage of her efforts to do what was needed for Sedrick. They were upset with her for not being able to do it herself, for not being able to stop her baby's demanding wails, for not having a place of her own—no one else would feed Sedrick, even occasionally. Margrete lost custody of her son, and her family continued to berate and blame her even while they had refused to help.

As Margrete laid out the story of her time with Sedrick, I worked hard to help her pace these difficult memories, giving her the power to go only as far as she wanted each time. My questions were gentle and infrequent. I listened carefully and occasionally reinforced her story with a recollection of something related that she had shared with me earlier—Margrete was amazed that I had remembered. With Margrete in control of the exploration of her past, she began to trust me and the process of the journey we had embarked on together. She began to sit closer to me, and the window shades were no longer drawn low to the sill. "I messed up," Margrete admitted as she filled in the details of Sedrick's illnesses and her response to them. "But I was so young and no one would help me. Sometimes I knew that he needed a doctor, and no one would take me to the appointment. Sometimes I wasn't allowed to use the phone."

She expressed dismay that she might have done to her son what her family had done to her. She sometimes could imagine that he was in a loving home, hopefully adopted, although she did not have any information on his current situation. She often took out of her wallet a worn newborn picture of him and a photograph that someone had taken in his second month, just before Protective Services had gotten involved, and she would lovingly caress the images. Gradually, she was rubbing her own tummy, investing some of her wishes and imaginings for her next baby. Then there would be an occasional day when she would rant and carry on about how angry she was, less at herself and more at her mother, her aunt, her sister, and those who had left her so alone—whether with Sedrick, before Sedrick, or after Sedrick. She had felt even more alone when Sedrick was taken from her. Eyes filling with tears, Margrete cried, "I am so stupid!" I responded, "Margrete, I think you sound like the only one who was trying to care for Sedrick. You were the smart one who knew what was needed but could not get the help you needed to do the right things for him." Margrete calmed and vowed to make things different for the baby she was now carrying.

Sometimes, when she remembered her first baby, Margrete became very stuck in her sorrow and blame. Reminders of what had worked against the relationship with her son had no impact whatsoever. It seemed, at those times, Margrete could not recall the emotional and cognitive processes that had brought her some peace about losing Sedrick. She was mired in an earlier time and could do nothing but clutch her sorrow close to her chest, unable to break loose its stronghold on her. There were other times that Margrete seemed to have totally misplaced a connection to her firstborn son, including the grief that ensued with her loss. She was almost too easily rid of her loss and did not seem to need to grieve. These were frustrating visits, which left me feeling powerless to help. The apparent limitations of Margrete's cognitive and emotional abilities sometimes seemed to permit her to forget her loss altogether. At other times, her limitations seemed to keep her from fully experiencing the loss in a way that would have led her to resolution. There were also stretches of time when Margrete seemed to have achieved a reasonable understanding about her losses and the abuse that she had suffered in her family. Working with Margrete's sharply opposing or shifting perspectives was an ongoing puzzle for me and our program and sometimes made clinical work inevitably unsettling or impossible. It was not that her limitations prevented any clinical advancement, which is sometimes the case when a person with cognitive deficits is concerned. I believe that there were cycles of disabling depression that would instigate her regressive states. I found that I had to ride out those periods. My role needed an adjustment of function; it demanded flexibility and patience. Occasionally, I necessarily decided to cut short a visit, with Margrete's full agreement. Sometimes, Margrete would become uncommunicative for a couple of weeks. I would call every few days, and usually we would reschedule in the next week or so.

During this pregnancy, I worked with Margrete, the FSW, and her public health nurse to develop an Individualized Family Support Plan. I remember how pleased Margrete was to have a meeting called just to focus on her and her needs. At about this time, she realized that sometimes our team meetings involved discussion about her and her baby. "You talk about me? And my baby?" She smiled broadly and expressed real pleasure and reassurance that we had discussions about her.

Jeree Pawl (1995) has reflected upon the concept of holding another person in mind, which seems to apply here. I am once again reminded of our program's importance to Margrete in offering her a holding environment, stretching Winnicott's concept to include keeping her present in our minds even when she was not with us. I believe we helped her to know that she was real and valued, not forgotten or obliterated as her family had often left her feeling. Much as a supportive parent would do with a child, we held Margrete's stories and her feelings, helping to contain those that otherwise threatened to overwhelm her. Even when she was less able to make decisions that would move her toward her goals, she usually was confident that we would hold her interests and needs in mind as we met, and she asked us if we had discussed her situation.

A Baby To Keep, Maybe

When Brigette was born, she was a robust and lovely baby who weighed 7 pounds, 4 ounces. With the assistance of her FSW, Margrete was settled into a plain but clean and relatively modern apartment, which she always kept neat as a pin. The labor and delivery were unremarkable (if it is possible to describe it so), and Margrete was so pleased to have a little girl. Brigette had her mother's intense eyes, a lovely tawny complexion, and an abundance of curly hair, much like her brother in the newborn photo her mother carried. During the first few days after they went home from the hospital, I would arrive for a home visit and often find Brigette asleep in her car seat, facing in the direction of her mother. Margrete was proud of her little beauty and nursed her with great tenderness, careful to cover herself modestly each time. A baby who alertly observed the activities around her, Brigette was easily contented and fairly passive. There was a brief scare about a hole in Brigette's heart, and, even when the doctor was certain it was healing itself, Margrete remained panicked and seemed unable to contain her fears.

One of the few early memories that surfaced as I met with them, other than her mother's hateful words about Margrete's inferiority, was how afraid Margrete had been as a little girl whenever she was ill or when her mother or sister became ill. During several home visits, I heard of other trips to the emergency room because Margrete feared she could not understand what was wrong with Brigette and could not make it better. Although the remembered evidence was subtle, I thought that Margrete was made to feel both that she was at fault when she or anyone was sick and that she was also supposed to make it right again. As a child, she was responding egocentrically, which was developmentally appropriate, and of course she could not make everyone all better, although she probably tried her best to do so. A child likely would internalize these experiences, feeling incompetent and unworthy, and perhaps also traumatized. She may also fear the loss—or maybe wish for the loss—of an abusive parent. Our conversation about these episodes, which in her memory had occurred quite frequently, led me to speculate that she may have been re-experiencing the panic associated with posttraumatic stress disorder when her babies became ill, necessitating medical professionals to take over the judgments about what to do. Margrete's panic and anxiety surfaced many times over those months, but she always refused to seek pharmaceutical treatment or further evaluation, regardless of our considerable efforts to encourage just that.

Unfortunately, another complicating factor in these early days of Brigette's life was her father. Like the father of Margrete's first child, Brigette's father was a man scarred by life and quick to take advantage of his relationship with Margrete. His efforts were often verbally and emotionally abusive, and Margrete was easy prey for his manipulations and the inappropriate use of her money, good heart, and good credit. Margrete began to separate herself from him and tried to withstand manipulations related to their baby. Brigette was not endangered, but her early life was impacted by such events as the telephone being cut off because her father had made many long-distance calls on Margrete's telephone, resulting in a bill which Margrete could not pay and which he would not assume. Margrete was disturbed by his inappropriate and misguided behaviors yet seemed powerless to protect herself from them. She would become outwardly angry that he did not follow through on his promises of assistance and maintenance of a good relationship with his tiny daughter. Yet, ultimately, Margrete agreed that she was mad at herself for getting involved with yet another undependable male. Each time she resolved to stop seeing him, however, she would eventually consent to another opportunity to be let down—and she was, again and again. The FSW and I tried to help Margrete step back and see her pattern of behavior and its destructive power. As with her grieving, she vacillated in her understanding about this behavior and resumed a position of powerlessness and victimization.

Baby, Interrupted

Quite unexpectedly, I learned that Margrete was planning to move with her baby and her belongings to Texas, where her father lived. She imagined that, at last, her father would take care of her and help her get established and she could be warm and able to escape her latest disappointing relationship. At first I thought Margrete was just daydreaming. Then I realized I was mistaken. This plan seemed to have emerged from nowhere, although Margrete apparently had thought about it for several years, on and off. No amount of conversation swayed her. My countertransference threatened to disrupt my ability to assist Margrete, since I was unhappy about her choices. I regarded this as a decision that would probably bring her much difficulty, and it reminded me of our many families who believe that a new location will take away their current troubles. However, the plan seemed to be her hope to grow up, to be independent of the Healthy Start staff in much the same way as a teen leaves home to test her independence.

She was seriously planning what she could take and what she had to leave behind. Driving to Texas with a baby would be a daunting task for anyone to do alone. She tried to figure out who might drive with her and began to scour her relative list, describing each as undependable as she told me her experiences with them. Then she began asking for a volunteer driver in her apartment complex, and I heard about several other shady-sounding characters. Each time I would ask if she and her baby could rely on the potential driver and trust that he had her interests in mind, not simply his own. Although this was a discouraging process, Margrete remained steadfast in her goal.

I came to believe that this was her dream, real to Margrete, even if unlikely to be actualized; and no one had the right to dismiss it. In fact, I quite admired how courageous she was in daring to act on this long-held dream. I so wanted to believe that she would find her rapprochement with her father and be able at last to feel some security and love within her family, although that was unlikely. She knew that her father had remarried, and she imagined that she might at last have a real mother as well. So Margrete set out without a second driver one early fall day, after we had discussions about how to map out her drive, planning how she would help Brigette survive those days on the highway in her packed car with a trailer tagging behind. We talked about how she would seek help if her car broke down or if she ran out of money. I listened as she dared to believe her father's words that he would help her find a place of her own, and that she and Brigette could stay with him for a few weeks.

Margrete came to our Healthy Start office to say good-bye to all of us, and I was reminded of my own early partings from my parents as well as the partings of my own child. She agreed to let us know that she had arrived safely and to send her new address. She gave us her father's telephone number. We told her about the Healthy Families program there and gave her the numbers to call. Then, with a broad smile on her face, she left. Brigette was 4 months old and just happy to be near her mama.

In the next 3 months we heard from Margrete twice. The first time she called, she was elated at her new start and hopeful about being on her own, although she hinted that things were not so wonderful between her and her father. Then, about 2 months later, we received a call that she was headed back. She sounded emotionally broken and almost out of money.

When the mother and daughter came into my office on their return, Margrete's face told the unfortunate, though perhaps inevitable, story. Her dad was still a hard-edged man who was bitter and angry most of the time, whether he was drinking or not. He could not deliver what Margrete had so hoped to get from him. He had been unable to tolerate the crying of his new grandchild, and his new wife was relentless in her critique of Margrete's caregiving, especially the fact that she continued to nurse Brigette.

The mother and infant who presented themselves in our office were desperate. Brigette was now 7 months old, and we hoped to see her interested in getting around to explore. Instead, she was clingy, made no effort to move around, and seemed passively content on her mother's lap—but only on her mother's lap. Brigette had been uprooted from the familiar and was expected to settle into an unfamiliar house with people entirely new to her who were none too sure that they wanted a baby in their home. Brigette's base was her mother. She was unable to move even 2 feet from her mother's body. Margrete herself seemed an orphan with a small baby to whom she clung. The sense of abandonment was as profound and unsettling to Brigette as it was consuming to Margrete. Unable to consider what had happened and what might be learned, Margrete carried around a mental whip with which she flogged herself many times for making such a terrible mistake as to think she might have been able to make her dreams come true. Each had lost her stable base from which to gather energy and the confidence to be able to regroup and tackle the next challenges. Gone was any sense of a holding environment.

Homeless and Rootless

What followed were 6 enormously troubled months of homelessness for this pair. With no apartment to return to, Margrete and Brigette moved first from one relative's home to another. Each was as bad as the last, reinforcing the many past and occasional current messages from Margrete's mother that she was a bad, incompetent person. There was even a week with Brigette's father, with the usual consequences. Then they moved into a shelter for women and children, but there was a 30-day limit for this arrangement. Another shelter, more bereft of home-like amenities than the last, became the roof over Margrete and Brigette. They stayed there for about 5 more months, surrounded by families in disarray for many reasons, most often substance abuse, frequently accompanied by mental illness.

I truly do not know how Margrete or Brigette survived. The costs were enormous to Margrete's state of mind, which was trapped in deep depression as might be expected. She could focus her mental energies only briefly and only at times. Brigette became all the more wary and insistent upon her mother's constant nearness. With so many other people around them, Brigette had persistent trouble sleeping; her frequent waking and crying jeopardized their stay more than once.

Although together virtually always, Margrete's preoccupation with the need to find her own place left her without the emotional energy to be attuned to Brigette. Therefore, Brigette began to look enervated and increasingly dull, as an infant with a depressed mother often does. The shelters required the residents to be out looking for homes or work or both during the day. By about 9:30 a.m. each morning, Margrete and Brigette were out in their car (when it was working) or at the mall or dropping by other lonely acquaintances' places or trying to fill out applications at various apartment complexes or agencies that served the homeless. I usually saw them twice a week for an hour in our playroom, trying to provide a brief respite from the anonymity of the streets, lines to wait in, and the lines of cots that dominated their grim days. In part, I had set up these appointments to help bring a small amount of continuity to these long weeks that Margrete and Brigette were staying in shelters. This was far less than either needed, but it appeared to help stabilize Margrete. She generally let out a sigh of relief each time she entered our door, greeted by some welcoming and familiar people. Margrete used our phones, and we tried to help both mother and daughter feel safe and nurtured, advocating with numerous support systems. Children's Protective Services was notified and monitored the situation to some extent.

During this homeless period, I became more worried about Brigette's passivity and the lack of motor advancement expected for her age (from 8 to 13 months). When they came in to see me, Margrete would update me on her recent days and any progress in the apartment search. She and I sometimes simply observed Brigette's limited play, and Margrete would occasionally engage her baby in a pleasurable exchange. Neither had great expectations of the other except physical presence. Margrete, herself, needed lots of emotional holding and containment through active listening and empathic validation for how difficult this time was for both of them. Although Brigette was always clean, dressed, and well fed, her expression became blanker and her silence was noticeable. Brigette had no word except "mama"—only grunts, cries, an occasional chuckle, and few other vocalizations. She seemed to understand a few of her mother's words. She did not crawl until after her first birthday and made no efforts to stand up. Brigette seldom was tempted to explore or reach beyond a toy that was offered to her.

As in our earliest service to Margrete, we functioned as her family base, albeit a meager one. We learned how the lack of an address impeded accessing mental health and other services. We learned that there were no integrated services for adults with cognitive limitations who were parents, although there were agencies that were ostensibly created to assist with their basic living needs. None of the sheltered environments that might be appropriate for Margrete would allow or accommodate a child. Similarly, without an address, services for a baby were limited to where the parent could transport her. Other than our program, Brigette was seen by a pediatrician several times and attended a playgroup to which her mother took her.

Home, at Last, and a Toddler Emerges

Finally, there was a call for Margrete with the message that a subsidized apartment had opened up for them. All of our Healthy Start staff felt the same deep relief that Margrete expressed. As soon as she and Brigette had had a few weeks in their very own apartment, we witnessed a transformation in both mother and child. Margrete's depression lifted, and she went about the business of finding the furnishings the apartment needed. Brigette began to look more like a toddler, with a safe and clean environment to develop her motor skills and let loose her curiosity. She remained extremely wary of other adults and, for a long time, was unable to let her mother out of her reach, much less her sight. A new FSW was assigned, since her former FSW had left the program, and she began to help Brigette and Margrete to play more freely together as well as to practice ways other than nursing to feel close and connected. Margrete became more invested in helping her daughter expand her horizons. Slowly their communication improved. With our support and encouragement, Margrete made efforts to talk with Brigette and to explain things to her as well as to encourage her to use words instead of whining or throwing things. Margrete continued to need considerable prompting to be consistent in these matters, though she was, as always, attentive to Brigette's basic needs. Learning how to support her child's language development has been a continuing goal for Margrete and the Healthy Start FSW in our work since.

Toddlerhood: The Difficulties of Discipline

Brigette grew more fully into her toddlerhood, her wide-eyed, tawny face capturing the notice of many. Still, issues surfaced that seemed to thread back to early, consciously lost traumatic experiences. The most prominent one involved toilet training. As with a number of our parents who have cognitive limitations, Margrete has great difficulty in being firm and consistent with general limit-setting, expectations, and body regulation practices that will allow a toddler to feel competent and in charge of her body. This often translated into inappropriate behaviors that Brigette tried out with her mother and any other adults who were present. Of course, this often left Margrete feeling embarrassed and in need of punishing her daughter.

We were often Margrete's alternate memory when she retreated from the trauma of the moment. When the FSW and I saw a belt in her apartment, we repeatedly had to remind her about the consequences of using "whoops" as a way to stop "bad" behavior in a child. Several times, we came across evidence of a resurfaced struggle with corporal punishment after Margrete's contact with her relatives, who had criticized her inability to control her toddler and goaded her to spank or whoop Brigette. Margrete once tearfully stated, "When my mama hit me I hated myself and her. I don't want Brigette to be scared of me like I was of my mother. Every hit made me feel humiliated."

This issue resurfaced time and time again. When Brigette lost control or tested her mother at a vulnerable moment, Margrete lost her capacity to respond firmly and appropriately. At those times, we witnessed an unraveling of empathy and reasoning. I believe that her cognitive impairment or the trauma-induced state overtook Margrete's better judgment at such times. Our program's role sometimes included serving as her back-up memory (holding her emotional sensitivity and her sound judgment or her more reasoned response) as well as a repository for the cognitive and emotional process she uses in nonstressed times. These are processes that a good parent might attempt for a temporarily out-of-control youngster or for an adult child with cognitive/memory problems—something no one in Margrete's family has ever been willing or able do. This role definition may seem unusual but might be viewed as a variation of offering Winnicott's (1972) holding environment, which may be experienced in a therapeutic setting, if not within a family.

The consequences for Brigette remain to be seen. With Margrete's fluctuations in consistency with her toddler, Brigette progresses developmentally primarily during Margrete's more stable stretches of time. When Margrete is in another depressive or regressed cycle, Brigette hunkers down and tries to tend to her own needs with less reliance on her mother's help. As her mother moves out of these periods, she leaps forward in several domains of development. Probably the most obvious cost is that Brigette is not emotionally well regulated, either; she lacks the skills to gain self-control. For both mother and daughter, anger is a dangerous and frightening emotion, and, like Margrete, Brigette will probably need help with it periodically throughout her life.

A Family Grows: Can It Thrive?

The last 18 months of work with Margrete evolved in several ways, as did her life. Not long after settling into her new home, Margrete met another man, Al, and soon they were living together. Al and Margrete began to discuss marriage, and he often participated in the home visits. Al seemed genuinely interested in both Margrete and Brigette. He frequently spoke of making Brigette a brother or sister. By the time of the wedding, there was another baby well on the way. Margrete wanted to continue with Sally, her new FSW, and she also expressed interest in the new groups Healthy Start was initiating. Together these seemed a good fit for her, with her expanded family commitments.

This became a natural point for me to take a background role with Margrete, and she agreed. Together we agreed that she could still call me whenever she needed, and she has regularly stopped by my office since then. But my role became more indirect, supporting the FSW as clinical supervisor and promoting regular communication between the group facilitators and the FSW.

The weekly group Margrete joined was for parents with learning difficulties and their children from birth to 5 years of age. Based on the Bavolek and Bavolek (1996) Family Nurturing Program, this group opened a new door for Margrete. Here she has been able to expand her social supports and get regular reinforcements for the nurturing she has tried so hard to offer and for the positive discipline methods she has tried to acquire. Additionally, this group has been more able to understand and accept her, because each member has some kind of mental or emotional difficulty that makes parenthood and decision making more problematic. While Margrete was in the parent group discussions, Brigette (and eventually her baby brother) were in a children's group. There they received abundant adult attention (the adult-to-child ratio was at least 1:2), were offered developmentally appropriate activities, and had the opportunity to develop their own social skills and friendships with other young children. Both the parents' group and the children's group had at least one IMH professional during the discussion and play-based activities, ensuring appropriate follow-up for each family. Each session concluded with a fun parent-child activity, an opportunity for further "coaching" in positive interactions.

This has become the center of the services for Margrete and her family. It has become apparent that Al also has cognitive limitations, though he has been able to maintain a job for several years. At times, he has joined in with the FSW during home visits, and, on at least one occasion, he came to a group meeting with Margrete. Our staff has also tried to assist her in gaining Al's cooperation and understanding of the consequences of corporal punishment, a practice his family advocated. Collaboration between the FSW and the group facilitators has been essential, as much to reduce our frustration over the temporary nature of changes in Margrete's and Al's disciplining decisions as to ensure that we provide simple and consistent messages of support to this family unit.

The relationship between Margrete and Al has frequently been very strained, since Al has placed unrealistic expectations on Margrete and Brigette and has tried to assuage his own wounded ego through controlling behaviors that border on abuse at times. Still, he has been very invested in his newborn son and has often appropriately addressed concerns about Brigette's lingering toddler behaviors. These relationship issues have been included in the group discussions, and the FSW has developed enough of a trusting relationship with Al that she has succeeded in connecting him with a professional from the fathers' program. We hope this will offer him a masculine model for nurturing his children and supporting his wife. We also hope it will eventually lead him to his own mental health support.

Brigette's little brother, Tim, is now a fairly competent 8-month-old baby. He has strong attachment behaviors and shows considerable trust that his mother will meet his needs. He has already experienced a period of about 2 months, during which Margrete performed her perfunctory duties but was depressed and depleted. She resisted considering medications, ostensibly so she could continue to nurse Tim. During this time, she shut out the FSW, blaming it on Al's wish to get everyone out of their business. Amazingly, she pulled herself out of this bout of depression. She stood up to her husband, told him she needed to have these services, and began to have home visits again. With our continued urging, she began to see a therapist in a local adult mental health clinic. Brigette is signed up to begin Head Start in the fall and will soon be evaluated for possible speech and language services through the school system. Brigette wavers in her relationship with Al, sometimes clearly feeling comfortable with him and sometimes retreating to her room to avoid him.

Where will this family be in the next month, year, or beyond? Healthy Start can offer about 2 more years of support services to this family. Probably Margrete will want us to remain longer. In our community, there is no other comprehensive family support program that can offer services to this family when Brigette reaches school age. However, Margrete is resourceful in accessing many kinds of help, and she does so except when her depression takes over. She has surprised me many times before, and I expect that she will do so again. We all wonder whether her marriage with Al will survive the many trials that lie ahead. Whether Margrete has another baby to tug on her frailties will also affect the probability of their survival as a family together. What we do know is that our program has made a difference in the lives of Margrete and her family, a difference that has allowed her to raise her second and third children until now. Healthy Start, with its unique combination of supports and an IMH perspective, has adapted and stretched considerably to try to hold Margrete and her growing family in these last 3 years. Yet we wonder: Will there be others to hold them when we must let go?

References

Bavolek, S., & Bavolek, J. (1996) *The nurturing program for parents and children, birth to five years.* Park City, Utah: Family Development Resources, Inc.

Kirshbaum, M. (2000). A disability culture perspective on early intervention with parents with physical or cognitive disabilities and their infants. *Infants and Young Children, 13,* 9-20.

Pawl, J. (1995). The therapeutic relationship as human connectedness. *Zero to Three, 15,* 1-5.

Winnicott, D. W. (1965). *The maturational processes and the facilitating environment.* Madison: International Universities Press, Inc.

Winnicott, D. W. (1972). *Holding and interpretation: Fragment of an analysis.* London: Hogarth Press.

Discussion Questions

1. What additional considerations might the IMH clinician keep in mind when assessing a parent with a cognitive impairment? What adaptations might be useful in planning an intervention?

2. Is the role of the clinician/practitioner likely to be different in families with parents who have special learning difficulties? Explain why and how.

3. How can a practitioner assist a family, such as Margrete's, which has no reasonably reliable family support network?

4. What are the special risks for infants and young children of cognitively impaired or mentally ill parents? What additional supports might be put into place to help reduce those risks and improve the quality of life for these children?

5. What were the strengths and risks that Margrete and Brigette each brought to the formation of their attachment relationship? What else might have been helpful to this intervention to better assure a healthy attachment?

6. Given the task of designing and implementing a coordinated community service plan for families with impaired parents and young children (and the continuous funding stream to do so), what would you envision to ensure that parents with cognitive impairment and their children are adequately nurtured and protected? What would you have to change about your community to be able to realize this goal?

Scaffolding Parental Functioning in the Context of Serious Mental Illness: Roles and Strategies for the Infant Mental Health Specialist

Kathie J. Albright

Summary

A pediatric clinic becomes the setting for an infant mental health (IMH) specialist's intervention with a mother and baby at high risk. The mother had suffered a psychotic break during her pregnancy and continued to show signs and symptoms of psychotic functioning following the birth of her baby but refused psychiatric care for herself. The pediatrician and social worker, feeling very much in need of support in interacting with a mother with serious mental illness, ask the IMH specialist to join them in providing ongoing pediatric care. Building on the mother's clear investment in her daughter's development, the therapist identifies herself as a specialist in the area of infant development. She uses a developmental and interaction guidance model to help the mother establish realistic expectations for her young child's development, and provides information about appropriate interactions. The chapter includes specific guidelines for working with parents whose ability to perceive their babies accurately and respond appropriately is compromised by psychosis.

The Referral

Worry and anxiety were palpable when I first learned of Angela's plight during a telephone call from a pediatric social worker from elsewhere within the University of Michigan Health System. I had never met this social worker, yet she was calling to ask if there was any way that I might be able to help her help Angela, a 2-month-old baby severely at risk because of her mother's psychiatric condition. She told me that she had been given my name by another social worker from Mott Children's Hospital, where I often served as a consultant concerning hospitalized infants and children through the Pediatric Consultation Liaison Service in the Division of Child and Adolescent Psychiatry. She went on to say that she was playing a supportive role in Angela's care during outpatient, well-baby visits at the Pediatric Continuity Care Clinic. She described how she and Angela's pediatrician both were alarmed by the mother's bizarre behavior and thinking, which she characterized as psychotic. Together, they felt that it was only a matter of time before Angela would be in extreme peril of some sort; they feared that she might be neglected, abandoned, injured, or even killed. They were also frustrated by their failed attempts to secure support for this mother and baby through Child Protective Services, for something more alarming needed to be reported before the situation could be investigated. They were feeling a tremendous burden monitoring Angela's progress themselves without benefit of knowing how she was doing at home between clinic visits, visits that were being scheduled more frequently than routine as a safety measure.

Although Angela was not yet failing to thrive, it was feared that she was on such a trajectory because she had not gained much weight during the month prior to the last clinic visit. At that visit, it was recommended that Angela's diet be supplemented with formula. Despite her baby's slow weight gain, the mother rejected this suggestion, stating that her live-in companion was opposed to bottle-feeding and wanted her to breast-feed only. Because the mother looked like a thin young girl, rather than a woman in her early twenties who had just recently given birth, it was suspected that she might be anorexic and using breast-feeding as a way to lose weight. It was also feared that she might be consciously or unconsciously under-feeding Angela as well. Besides the concern about Angela's nutrition and growth, the mother's beliefs about Angela were so unusual that she seemed out of touch with reality and unlikely to be caring for Angela appropriately in other ways. The mother's unreliability as an observer and historian highlighted for clinic staff just how little they knew about Angela outside of her visits to the clinic.

When I asked the social worker how she hoped I could help, she replied that she was open to any and all ideas. To start the thinking, she offered a few possibilities: serving as an on-site consultant to her and the pediatrician to help them when dealing with the mother during clinic visits; determining if the mother required psychiatric hospitalization and helping to make a formal case for this if needed; conducting a baseline developmental assessment that might be used later to document the mother's deleterious impact on her baby; or providing parental guidance, especially about handling and feeding, in a manner that this mother might somehow accept. I agreed to help, noting that it was certainly a difficult case requiring careful thought. Because Angela and her mother would not be returning to the clinic for almost 2 weeks, I suggested that we meet in person, along with the pediatrician, to discuss the case further and figure out how we might best collaborate. I wondered to myself whether we could find a way to salvage a relationship between a frightened mother and her vulnerable baby.

Learning More About Mother and Baby and Planning to Collaborate

After coordinating with the pediatrician about times, the social worker called me back, and we set up an appointment to meet right away. During this meeting, I was told what was known about Angela and her mother, Ms. Drew, who was a first-time mother in her early twenties. Ms. Drew had been hospitalized on psychiatric units, on an involuntary basis, on at least three different occasions over the course of the past year and a half. The first two inpatient stays were for about a month each at two different public hospitals in Chicago. This was before Ms. Drew became pregnant with Angela. Ms. Drew did not receive prenatal care until late in her pregnancy, when an older man, Mr. Staples, took her in off the street when he realized that she was homeless, pregnant, and in jeopardy, for she was prostituting herself. The details of how and why she came to Michigan were not clear. Due to her prostitution, Ms. Drew was not sure who had fathered Angela. Mr. Staples had been instrumental in obtaining prenatal care for Ms. Drew and provided transportation. During a check-up late in her pregnancy, it was evident to clinic staff that Ms. Drew had become psychotic. She was transferred directly to psychiatric emergency at a public hospital in Detroit and from there was hospitalized at a regional psychiatric hospital, again against her will. Here, she was hospitalized for about one month and then released to the care of Mr. Staples, just prior to giving birth to Angela.

During the three hospital stays and visit to psychiatric emergency, Ms. Drew had been given various diagnoses and provisional diagnoses: paranoid schizophrenia, atypical psychosis, catatonic-type schizophrenia, bipolar disorder, and schizoaffective disorder. Some of her worrisome symptoms included unsound reality testing; impaired judgment; burning of religious books; suicidal ideation; responding to auditory and apparently persecutory hallucinations; severe mood swings with profound crying spells; impulsive and hostile behavior; and catatonia, with an inability to attend to basic needs late in her pregnancy. She was considered to be potentially violent and at risk of fleeing or committing suicide. Immediately following discharge from the regional psychiatric hospital, Ms.

Drew refused further psychiatric care and stopped taking the psychotropic medication that had been prescribed to target her psychotic symptoms. Other details about Ms. Drew and her history were sketchy. However, it was known that she had stayed temporarily with an older sister in the Chicago area before coming to Michigan, had very little contact with her father throughout her life, and was currently estranged from her mother. It was also known that Ms. Drew's mother was schizophrenic and had been actively psychotic at times when parenting Ms. Drew during her childhood.

Although she shunned continuing medical care for herself, Ms. Drew brought Angela for regular pediatric visits with Mr. Staples' help. During these visits, Ms. Drew exhibited very odd behavior. For example, she once pulled down her underwear to show that she no longer had any menstrual flow. At other times, without warning, she would abruptly leave the examination room or hand Angela over to clinic staff. Ms. Drew also exhibited a pattern of marked interpersonal withdrawal in response to unwanted inquiry about her family, her history of psychiatric care, or her experience as a first-time mother. Her unusual behavior and pattern of response to questions alerted clinic staff not only to her continuing psychiatric difficulties but also to the possibility of inappropriate, if not destructive, interactions with Angela at home. Although Mr. Staples was certainly providing much needed financial and housing support, the exact nature of his relationship with Ms. Drew was not known. He was also described as quiet, socially awkward, and very odd. Because he did not participate in the clinic visits, it was up to Ms. Drew to incorporate the feedback and follow the advice given her, which the clinic staff felt she was unable or unwilling to do in a consistent manner.

Prompted by such observations and concerns, the social worker made several attempts to arrange for in-home support services, such as regular visits by a public health nurse or an IMH specialist. However, Ms. Drew refused all proposals for such support. She appeared threatened and paranoid, possibly fearing being hospitalized again against her will or having her baby taken from her. This meant that voluntary intervention would have to take place within the circumscribed scope of outpatient pediatric visits. Child Protective Services had already been contacted and apprised of the situation. Despite the reported concerns, including Angela's recent failure to gain adequate weight, there was insufficient evidence to warrant an investigation. This determination was made because the mother brought Angela for regular medical check-ups and Angela did not show any clear signs of maltreatment or neglect based on the observations and medical examinations made during these visits. Although Angela had not gained at the time of the last check-up, she had a good birth weight, she had not lost weight, and she was still within normal limits for her age.

It was not easy to identify positive aspects of Ms. Drew's relationship with her baby. However, by the end of our meeting, the social worker and pediatrician agreed that Ms. Drew appeared highly invested in her daughter's development and well-being. This was evidenced by her heightened interest and engagement when talking about Angela. Ms. Drew also provided excellent overall grooming and physical care of her baby, and was well equipped with all the expensive trappings of babyhood.

After much discussion, it was decided to move quickly to involve me directly in seeing Angela and her mother. This decision was made partly because the pediatrician and social worker were feeling very much in need of support in interacting with a psychotic mother. Despite her rejection of in-home services, Ms. Drew seemed to have established a fairly trusting relationship with the social worker, so I suggested that she incorporate me into the positive alliance that she had already formed. It was decided that she would introduce me as an infant development specialist and then stay in the room during my entire contact with the family. She would emphasize that I could help in ways that she could not, and I would offer to join in clinic visits to discuss Angela's developmental progress. This narrow emphasis on what I would offer was considered crucial because of Ms. Drew's guardedness, refusal of mental health services for herself, and resistance to receiving additional help in caring for Angela.

Since the pediatric setting was the only arena for monitoring how well Angela and her mother were doing, we agreed that my involvement would have to be acceptable to Ms. Drew and gently assimilated into the existing structure of ongoing pediatric care. The pediatrician had the practice of meeting with the family after the social worker, so this would continue. We would establish the procedure of meeting all together before her contact with the family so we could share our observations, alert her to any worrisome developments, identify important themes to reinforce in talking with the mother, and collaborate in other ways as needed. I also recommended that we try to involve Mr. Staples as a participant in clinic visits. Mr. Staples was a very important source of support for Ms. Drew and her baby. He had helped orchestrate Ms. Drew's prenatal care, provided support during her most recent psychiatric hospitalization, was continuing to let her live with him, and was financially supporting her and her baby. By involving him more, we could possibly multiply our intervention efforts and stay better informed about what was occurring at home between clinic visits.

The First Encounter: Creating a Reality-Based Focus

During the next clinic visit, I was introduced to Ms. Drew. She was an attractive but thin and fragile-looking woman, with long jet-black hair and dark sunken eyes. Her eye gaze was avoidant and fleeting, and she looked frightened, not just anxious, when averting her eyes. She looked more like a young teen than someone in her twenties. At the time of this first meeting, Angela was 2½ months old. Like her mother, she was thin and her eyes were not very engaging. I explained to Ms. Drew that I could meet with her regularly during clinic visits in order to follow Angela's developmental progress, discuss any questions she might have, and make suggestions about ways of interacting with Angela to further her development. I shared my finding that many first-time parents like a chance to meet with someone who knows a lot about babies because, of course, they have a lot of questions as they watch their baby change and learn to do new things. I further explained that I would come to clinic visits as long as she thought the time we spent together was useful to her. I clearly let Ms. Drew know that our meetings would be voluntary, hopefully setting the stage for a positive alliance based on mutual interest in Angela's development. I also offered myself as an expert, normalized the experience of having questions and concerns about being a parent, and established that we could share observations of Angela and talk about the kinds of things that parents and babies can do together.

Observing mother and baby. Although Ms. Drew accepted me as a member of the clinic team by agreeing to accept my services, the observations that I made during this first contact with her and Angela were extremely worrisome. Ms. Drew was difficult to interact with in that her exchanges were not very reciprocal. Often she did not respond to my questions and appeared to be attending to internal stimuli. Sometimes she made comments, out of the blue, that were totally unrelated to the topic being discussed. In one instance, she abruptly held out her hand to shake hands with me, when this was not at all socially appropriate in the sequence of events. In terms of caregiving ministrations, such as diapering and feeding, Ms. Drew was perfunctorily competent but very mechanical and wooden in her overall manner of relating to her baby. For example, she would change Angela's diaper quickly without talking to her or she would talk to Angela without changing her facial expression, moving her head, or providing vocal repetition and interest. Consequently, it appeared that Angela was not experiencing the kind of attuned, multimodal interactions that would engage her through a combination of her senses of movement, touch, sight, and sound and thereby enrich her social exchange with others.

Ms. Drew's behaviors while interacting and communicating with Angela were also lacking in meaningful responsiveness to Angela's affective states. In this regard, interpersonal exchange had already become negatively tinged and something to avoid for Angela. For example, Ms. Drew insisted that Angela liked a bumblebee rattle and continued to rapidly "buzz" the toy toward Angela's face despite her flinching, fussing, turning away, shutting down, and then drifting off to sleep. Ms. Drew chased Angela with the toy despite obvious cues that the baby was trying to disengage. During this extended bumblebee encounter, Ms. Drew misread or distorted Angela's personal experience of the exchange. For instance, at the height of Angela's protest and active turning away, Ms. Drew commented: "See, she likes the bumblebee. I like the bumblebee." It appeared that Ms. Drew's tendency was to overstimulate and intrude when she tried to engage with her baby and that Angela, in turn, was prone to withdraw or avert when overwhelmed by such interactive input. Despite Angela's apparent normal progress in terms of sensorimotor functioning, she seemed somewhat withdrawn and displayed a potent behavioral indicator of social apprehensiveness: staring at people with a vigilant, fixed gaze. It was worrisome that Angela was beginning to perceive the world as potentially overwhelming and something to shut out, instead of organizing herself to seek out further social engagement.

Ms. Drew's description of Angela's developmental achievements during this first encounter also reflected distortions in her perceptions of her baby's behavior. Although the distortions were generally positive, they were sufficiently gross that they indexed ways of handling and interacting with the baby that exceeded her capacities. For example, Ms. Drew maintained that Angela was trying to talk and imitate words, was close to crawling, and was on the brink of being able to stand alone—all at 2 months of age. These reports were clearly inaccurate. Further inquiry about practices at home revealed that Ms. Drew, along with Mr. Staples, had inappropriately established as priorities teaching Angela French and preparing her for gymnastics. Playing foreign language tapes was reported as one method being used to teach her French and holding her upside down was an activity provided as an example of the gymnastics program. All of this told me that, not only were Ms. Drew's observations distorted by powerful desires to have her baby excel, but that the activities selected as a means of stimulation and interaction were inappropriate from a developmental perspective. Obtaining a report from Ms.

Drew about realistic and appropriate ways of her interacting with Angela at home felt like looking for a needle in a haystack.

During my encounter with her, Ms. Drew frequently jiggled Angela in an effort to bring her to an alert state when she closed her eyes and seemed to drift toward sleep. When asked about this, Ms. Drew admitted to the practice of not allowing Angela to sleep during the day as a technique for helping her establish a pattern of sleeping through the night. When asked about feeding practices, Ms. Drew told me that she decided to breast-feed her baby primarily because of Mr. Staples' strong belief about the matter. This decision to breast-feed, as it turned out, was linked to her discontinuation of the antipsychotic medication that had been prescribed on discharge from the psychiatric hospital. Ms. Drew subscribed to a rigid but meager feeding schedule despite Angela's slow weight gain and clear signals of wanting to eat more often and for longer periods of time. Although she offered her breast when I talked about how Angela's rooting behavior was a way of saying she's hungry, Ms. Drew did not cradle her or hold her close. She also ended the feeding as soon as Angela paused or began to suck more slowly, as she explained was her method at home. In sum, not only were Ms. Drew's caregiving practices inappropriate from the perspective of realistic developmental expectations, but, more critical than this, they appeared to place Angela in jeopardy with respect to basic regulatory functions of arousal, sleeping, and feeding.

Discussing realistic expectations. During this first meeting, I tried to capitalize on several entry points for intervention. In two instances, when Ms. Drew suddenly thrust Angela out toward me with rigidly extended arms and without comment, I acknowledged that Angela was a nice baby but declined the opportunity to hold her because I was sure she would much prefer to be held by her mamma. Because Ms. Drew's previous rejection of in-home intervention was probably due to her fear of Angela being removed from her care, I tried to let her know that I thought she was the most important person in her baby's life and that I was not about to snatch her baby. I also tried to reframe some of her distortions of Angela's behavioral capacities and communications within a more realistic developmental framework. For example, I discussed Angela's mouthing movements within the normative context of the importance of sucking for a newborn and the use of the mouth as a way to first connect with the world. Along these lines, I commented how "all the mouthing a baby does can certainly look like talking." Then I tried to reset expectations by stating that "babies usually go through a period of babbling and then jabbering before saying their first words at around one year." In this way, I singled out a reality basis contained within the type of observations made by Ms. Drew that led to her distortion that Angela was almost talking, reinterpreted the meaning of her observation, and sketched out the expectable transformations along this developmental line. Ms. Drew's direct question about how to teach Angela to crawl better provided me with an opening to establish realistic expectations and goals in the area of motor development as well. The discussion about crawling led into a general discussion about the importance of starting where a baby is developmentally and providing opportunities for play and interaction and allowing new abilities to unfold naturally. I specifically advised Ms. Drew to stop holding Angela upside down and standing her up in a walking position because such activities were getting way ahead of the developmental timetable. I was careful to counterbalance this direct advice to Ms. Drew by registering that I could tell how proud she was to be Angela's mother and how she seemed eager to help Angela develop in the best possible ways.

I then offered to conduct a mini developmental assessment to give her a better idea of the kinds of things Angela should be able to do at her age. I used the assessment process not only as a means for reassuring Ms. Drew about her baby's normal progress but also for massively refocusing her attention to the kinds of exchanges that were appropriate with a 2-month-old infant. I showed Ms. Drew how Angela could visually regard and look for objects, search for the source of sounds, and be engaged in soothing face-to-face exchanges. To help Ms. Drew establish more realistic goals, I predicted for her the kinds of accomplishments she could look forward to during the 3 or 4 weeks before we would meet again. I described how, with experience, Angela would become more interested in face-to-face play and would become more expressive with social smiling and vocalizing. It was through face-to-face exchange that Angela would get to know her mother better. I suggested that Angela might become more interested in holding on to objects and exploring them with her hands and mouth. I also told her not to worry about the pauses in sucking during feeding because this was normal and emphasized how this time with mother is important to a baby. I then warned that breast-feeding might start to take even more time, as Angela took longer pauses to look at her mother, reach out to touch her, vocalize, and even become more playful.

During the entire interview, I also tried to help Ms. Drew understand her baby's signals by talking out loud about the meaning of Angela's behavioral cues, especially in relation to states such as sleepy, still hungry, frustrated by teasing, interested, and content. The other major intervention during this first encounter was to extend an invitation for Mr. Staples to attend our future meetings, because it seemed that he was also involved in parenting Angela. Ms. Drew liked this idea, so I offered to introduce myself to him while she and Angela were meeting with the doctor. She agreed and told me how I would find him in the waiting area.

Finding temporary closure. As planned, my meeting with Ms. Drew and her baby was held first to afford an opportunity for sharing observations and consulting with the pediatrician about important points before her contact with the family. During a brief, rapid-fire contact with the pediatrician, I emphasized my observations and recommendations concerning basic regulatory issues of arousal, eating, and sleeping, so that these could be addressed again from a medical standpoint. Since Angela was still slow in gaining weight, liberal breast-feeding on demand was going to be recommended by the physician. She would also reinforce the idea that a pause in sucking was not a reason to stop breast-feeding but was a cue to touch or talk to Angela to gently reengage her. I also told the physician that I had obtained Ms. Drew's approval to meet with Mr. Staples and invite him to participate in future clinic visits.

After talking with the pediatrician, I located Mr. Staples in the waiting area and told him about our plan to meet during clinic visits to talk about Angela's development. I explained how Ms. Drew thought it would be a good idea to include him, since he was helping her to parent Angela. Mr. Staples said he would be glad to join in and acknowledged that he was trying to help. Mr. Staples had an odd manner of engagement: his speech was slow and hesitating, his affect was quite flat, and he seemed uncomfortable relating socially, yet his eye contact was riveted. I told him that Ms. Drew seemed very interested in how to help Angela develop and mentioned a few good books for parents that might help to guide them in what to expect of Angela at different ages. I also provided a summary of the key recommendations that I made to Ms. Drew, emphasizing that Angela wasn't ready for gymnastics but that she needed help with establishing good eating and sleeping patterns. Although Mr. Staples was cordial and agreeable during this exchange, he did not spontaneously reveal much about himself or his thinking about Ms. Drew and her baby. It was difficult to determine to what extent he would become involved. Like Ms. Drew, however, he seemed positively invested in Angela and her development. Before she left the clinic, I made a point to tell Ms. Drew that Mr. Staples had agreed to join us during the next clinic visit and that I looked forward to seeing her and Angela again.

Although the first meeting with Angela and her mother went better than expected and Mr. Staples agreed to become more involved, the future for them and my work with them felt tenuous. It was true that Ms. Drew accepted me by agreeing to meet during future medical check-ups. However, I was not successful in engaging her in any extended interpersonal give-and-take, and therefore the meaning to her of our encounter was not really clear. The possibility that our exchange had unique meaning for Ms. Drew was suggested by her rather enigmatic behavior of abruptly introducing herself and offering a handshake in the midst of a discussion late in our meeting. I wanted to take this as a positive sign of acceptance, but this felt like a leap of faith on my part. I had serious questions about Ms. Drew's capacity to incorporate and use feedback, and any future success would hinge on this. Her recent history of shunning psychiatric care, discontinuing her medication, and refusing to allow a visiting nurse to see her baby at home underscored that this was a high-risk case in which intervention efforts could easily be thwarted. In a letter to the referring social worker and pediatrician, I summarized my observations and impressions from this first encounter. In this, I recommended that Angela required continuous close monitoring from a child protection standpoint.

A Second Meeting: Allying to Establish Dependable Ways of Relating

It was a long month until the next clinic visit. On my way to the clinic, I ran into Ms. Drew, Mr. Staples, and Angela, who were also on their way to our meeting. I was delighted when their faces lit up when they recognized me. Even little Angela beamed with a smile when I approached her in the stroller. "Something good is happening," I told myself. "Everyone is smiling!" On assessing Angela, I was also quite pleased about her developmental progress, for she had made clear and impressive gains in motor, social, language, and cognitive development during the intervening month. Overall, this second meeting was very encouraging, and my newfound but tempered optimism at the time was expressed in a letter to the referring social worker and pediatrician. This letter and other such letters served a liaison purpose, in addition to satisfying the need for clinical documentation. They included detailed information about what I expected to see, what I observed, and what I hoped to see at the next visit, highlighting key infant capacities in the usual developmental sequence. In that particular letter, I emphasized themes of self-regulation, attentional capacities, and social interest, and I described what I observed of Angela along these lines. Angela was looking at other people's faces for longer periods and was listening intently when they talked. She was turning her head to search out the source of a voice and was seeking out other people's eyes from a distance. She was also responding facially to perceived changes in the facial expressions of others and was showing patterns of social initiation through social smiling and expressive vocalization. In addition to such gains, Angela's mood was generally content; she was alert throughout my entire contact with her, and she showed good state-recovery by quickly calming herself after two instances of becoming upset. I summarized in the letter how Angela now appeared to be developing in the direction of becoming an increasingly vigorous and robust infant who was also very interested in interacting with people.

In addition to the positive mental status findings with respect to Angela, I was pleased to find that Ms. Drew and Mr. Staples were quite amenable to feedback. As a way to let me know that they had reset their developmental expectations, Mr. Staples jokingly commented: "Everything's fine, except Angela's not developing fast enough—she's not walking and talking!" He also informed me that they "dropped the gymnastics program" in response to my advice that the kinds of exercises they were doing with Angela were inappropriate. In addition, Mr. Staples and Ms. Drew made a point to let me know that they had bought Dr. Spock's book on infant development as a way to educate themselves. During the course of our meeting, Ms. Drew asked several questions about Angela's development and reported her own behavioral observations. Not only did her questions reveal increased acceptance of my role as a guide, but her observations also demonstrated enhanced skill in realistically perceiving and reporting Angela's behavior. In general, it appeared that once Ms. Drew was guided about what to look for and her anxieties were alleviated with respect to Angela's rate of developmental progress, she became more apt to exchange information, report reliably, and seek further guidance.

My observations of mother-infant transactions during this second encounter told me that Ms. Drew still had a tendency to overstimulate Angela and handle her abruptly. However, Angela was vocally protesting inappropriate handling now, and Ms. Drew was altering the form of her interaction in response to her daughter's protests. Also, Angela was displaying good capacity to soothe herself and recover to a calm state quickly, once her mother responded in a contingent way. It was really nice to see that Ms. Drew seemed very invested in keeping Angela's affect within a tolerable range and was allowing herself to be trained, so to speak, by Angela's communications about what she liked and did not like. I told Ms. Drew that Angela's vocal protests seemed to be her way of letting her mother know that something needs to change. As in the first meeting with this family, I predicted the next developmental agenda facing Angela, and I tried to convey a sense of excitement in antici-pating little developmental changes, as opposed to big developmen-tal leaps. As I conducted my assessment of Angela, I verbalized exactly what I was looking for in terms of her behavior and respons-es and demonstrated appropriate ways of interacting with Angela. Ms. Drew and Mr. Staples appeared quite interested in this verbal commentary and asked questions as we went along. I agreed to con-tinue this practice of talking about my observations and suggesting ways of interacting to bring out Angela's best during future meet-ings with them.

By the end of the second encounter, I felt more optimistic about Ms. Drew's capacity to utilize feedback and guidance, especially with Mr. Staples' functioning as a source of social support. It was also encouraging that Ms. Drew was accepting direct advice about how to interact with her baby, now that it was quite explicit that I could guide her interactions with Angela as well as track Angela's development with her. Despite these important gains, I thought it important to temper my enthusiasm in feedback to the social work-er and pediatrician because of Ms. Drew's variable functioning and potential for distorting or breaking from reality. Therefore, despite my favorable observations and the impression that Angela's good temperament was serving her well in relationship with her care-givers, I strongly recommended continued close monitoring with monthly pediatric visits.

The First Year:
Buffering the Attachment Between Mother and Baby

Throughout most of Angela's first year, the intervention proceeded in the same manner and with the same structure. Before clinic vis-its, which continued to be held on a monthly basis, the social work-er and I would meet to discuss the case. We would review our notes about the previous visit and predict what developmental achieve-ments might have emerged. We would also anticipate the next-step predictions we might want to make concerning Angela's develop-ment and forecast transactional issues or problems that might be on the horizon, exploring ways to positively influence parental repre-sentations and behavior in a prospective way. All of this discussion was not to generate a script for the sessions, but it was a mechanism for anticipating the probable developmental and transactional themes that we were likely to encounter. In this way, we would be optimally ready to perceive and then capitalize on naturally occur-ring opportunities for intervention as they unfolded in the session.

Ms. Drew obviously looked forward to our meetings. She came in with questions and realistic observations of her baby, became much more relaxed and lively, displayed pride in her expanding mothering abilities, and became increasingly dependable and empathetic in her manner of relating with Angela. Angela proceeded to grow and develop in expectable ways and began to excel, especially in communicating and relating socially. She was an engaging baby who became increasingly exuberant. In maintaining a consultation role, the social worker and I continued to meet with the pediatrician before her contacts with the family. More and more the discussions with the pediatrician became opportunities for remarking on how well Angela and her mother were doing and opportunities for talking about resiliency and strength. Worry about not knowing how Angela was doing between clinic visits had been transformed into positive anticipation about what she would be doing next and hearing about this from Ms. Drew, herself, now that she could provide realistic between-session updates.

Eventually, because of how consistently well Angela and her mother were doing, it was decided that only routine check-ups were required. Consequently, the developmental and interaction guidance sessions had to be separated from the clinic visits, if they were to continue on a monthly basis. Since the alliance with the family appeared strong enough to weather a transition, the issue of fewer medical visits and what to do about scheduling guidance sessions was raised. Ms. Drew and Mr. Staples readily accepted the invitation to keep meeting regularly elsewhere. The pediatrician, social worker, and I were delighted that the family felt prepared to make this transition.

Angela was close to a year old at the time of our first meeting in the Outpatient Clinic for Child and Adolescent Psychiatry. The referring social worker participated in this meeting, although her involvement in the developmental and interaction guidance sessions ended after this. This transitional session included a formal developmental assessment. I had asked Ms. Drew if I could conduct an assessment of Angela that would be recorded on videotape. I emphasized that Angela could help me make a good training tape about conducting developmental assessments because she was such a happy baby and was doing so well developmentally. Ms. Drew was delighted about the invitation and looked forward to getting a copy of the videotaped session to keep. For the actual occasion, Ms. Drew dressed Angela even better than usual in a blue velvet dress with a white lace collar, white tights, and white shoes. Ms. Drew and Mr. Staples were also dressed nicely, but clearly it was Angela who was dressed as the star of the show.

As had become our routine, Ms. Drew would report on her latest observations, noting if Angela's accomplishments matched our predictions of what she might be doing by the time we saw her again at the next scheduled visit. At the start of this session, Ms. Drew smiled from ear to ear and exclaimed, "Angela has a new word: mamma!" I matched her excitement: "She does?" Ms. Drew shook her head affirmatively and jutted out her chin, conveying pride and confidence that Angela was meeting expectations and possibly exceeding them. Ms. Drew reported that Angela had started walking, too, but she was still crawling when she wanted to get somewhere fast.

The joy of discovery was very much a part of all our sessions. This was the case in this session when we realized that Angela had added yet another new word to her vocabulary: "see." Early into the session, Angela showed much interest in the camera and videotaping equipment in the corner of the room. At one point, she transferred from a sitting position to a crawling position and aimed herself in the direction of the equipment. Instead of crawling toward the corner to investigate, she balanced on three points and lifted her right arm to extend her hand and index finger in a precise point toward the equipment. Angela also verbalized something that was a little difficult to make out, but, given her postural and gestural communication, I was able to discern that she was saying, "See." Ms. Drew enthusiastically confirmed that this was her impression, too: "That's it! That's it! That's what she's been saying!" She then remarked that Angela had been saying this word, sometimes repeatedly, when she pointed. Now, for the first time, it was finally clear to her what Angela had been trying to communicate. Ms. Drew proudly concluded that Angela was imitating her for she would often point things out to Angela and say "see" at the same time.

Now that Angela's focus of interest was made so clear, I encouraged her mother to help her investigate the equipment: "She can go over to see it, if you hold her." Ms. Drew carried Angela across the room so she could see how the rest of us could be viewed on the monitor: "See, they're on TV." What was so fun about this situation was how Angela's interests and communications were orchestrating adult behavior. With her mother's help, Angela soon had everyone looking, pointing, and waving for the camera so she could see the results on the monitor. Refinement of Angela's ability to point had been predicted in the previous session when she extended a limp hand at the end of an outstretched arm. Now she could point more precisely and was finding power in this for directing everyone's attention and behavior. As we talked about what was happening in the session, I also learned more about what was happening at home, how developmental accomplishments manifested themselves, and how they were noticed and then incorporated into family life. On their own initiative, this family had also amplified the developmental accomplishment of pointing into "the ET game," an interactive game of touching index fingers to extend moments of shared attention. At Mr. Staples' prompting, Angela joyfully cooperated in playing the ET game with him, revealing the well-rehearsed magic of touching index fingers together. Mr. Staples chuckled, "That's our little game."

In this session, Ms. Drew tried to persuade Angela to show me another new accomplishment—clapping her hands together. When Angela failed to cooperate, Ms. Drew was clearly disappointed. I tried to counterbalance the disappointment by remarking how Angela must be saving her best for her family at home. I then drew attention to how she seemed to have her own ideas about showing off, for she was trying to get our attention by pointing with her magic finger again. I also emphasized the intersubjective aspects of Angela's behavior, such as when Angela rang a bell but then seemed mostly interested in sharing how the bell worked with her mother, instead of just having fun ringing the bell on her own. Given her very broad smile, it was evident that Ms. Drew was delighted by my interpretation of how Angela's behavior revealed her strong and primary desire to connect with her mother.

Across all the treatment sessions, a major emphasis was on helping Ms. Drew perceive that Angela's behavior reflected specific internal states or needs, accurately read these states and needs, and then respond to them with empathy. With this emphasis, Ms. Drew had become very invested in keeping Angela in a positive state of arousal and in a positive interactive frame. She had also become quite confident in interpreting what Angela was reacting to and how she might be feeling. Whereas I was the one, early on, to profusely interpret Angela's behavioral signals as indices of internal states and then speak for her, Ms. Drew increasingly took on this role. For example, I successfully captured Angela's attention by shaking wooden beads in a plastic box but, before handing the box to her to investigate, I secretly removed the beads. This was done a couple of times, and, each time she was handed the box, Angela inspected it and then looked up at me with surprise, for she could not find what was making the rattling sound. Ms. Drew watched this exchange intently and then spoke for her baby, empathetically interpreting and giving voice to Angela's internal response: "Hey, ah, come on, give it to me."

A rather extended discussion ensued later in the session about Angela's attachment behavior and intense focus on her mother. Mr. Staples was concerned about Angela's fussing over little separations from her mother because this might foreshadow the development of a mother-daughter relationship that was too close. He thought that this had been the case with his own mother and grandmother. I framed Angela's fussing behavior within the context of a realistic expectation that this is what babies do when they succeed in forming a primary attachment relationship, a critical developmental task. Mr. Staples was emotionally supported by talking about how even the best soothing can fail when a baby Angela's age thinks that fussing might bring about a reunion with her mother. For Ms. Drew, Angela's intense focalization was not the problem; interference with this process was the problem. Mr. Staples was orchestrating little separations for the sake of getting Angela used to being apart from her mother, undermining Ms. Drew's opposing desire to be readily available. To help buffer the mother-infant attachment relationship from Mr. Staples' anxiety about its becoming too close, I explained how a baby naturally seeks out others and abandons an exclusive focus on the mother after feeling confident in the relationship with her, after learning that reunions always follow separations. I suggested to Mr. Staples that the practice separations were not really necessary because Angela would be naturally drawn to explore the world away from close proximity to her mother. I speculated further that the practice separations might actually be serving to intensify Angela's focus on her mother and briefly described the outcomes of attachment research.

The idea of Angela moving away from her to explore the world and to seek relationships with others was clearly uncomfortable for Ms. Drew. At one point in our discussion, she stood up with Angela, clutched her, and carried her away from the social circle. Ms. Drew's nonverbal behavior conveyed that, as hard as it had been for her to form a real emotional connection with her baby, it could be equally difficult for her to negotiate Angela's eventual striving for autonomy and separateness. Obviously, just the thought of it was threatening to her. I attempted to buffer the mother-infant attachment relationship from stress again by echoing the concepts with newly chosen words. A baby's ability to make new relationships was a sign of security; it was a sign of good mothering. In this way, I hoped to alleviate Ms. Drew's anxiety by establishing for her an internal link between feeling positive about being a good mother and recognizing that Angela would go about forming important relationships with other people when she was ready. Ms. Drew listened but said nothing more about the topic. However, she seemed to accept what I was saying because she returned to the social circle and sat down with Angela on her lap. Mr. Staples seemed to register the importance of what was happening in the session and acquiesced: "Yeah, now it's got to be mamma."

Angela continued to progress extremely well from a developmental standpoint. Her temperament continued to serve her well also, and she continued to be lively and happy. When she was close to 18 months of age, a formal assessment using the Bayley Scales (Bayley, 1969) yielded a developmental index of 122 on the mental scale. This placed her cognitive functioning within the superior range. During this same session, Angela spontaneously began to "play mamma" with a baby doll. Her play reflected internalization of an experience of nurturing care. She first enacted an organized diaper change, using tissues to wipe the doll's bottom and other clean tissues as pretend diapers. She then cradled her baby and breast-fed her, patting her gently as she vocalized softly, "Ah." This "ah" was clearly in imitation of the quality, tone, and downward modulation used by her mother when saying "ah" for comfort when calming Angela during breast-feeding and also for expressing affection when playing their new game: "little love pats." Ms. Drew prompted Angela to further express her sentiments by including me in their special game: "Give Kathie pats, Angela. Give Kathie little love pats." Angela responded cheerfully and walked over to give me little love pats on my arm. All together, we chorused, "Ah."

Toward the end of our meeting, when it came time to schedule our next session, Ms. Drew brought up the subject that she and Mr. Staples were taking a trip to Texas to help her mother. She was vague about the reason for this but shared that it involved a family crisis. When she said "crisis," she looked quite frightened, a powerful look I had not seen on her face since the first day we met. I offered to take extra time to talk with them about the crisis but this was clearly not something Ms. Drew was prepared to do, for she said, "That's all right," and abruptly stood up in getting ready to leave. Because of this turn of events and being unsure of when they would return from Texas, Ms. Drew and Mr. Staples did not schedule a next meeting with me. This was the first time since beginning our work together that this was the case. The plan was for them to call.

As it turned out, this was the last time that I saw Ms. Drew, Angela, and Mr. Staples. I found out that they had returned from their trip when Mr. Staples called almost a month later. He called to tell me that Ms. Drew did not wish to schedule any more meetings. I could hear her in the background telling him what to say during this call. She sounded very distressed. He seemed distressed, too, because of how upset she was. I had never heard her talk loudly or sound this upset. She had usually been very soft-spoken. She directed Mr. Staples to tell me: "Things have gotten too personal."

Because of this, she no longer wanted to meet with me and be reminded of things, things she left unspecified. She also told him to tell me about the agreement with her sister that, if Ms. Drew ever became too upset to take care of Angela, her sister would watch over her until the situation improved. From what Mr. Staples said, I gathered that this agreement was made between the two sisters because Ms. Drew was not doing very well after seeing her mother. Ms. Drew would not come to the telephone to talk with me directly. I asked Mr. Staples to tell Ms. Drew that she could call me at any time in the future if she changed her mind about our meetings or thought I could help in some way. When he told her this, she became more upset, and we agreed to end the call because it was no longer productive and was only serving to upset Ms. Drew. Mr. Staples concluded: "Things are difficult, but her mind is made up." For now, he was willing to go along with whatever she wanted, to appease her.

Fairly soon after this call, I sent a letter to Ms. Drew to offer, once again, to meet with her if she decided that this was something she would like to do. I was positive in the letter about the times we had met together in the past and what we could focus on in the future concerning Angela. I trusted that Ms. Drew received the letter, although I never heard from her or Mr. Staples again. Through contact with the referring social worker, I knew that Angela had been seen, along with her mother and Mr. Staples, for routine pediatric care at 18 plus months of age, and that she continued to do well. It was good to learn that it appeared as though Ms. Drew would be continuing to bring Angela for clinic visits. Nonetheless, the abrupt end to my work with Ms. Drew and Angela was difficult to accept.

I speculated about Ms. Drew's inner workings and her possible unease about getting too close after linking me in a circle of love pats. I wondered, too, about the crisis-related contact with her mother and what this might have stirred in her. I suspected that the crisis had something to do with her mother's mental illness and that contact with her mother had threatened her stability, reminding her of her own experiences with psychosis. I also guessed that coming to see me and, with this, seeing numerous signs containing the word "psychiatry" were being avoided for fear of triggering bad memories of psychosis and hospitalization. However, I found comfort in the thought that Ms. Drew had come to the realization that she needed to have a back-up arrangement for Angela's care, in the event that she might not be able to care for her herself. I was impressed that Angela had become this much of a person in her own right to Ms. Drew, a person with needs separate from those of her mother. Although I had envisioned working with Ms. Drew and Angela for a much longer time than how things turned out, I am thankful for Angela's good start in life, the positive experiences as a mother for Ms. Drew, and for the relationship that grew between them and that helped Angela to develop an internalized image of motherly love and care.

Concluding Case Remarks

Early on, the primary goal in this case was to extricate the baby from maternal distortions by establishing realistic expectations about her development and providing information about appropriate interactions with her. This treatment strategy was based on the operating assumption that Ms. Drew's psychotic break late in her pregnancy was linked with profound and disorganizing fears about becoming a mother, including terrorizing self-doubt about her capacity to function as a good mother. It was also considered that her odd behavior and unrealistic beliefs about her baby following her birth were serving to defend her from these fears, however tenuously. Given potent signs of continuing disorganization, with mental and emotional turmoil, focal attention to Ms. Drew's thought process and affective life was contraindicated. Instead, what was required was a reality-based scaffold on which a sense of predictability, competence, pleasure, and confidence could be built for both mother and baby. Angela became a link to reality for her mother, and Ms. Drew gradually was able to perceive and respond to her baby appropriately and lovingly. The mother's significant reconstitution and the baby's excellent developmental progress are viewed as forms of organizational coherence derived from the corrective modes of relating and communicating that came to connect one to the other.

Practice Points Concerning Work With Psychotic Mothers

It is critical that a mother be able to read and respond appropriately to her baby's signals and that caregiving exchanges be reasonably suited to the baby's functional developmental level. The development of the baby's sense of self is further dependent on the mother's ability to respond with a reasonable degree of affective attunement and empathy. These are primary requirements for a mother to meet during the first year.

When a mother's ability to perceive accurately and respond appropriately is compromised by psychosis, the baby's development is at severe risk. There are several related dangers, all involving the risk of neglect or abuse:

1. The baby may become incorporated into the parent's delusional system, which at the very least results in the mother's misinterpretation and idiosyncratic responses to the baby's behavior and

initiatives or, in the extreme, may result in severe distortion and maltreatment.

2. Due to delusions and ignorance, the mother may also have extreme expectations of the baby's developmental capacities, leading to grossly inappropriate caregiving practices and modes of interacting with the baby.

3. The mother's efforts to avoid overwhelming affects and the regressive pull of the maternal role may lead to a wooden or mechanical stance vis-à-vis the baby.

4. Alternatively, if the mother becomes more affectively labile, the baby may be subject to affective storms and chaotic care.

Although the risks to the baby loom large in such a situation, the clinician's leverage may seem slight. This is especially so if the mother is steadfast in refusing treatment for herself or if protective and supportive resources to keep mother and baby safe are difficult to mobilize. The frontline clinician is then faced with a psychiatric emergency of having to find a way to monitor and protect a severely at-risk baby in a context of maternal guardedness and suspiciousness. As highlighted in the reported case, a possible way out of this clinical dilemma is to purposefully avoid making the mother's psychopathology the focus of attention and instead to ally with the mother to make the baby's developmental progress an organizing focus of reality. The clinician who is identified as a specialist in the area of infant development can use this expert status as a vehicle for forming a relationship with the mother that is analogous to forming an apprenticeship. By imparting a normative, developmental, and transactional framework for the kinds of things that parents and babies do together and by taking a prescriptive approach, the clinician is in the position to scaffold the mother's role as primary organizing interactor with respect to her baby. This predictive extension of a developmental and interaction guidance model is especially useful in working with psychotic mothers, for this feature helps build continuity across sessions in terms of perception, expectation, and experience.

Summary Checklist of Aims When Working With Psychotic Mothers

1. Assess the mother's capacity to separate the perception and representation of her baby from psychotic processes and assess her ability to respond appropriately, despite possible psychotic perceptions and notions about her baby.

2. Create a working alliance in support of the mother's development of a sense of competence and positive self-esteem as a mother.

3. Focus on the baby's behavior, not the mother's psychosis, and create a context for collaborative observation of the baby.

4. Support and expand the realm of the mother's realistic perceptions of the baby through shared observation of the baby and provide developmental information and guidance, countering distorted perceptions and unrealistic or delusional expectations.

5. Endeavor to facilitate the mother's evolving relationship with the baby to become an "island of reality" and a primary organizer of her experience, again countering psychotic processes.

6. To the extent that early case finding makes it feasible, join as early as possible with the mother on the baby's behalf and begin to intervene during the neonatal period, while representations of the baby are more pliable.

7. To the extent possible, identify and mobilize family members, friends, professionals, and paraprofessionals in an active system of support for the mother and baby, including a focus on tracking and diluting the impact of the mother's psychotic functioning on the baby.

References

Bayley, N. (1969). *Bayley scales of infant development.* New York: Psychological Corporation.

Discussion Questions

1. Both the pediatrician and social worker were alarmed by Ms. Drew's bizarre behavior and thinking. They called upon the author as a resource. What resources are available in your own community for support or consultation regarding infants who are at severe risk and their families?

2. Ms. Drew had an extensive psychiatric history including refusal of psychiatric care, psychotropic medication, and medical care for herself. Despite this resistance to treatment, the author successfully engaged Ms. Drew and developed a therapeutic alliance with her. What were the author's strategies? Give specific examples of strategies put into place.

3. In the Summary Checklist, the author recommends assessing the mother's capacity to separate the perception and representation of the baby from the psychotic process. If the mother was unable to separate the baby from her distorted thinking and there were serious concerns about appropriate maternal response, how would the treatment plan be altered?

4. The author gives several examples of developmental guidance. At 2 months, for example, she predicted that Angela would soon be more interested in face-to-face play with social smiling and more vocalizing. Considering the first year of life, what other developmental milestones might be important to predict to parents? Which of these milestones might significantly impact on the infant-parent relationship?

5. Considering a parent and infant you are working with, how can you use the relationship with the baby to be an "island of reality," or primary organizer for the parent's experience?

6. This intervention strengthened the infant-parent relationship during Angela's first year. Consider how this will help buffer Angela for the inevitable challenges she will yet face.

No Longer Risking Myself: Assisting the Supervisor Through Supportive Consultation

Brooke Foulds and Kendra Curtiss

Summary

The relationship-based approach that is the hallmark of infant mental health (IMH) intervention can also characterize personal and professional supports to program staff. Many agencies do not build in support for their supervisors and managers, who are called upon to support their staff as they bear direct witness to the chronic pain and need of others. They may also lack support when they find difficult parallels between their work and their personal histories. The authors of this chapter observe that "relationships are the means through which we best teach about the role of relationships in the optimal development of children." In this collaborative story, a consultant, trained for many years within the field of IMH, provides an opportunity for a program supervisor to reflect on the connection between her personal and professional life. Through their relationship, the supervisor considers how her own history affects her ability to understand and relate to her staff.

A Consultant's Dilemma: Brooke's Reflections

As I think about how to respond to a request to write about my work as a supervisor in IMH, my mind reaches back over the years, remembering a series of moments, scenes in meager apartment living rooms and sparse public offices. Many of those moments are with families, most consisting of mothers and their babies. So many lessons were taught to me in those rooms by the many fragile yet stalwart women clinging to their young children, struggling to find their way despite the drag of poverty, violent environments, numbing loneliness, and childhood histories of uncertain parental love and protection. Then there are the moments, adding up to years, knee-to-knee with my many colleagues, mostly women younger than me, who were struggling through similar lessons taught by similar families, in similar rooms. The lessons I learned in my years of delivering IMH services, mentored by more experienced colleagues, ground me as I consult with others, knowing that supportive supervision is the true bedrock of high-quality service for children from birth to 3 years old.

As a service provider in the field of infant-family work for more than 30 years, I am completely committed to the concept that relationships are the means through which we best teach about the role of relationships in the optimal development of children. Although I still consider myself an IMH professional, I no longer provide services or clinical supervision to IMH specialists. I am uncertain that I am in a position to discuss the issue of supervision in a helpful way. Yet just this week, in my current position as a consultant to programs that serve children from birth to 3 years, I found myself reaching back for the message of those living room lessons, as I listened to another young woman talk about her work.

A Colleague Under Duress

Kendra is a supervisor in a program that provides comprehensive services to low-income families, including pregnant women and their infants and toddlers, who are scattered in homes over five predominantly rural counties of northern Michigan. I have known Kendra for nearly 5 years, since the inception of our program. She has provided quiet, competent leadership in the development of the program, steadily identifying gaps in services and developing partnerships with other community agencies to improve the quality of services the agency offers to families. I respect her dedication to children and their families and like her for the delight she finds in caring for her staff as they care for others.

Looking for guidance in addressing the program's needs, I began consulting with Kendra. When I saw her for the first time that day, I immediately reacted to her appearance. As I attempted to keep my visceral reaction to myself, I moved to two levels of thought. On one level, I focused on how I might address what I was seeing and becoming aware of in Kendra. On the other level, I thought about the status of the program, the business of assessing staff development needs, and the maintenance of the program standards expected by the program's funding source.

Kendra had battled a physical illness for the better part of a year; at the same time, she was trying to expand the desperately needed service to families while maintaining the quality of these services. She is also a mother in the center of her own growing family. I first asked about her and her family. "Kendra, how is your son? Is he still having difficulty with his asthma? And your girls, what are they up to these days?" We chatted about the health and antics of her younger children and the volleyball games of the daughter in her middle teens. I knew from previous discussions with Kendra that the illness, undiagnosed for many months, had added an additional drain to the energy and enthusiasm she always exuded when I saw her. As we settled into a modestly furnished public meeting room, I noticed that she was many pounds lighter than during the previous year, and she seemed far more fragile. In this room we would spend the day, talking about her program and identifying the needs for which I might provide supportive consultation.

This is very demanding work, but I couldn't help wondering, "What is happening with Kendra? Is there something, other than her illness, that I am sensing in her quieter mood and her more tentative interaction and eye contact?"

I inquired about the status of the program and the changes since we last met. "What have you been thinking about staff development needs this year?" I began. Because of our relationship, I felt comfortable asking, "Kendra, how have you been feeling?" She was quite open with me about her quest for a diagnosis, her chronic fatigue, and the need to reduce her hours in the office, simply to maintain her ability to function in her job and with her family.

Kendra then shared with me that she was better, but still not up to her previous energy and functional level. Out of respect for our history of straightforward and honest interaction, I commented on my observation of her appearance. "I see that you have really lost more weight. Are you still able to flex your work time?" I inquired about details, asking about agency support and what it was like to live with her level of fatigue. I was hoping she would share information that might help me ascertain if she was feeling less optimistic about her ability to manage it all. I asked about the staff and the work that they were doing with the families. I asked about the benefits she might have found in the IMH consultation I had been providing, which had focused on reflective supervision on behalf of the supervising staff. Her answer came quickly, "Well, the staff are providing reflective supervision to the family service providers. I can't say everyone is responding to my expectations with total enthusiasm, but they are doing it."

She responded to all my inquiries with a frank appraisal of the situation, noting that she was managing but that it was a very full load. Within a few minutes of the initial exchange about the program status and then her health, she matter-of-factly mentioned, "The reason I was late and you had to wait in the reception area was that Shirley pulled me aside to ask about Phyllis." She explained that Shirley, the Executive Director, had asked her about the situation of a former employee whom Kendra had supervised during the previous year. Phyllis, the former employee, died the previous week while the Executive Director had been at a conference. Kendra cast her eyes downward and explained that Phyllis had committed suicide, shooting herself in her brother's home while he was away.

My Cue to Ask More

My red flags warned me, "This is serious. This is a clue." Suicide, by someone Kendra had supported in supervision? I told myself, "Brooke, pay close attention." In response to my expression of concern, Kendra added, "I talked to Phyllis only 3 days before she died, when she called to ask if she might qualify for a newly posted position under my supervision." She then softly stated that she felt very badly for the children Phyllis had left behind.

This was my cue to ask more. I asked for more information about the family situation and then, sketching details about the incident, Kendra said again, "I really feel badly for the kids." The office had continued to function, and Kendra continued to function; everything went on as normal. I wondered how Kendra had dealt with her emotions? How did she manage to get through her days and nights? Because of her demeanor, I suspected that Kendra had removed and distanced herself from the mental images of Phyllis' death and the knowledge that Phyllis might have been contemplating suicide when she called Kendra about the job. I knew this was critical. "How significant it must have been for you to have to distance yourself from what Phyllis may have been telling those around her." Kendra looked at me and wearily acknowledged, "Yes, it was hard," and then went on to share with me her own childhood history.

Kendra Tells Her Story

She told me that her mother had, more than once, threatened to kill herself when Kendra was a young child. She remembers well how she, as a young teenager and the oldest girl, had finally decided that she could not make things different for her mother. To survive, she moved to her father's home, only to find that there, too, the responsibilities of parenting an alcoholic were too great for a 16-year-old girl. Subsequently, she moved into the home of a sympathetic, nurturing older woman to simply make it through high school. She could only imagine the feelings of the children left behind in Phyllis's tragedy, and she felt very, very sad.

"I wonder if you might be remembering what it was like when you were young. It would be very understandable if you were experiencing feelings from that time in your life." Kendra told me about feeling forced to choose between abandoning her parents and younger siblings and her own survival when she was a teenager. I observed that this recent tragedy of another woman, with whom she had had a nurturing role, might evoke memories of the imagined death of her own mother that she had carried with her for such a long time. "Those memories and feelings must be very present for you right now."

I think there was a tacit understanding between the two of us, that she, in no way, had responsibility for Phyllis's decision to take her own life. I knew, nevertheless, that she might feel guilt, while at the same time there might be angry feelings related to her identification with Phyllis's children. I remarked that often in our line of work we find ourselves trying to lighten the burdens and support the competencies of others, on the basis of discoveries of our own childhood struggles.

Following My Instincts

As I conversed with Kendra, I continued to ponder my role as a consultant, since I did not have a formal contract that allowed me to inquire about her personal life or her feelings. I decided, nevertheless, to follow my initial instinct that Kendra was going through some significant difficulty. This was based on my own experiences as a supervisor and, in part, because I was seriously concerned about Kendra's health and well-being. I trusted that she would let me know if I had overstepped my boundaries and that the relationship we had developed in the past years would carry us through any awkward moments. I weighed her need for privacy against what might be a breach of relationship if I did not offer her the best of my own experiences and knowledge. In the face of pressing emotional issues, often there is a tendency to become distant and task focused. I knew that the matter-of-fact statement about Phyllis's suicide meant more than she said. A quick assessment of our relationship led me to ask more about her emotional reaction. I knew it was more than "just facts," so I responded to the cues she provided me with when she spoke of her feelings about the children.

We Begin to Talk

As a professional, I am very concerned about the quality of care for infants and toddlers and their families. I am also very concerned about those who provide this care. Now, I felt especially concerned about Kendra. My internal voice was asking, "What about this young woman who works so diligently on behalf of very young children? Where does she find the energy to carry such a tremendous load? Has she asked herself to carry more than is possible for her to carry? Where can she sort out her own feelings about Phyllis's desperation? What will she experience when she thinks about how her former employee's suicide might affect the joy and confidence of the children she left behind?"

So we began to talk. We talked about the need for Kendra to seek support for herself and to consider options to alter the situation she finds herself in. Kendra reported that, while the agency has been very supportive during her illness, it had not built in support for its supervisors and managers when they find difficult parallels between their work and their personal histories. Like Kendra, most administrators of programs designed to meet the needs of infants and young children do not have protected time and support to understand or talk through the evocative nature of work with parents and vulnerable babies. This lack of clinical supervision is a potential drain on the best leadership skills and commitment of our most capable managers and supervisors. They need support as they support those who bear direct witness to the chronic pain and need of others.

Someone to Share the Experience With

On this particular day, just by coincidence, Kendra could share her experiences with someone who understood the possible interrelationships between abandonment, conflicted attachment, and maternal depression. Often we ask so much of our managers and supervisors but do very little to provide a safety net to sustain them in their very difficult work on behalf of infants and toddlers. Our managers and supervisors tend to be isolated within programs, with business days too full to manage and families who demand—and must have—their attention first. Nevertheless, it is important to convey the message that each must find a way to counteract the isolation and pursue personal growth. Each must find a way to be "held" professionally so that they can continue to hold and nurture a program and its staff, and so that they and their direct service colleagues can experience each of the normal developmental stages in the work that Bill Schafer describes as "the professionalization of motherhood." Schafer suggests that, by moving through stages, the practitioner will find that he or she "has grown personally, that one's professional work has left one calmer, warmer, more honest and wise" (Schaffer, 1992, p. 75).

Kendra's Reflections

As I reflect on my experiences as a supervisor of staff who provide services to low-income families with pregnant women, infants, and toddlers, I remember many cases where staff have shared frustrating, scary, or even tragic situations. I wonder, "Did I hear their concerns? Did I note the personal impact that the experience might have had on them? Did I respond only to the surface problem, or did I really help my staff understand the personal impact of those problems on them and their families?" This reflection comes after a moving experience happened to me.

It was just another day with too many things to do and the pressure of trying to juggle my many responsibilities. Don't get me wrong, I love my job. It can be very rewarding and fulfilling, but it also can be emotionally draining. Brooke, our program consultant, arrived just as I had planned. Brooke and I had known each other for almost 5 years then, so our morning greeting was warm and familiar. "How are things with you, Brooke? As busy as ever, I would imagine?" I noted how busy Brooke had been as a consultant for a rapidly growing, federally funded program—the pressure was always present. Brooke responded briefly about her previous few weeks of work and travel. I shared stories of my children and family. As we settled into our meeting, we discussed the condition of my health and how I have been feeling recently.

My health has been a major concern for me during the past year. Having been diagnosed with a relatively new syndrome, I have wondered many times, "Is the job the cause? Am I going crazy?" I question the medical profession and myself: "Will this ever end?"

The Focus Changes

The focus of the meeting changed from my health to the status of the program, or so I thought. "Overall, the program is going quite well," I responded to Brooke's inquiry. Together we reflected on the previous consultation and how it had impacted the program. I stated, "my line staff is benefiting from the reflective supervision that we have implemented, though we have not yet implemented it in all program areas." Brooke again voiced her concern for my health and for me and questioned whether not just the staff, but I, needed support. She asked, "What are you doing for yourself, Kendra? Are you taking care of yourself?" I responded that "I do what I need to do, the agency lets me come in late if I need to."

I knew that Brooke's question asked about care beyond the option to come in late. She was talking about taking care of myself emotionally, so that I can give what is needed to the employees I supervise and my own family. Though I believe that my agency is very supportive of their employees, reflective supervision is not part of our philosophy. Until that day, I guess I secretly believed that reflective supervision was very important for staff who work directly with families at risk but not for supervisors who just "push paper." Again, Brooke voiced her concern about my health and me and asked me to consider options I might have for more support. I remember feeling awkward and nervous, part of me thinking, "We should be focusing on the Program and not me. Why are we spending time talking about my feelings?" At the same time, another part of me was thinking, "I need to talk to someone desperately."

To move the conversation away from me, I agreed to consider my options. At that point in our conversation, I changed the subject to mention an event that occurred the previous week, believing we would no longer focus on my current state. Little did I know that my choice was, in fact, to move directly to the topic of my emotional well-being.

Brooke had waited for me to arrive in the conference room that morning. For some reason, at that particular moment, I felt the need to explain my tardiness and mentioned that I had been pulled into another office by my Executive Director to talk about an incident with a former employee.

"One of our previous employees committed suicide earlier this week. This was the first time since it had happened that my Executive Director and I were able to talk about what had occurred." I continued, "We were all shocked by the event." My Executive Director and I had worked closely with Phyllis during a very hard time in one of the programs I supervise. I told the Executive Director that I had spoken with Phyllis just 3 days before the incident. But then, as I thought about that conversation, I realized that Phyllis had not seemed like herself. In retrospect, I knew something had been different with her, but I just pushed the feeling away and hustled on to the next task. Brooke let me know her concern. She asked how I felt about Phyllis and how her suicide affected me. "Are you angry?" she asked.

Why Would I Be Angry?

I remember the shock I felt from those words. "Angry? Why would I be angry?" I quickly dismissed any personal impact of Phyllis's actions on my life. "I feel badly for the children and what they will have to live with." I was not angry with Phyllis. "I am just fine. My feelings about this incident are for her children; they are not for me." I did not even consider that Phyllis's act so directly affected what was embedded in my own past. But, for whatever reason— maybe it was Brooke's concern for me or my need to process this event—we continued to converse, and I continued to disclose my thoughts and feelings about my own experiences with suicide.

"When I was little, I witnessed my mother trying to slit her wrists and heard her threaten to end her life with a gun. I had a special aunt who committed suicide with a handgun." I talked about my alcoholic father and how that impacted my life. "I was lucky I found a significant family, at a time in my life that was so important."

With gathering amazement, I began to realize the impact that Phyllis's suicide had on me. I realized that my heart ached for the young girls who just lost their mother and for how they must feel. I realized that my heart also ached for me and how I felt, at age 16, dealing with my mother and aunt. I knew how much Phyllis's children needed support and nurturing at such a painful time. I thought to myself, "Let these children be nurtured through this event." Brooke and I talked on about these events from my past. Together, we observed how it so directly relates to what I do and how I react at work.

No Longer Risking Myself

Sharing this personal incident with Brooke definitely helped me reflect on my past and present experiences. It also helped me to evaluate the needs of my employees and consider how the events we experience affect us on so many levels. Overall, I think that we distance ourselves from the tragedies we experience with our coworkers. I realize that, as a supervisor, I also distance myself from events in the lives of the families we work with. I know that I have given a lot of care to reflecting with and supporting the staff I supervise, hopefully helping them process "events," both professionally and personally. But, when I distance myself from the tragedies that happen at work, I put myself at risk. For me to give to my staff and my own family, I, too, need reflective support. It is my responsibility to ensure that the components of the program are carried out to the best of our ability for the infants and toddlers we serve. If I do not protect the staff that carries out the program, I risk the program. If I do not protect myself, I risk the program. We need to make sure that we don't miss the ways that traumatic experiences may affect us personally and bring pain from the past to the surface. I understand that I must continue to learn and advocate for the staff and myself as we continue to serve the families in our program. It is only in this way that we will be able to separate our experiences as directors, supervisors, and consultants from the experiences of staff and families and, at the same time, be fueled to help others by the compassion that we have for ourselves.

Reference

Schafer, W. M. (1992). The professionalization of early motherhood. In E. Fenichel (Ed.), *Learning through supervision and mentorship to support the development of infants, toddlers and their families: A source book* (pp. 67-75). Washington DC: ZERO TO THREE: National Center for Clinical Infant Programs.

Discussion Questions

1. The author states that she learned many lessons from the young mothers she has worked with. What do you think this means? What lessons have you learned from mothers (and fathers) you have worked with?

2. What lessons has the author learned that she used in her role as a consultant?

3. What do you think the author means when she writes, "Relationships are the means through which we best teach about the capacity of relationships"? Why is the relationship the foundation of treatment?

4. How did Kendra's history affect her response to the suicide of a previous staff member?

5. Why did the author decide to focus on Kendra's feelings during their consultation? What was the risk of this response? What was the risk of a different response?

6. What IMH principles are present in this case discussion?

The Red Coat: A Story of Longing for Relationships, Past and Present

Deborah J. Weatherston

Summary

A pregnant young woman, alone and living in a shelter after her foster mother learned of the pregnancy, courageously enters into a therapeutic relationship with an infant mental health (IMH) specialist. The IMH specialist helps her make concrete preparations for the baby, helps her understand her own relationships with her biological parents and foster mother, and supports her in the journey as she learns to care responsively for her child. Home-based IMH intervention continues as mother and child live in a number of homes, establishing their own household for the first time when the little boy is 18 months old. When the mother enrolls in a job-training program with high-quality child care, the IMH specialist sets up a 3-month schedule for their "good-bye." Years later the IMH specialist heard from the family; both mother and son were thriving at work and in school.

The Importance of Relationships: From the Start

This case discussion provides examples of the importance of relationships, past and present, to a parent's capacity to provide warm and appropriate infant care. As Dee shared her stories, good ones and those more difficult, with me, the IMH therapist, she wove them into one strong cloth in which to hold and nurture her infant son. She took a great risk, trusting that I could help her and allowing me to be with her as she prepared for, delivered, and learned to love her child. I suppose I took a risk, too. It was an astounding journey that we took together. It was truly a preventive intervention, where a referral was made because a woman was pregnant, isolated, alone in the pregnancy, unprepared for the care of a baby, and ambivalent about the care she could provide. She had little support from her family, no support from the father of her child, appeared to be without friends, and was estranged from the woman who had taken her in when she was removed from her family's care by the child welfare system when she was 13. Poverty exacerbated all of these risks. What I could not know when the referral was made to me was Dee's capacity for relationship or her power to gather me into her world just as she gathered her baby when he arrived. She held on to us both—sometimes fiercely, sometimes joyfully, sometimes just barely. It was her tenacity that made the intervention work. She simply wouldn't let go. I saw this in her consistent availability to me and to her child, and also in her deeper longing for her mother, her family, and her foster mother. She would not let go of them easily either. But I am way ahead of the story.

Step through the entranceway of the shelter and meet Dee, as I did one cold winter morning. She was a large and strong young woman, 23 years old, wearing a blue-jean skirt and oversize shirt and a hat perched rakishly on her head. Although in her seventh month, she had successfully concealed her pregnancy from her family and, until very recently, from her foster mother. One might think that she was simply a little heavy. It was hard to tell. We sat in a stark, cold room for visitors—three chairs and a large desk filled the space. We were an unlikely match, some might say. How on earth would this work? What could I bring to Dee? Of equal interest, what would she bring to me? And, most poignant of all, what about her baby, who was so carefully concealed?

As Dee spoke to me, she stroked her abdomen and lifted her jersey as if to really confirm for herself that she was pregnant. She paused to watch as her belly moved with the easy rhythm of her own breathing. "Is that me breathing or the baby moving?" she asked, contemplating so seriously herself and, also, the baby as a real and separate little being. "What do you think?" I replied. "It's the baby, my baby," she said, with awe. Then, "I'm not sure I can take care of a baby all on my own. Mama would be no help at all. She doesn't even know about the baby yet. And Mrs. Hill (her foster mother) won't let me back in her house, saying, 'You shouldn't have gotten pregnant.' It was wrong," Dee admitted. "This is a confusing time, Dee. Maybe it will help to talk," I said. "You have 6 or 7 weeks before the baby is due, don't you? I can come again—every week, in fact—if you would like." Dee seemed to think it over. "Will you come back?" she asked somewhat hesitantly, in a little girl's voice. "Of course," I said, and we set a time and date for the next meeting. I left, contemplating the challenges that lay ahead. I didn't really know very much except that she had, in a single gesture, directed me to the baby and, in my presence, acknowledged the reality of the baby to herself. Ambivalent, she was uncertain about her ability to care for a baby. There was a lot of catching up for her to begin to prepare for a child.

"Who Am I?"

As is often the case in IMH work, Dee led the way. She didn't mention her pregnancy or the baby again for several weeks. Instead, she focused intensely on herself, sharing a great deal about her family—her mother; her father; her sisters, who had many children (many in foster care); and relationships that had been important to her as an adolescent and a young child. "Where was the baby?" any clinician could legitimately ask: hidden from view, behind the layers of anger and pain.

In my third visit, I found Dee pacing, anxious, barely able to contain herself. In answer to my question, "How was your visit with your family, Dee?" she unleashed a description of the conflict and confusion characteristic of her family for many, many years. She talked angrily about her mother "who was never home—she walked the streets!" and her brothers who "hurt us girls, thrashed us on the legs" and her father who "started the whole trouble, getting my sister pregnant and making the Children's Protective Services worker come and take us all away!" The visit to her mother's home had triggered memories of neglectful treatment and abuse. It was a painful reminder of her longing to recover what she had lost—her mother, her father, her family—when she was only 13. She told me stories in greater detail about how she had been taken away.

She was angry with all this, not able to think about anything else. It seemed to me that during these initial visits, as I was both assessing the situation and offering a relationship for therapeutic support, my task was to observe and listen and respond with empathy, following her lead. In a brilliant way, during that third visit, she explained why it would be difficult for her to take care of her baby: her relationship with her mother. "It's been a long time since Mama and I have really talked. I haven't stayed with her since I was a little girl. She left us with Daddy when I was 3 and took to the streets. They were both alcoholics." Her relationship with her father was no better. "My Daddy took care of us, raised us until he couldn't do it any more, and then there was the trouble with my sister. The old goat—he's really ugly. He got her pregnant." Then Dee was placed in foster care and her relationship with Mrs. Hill began. "Mrs. Hill took me in. She was real strict and a churchgoing woman. I took care of her father later. But she wouldn't let me have my own friends." The stories tumbled out as if Dee knew their importance to the baby and her ability to provide for his care. "Will you come to the hospital with me?" she asked. I gently replied, "Of course, if you would like. What do you have for the baby, Dee? Can I help you gather a few things?" So began our conversation about babies and what she might need and where she could get some help. I could bring a few things, a blanket, a crib, and other agencies would also help.

The Baby

Darrell arrived full term, healthy, and weighing 7 pounds, 8 ounces. His eyes were bright, and he searched for his mother's face as she held him for the first time. She kissed him softly and caressed his head. I had never seen a baby that new. His capacity for engagement and response, hours old, was remarkable. He was a strong and robust baby who would carry his mother along in the months to come.

Can I Be a Mother?

In the first months following the baby's birth, housing was a problem. Dee and Darrell moved around several times, carrying their belongings to the next stop and keeping in touch with me. It was a time of great uncertainty for me. Could I really do this? I knew that was Dee's question, too. I found a room for them in a small mother-baby residence, and they moved in when Darrell was 7 weeks old. At first, Dee seemed comfortable in her new role. Darrell was eating and sleeping well and smiling, organized in response to his mother's face and voice. She held him when she fed him and kept his crib close to her bedside. But Dee was clearly anxious and uncertain about her baby's care. She wondered if her mother might take care of him. "He cries all the time!" she said. "When does he cry, Dee? What do you think he needs?" I asked. "Well, when he's hungry he cries and when he wants me to hold him and when he needs his diaper changed." "Isn't he remarkable, Dee? He knows just what he wants and how to let you know." I wondered to myself if it were Dee who had been crying. She was new at this, and the job of caring for a baby can be overwhelming. I moved in a little closer, and she told me that the girls in the house told her she's a bad mother when he cries. "Your touch is gentle, Dee. You are able to comfort him on your shoulder right now. He looks so content there." She continued to pat him gently, and he fell asleep as we talked about her visit to her family, how noisy it was there, but also how her mother was able to comfort Darrell when he cried. "You would like your mother to help you here, wouldn't you?" She nodded. "But she can't."

Claiming Darrell

In the next week, we went to see Mrs. Hill, Dee's foster mother. She was cordial and curious about me, but not very warm. Dee had disappointed her by having a baby. On the way home, Dee laid out quite clearly how drawn she is to both her mothers and how rejected she feels. "It's time for me to take my baby home, Debbie, and settle in there. I've reached out to both of them, and now they can just come find me," Dee said, taking a brave and protective step. Just then, Darrell woke up, cooing and smiling. Dee pulled him close to her, "My little man," she said affectionately.

We visited the next week in her room. She told me about a dream she had in which a church lady called her up to the front and asked, "Who is THAT baby?" She said proudly and aloud, "That's my baby!" claiming him in public. "I'd like to do that, you know. Tell everybody, 'That's my baby!'" I said, "He is your baby, Dee. I can tell by the way you hold him and rock him and talk to him that he is your child. He follows your voice and face when you talk. He looks so comfortable in your arms." As we sat there, Darrell reached for Dee's finger and held onto her with his hand. "I think he's telling you that he belongs to you, too!"

Holding and Comforting

The stories Dee told me were important to understanding Darrell and Dee's ability to care for him. Dee rocks him to sleep, comforted by him and her new mothering role. "He woke up in the middle of the night, screaming. I went to his bed and picked him up, and he quieted right away!" "Do you think he needed to know you were there to comfort him? Babies do need comforting when they cry." She continued rocking Darrell and told me a little more. "When I went to the hairdresser, she told me what a good baby he was! I told her that I give him a lot of love and rock him to sleep!" The hairdresser told her not to do that, saying he should cry himself to sleep. Dee then asked me, "What do you think about rocking babies to sleep?" I didn't give her an answer, but asked her how she felt about rocking Darrell. She quickly said, "I love to rock him and be with him. No baby needs to fall asleep crying!" I nodded, and she went on to describe how nice it felt to hold him. "It is nice to hold a baby close to you, to feel how warm he is, and have him hold on to you." She smiled. "I like to hold him when I feed him." At this point, his little hand was curled around her fingers. I wondered where she learned that rocking a baby was important, and asked "Who took care of you when you were this little, Dee? Who do you suppose rocked you?" She was quiet and said, "I think it must have been Mama. She didn't leave us until I was 3." We both sat quietly.

I drove home, wondering about their resiliency. The baby was so sturdy. She seemed able to take care of his needs, protect him, and hold him. I would not have thought it would be possible. His responsiveness surely fueled their relationship. Active and healthy, he was able to contribute to their interaction and reinforce his mother's attempts to provide care. I thought about my role. It was rather like the "envelope." By being consistently present, listening, observing, occasionally commenting on the baby's development and "holding them both," I was able to surround them with my caring. This might have been bittersweet, however. In experiencing being cared about, Dee may have missed those who once cared for her.

Longings

In visits following, when Darrell was between 4 and 5 months old, Dee talked often and intensely about her foster mother. She missed her and was hurt by her open rejection. She hadn't heard from her in several months. "Please will you let us come to see you?" Dee wrote in a letter to Mrs. Hill. To me, she said she felt so sad her heart might break. "I just can't let go of her." As she watched Darrell playing on the floor, she said softly, "Maybe I won't be able to let go of him, either." Darrell, playing with stacking blocks that I had brought that day, entertained by their shape and size, cooed happily and offered spontaneous grins directed at Dee. It was a moment of quiet, but sobering, pleasure. "You care deeply about Mrs. Hill and Darrell and, of course, you don't want to let them go. Maybe instead of letting go, you want to figure out how to hold on."

One game we played during these visits, "teasing and taking away," was particularly instructive. Many feelings were aroused by this interaction. The game alerted me to important themes, ones that I hadn't fully felt or explored, such as teasing, taking away, losing, getting what you want, resilience. "I want him to learn he can't always have everything he wants." "That is important to you," I said. "He is a strong little baby. Like you, he doesn't give up. He keeps trying until he does get it, doesn't he?" Dee smiled.

A Mobile Baby

At 7 months, we watched Darrell roll happily on the floor, moving away and hunching up on his knees, flopping down and returning to Dee's feet. He repeated this, and Dee swooped him up onto her lap to hold before setting him down to begin again. "He not only moves away under his own steam now, but he can also return to you! What an important step!" Dee said she hadn't seen him crawl in just this way before—away from her then back to her. She beamed, calmer and more relaxed than in many weeks. For someone who had experienced so many leavings and so many losses of people important to her, Darrell's increasing ability to be separate as expressed in his mobility was especially meaningful. In Dee's world, leaving meant losing—not leaving to explore and then coming back again. Her baby would show her something different. She would not have to lose him as he grew more separate and independent. She would have to think of other ways to enjoy him and to hold on. It was my job to notice and support these things and also to return.

Playing

When Darrell was between 8 and 9 months old, the visits were often baby centered. Dee spread a large and colorful quilt on the floor and set Darrell down. I would occasionally bring a toy for him. On one visit, I brought a car with a chunky figure to play with. He banged and rolled it, chewed on it, and pushed the car. Dee watched him so proudly and then told me a story. "When I was little, I brought home A's and my mother was so proud she kissed me on the cheek." Dee felt, all over again, what it was like to have her mother be so pleased with her. She reached for Darrell and, again, observed how clever he was; he was a curious, playful, communicative baby. He could entertain himself and was a joy to watch. He could draw Dee (or me) in with an eager smile. "You have so much to be proud of. He is wonderful." Sharing the pleasure of this baby was an important part of the treatment. It was critical that Dee's pleasure was shared, that her interest in Darrell was not only observed, but also acknowledged.

Providing Enough

There were lows, too. One week was particularly hard. Dee had left her food stamps and wallet in a taxicab. She had no money for diapers and out of desperation had called her aunt. "Aunt B. helped us many times before. I remember it was Thanksgiving and there was no food in the house. Aunt B. asked us to her house. My father said a blessing at the table, tears rolling down his cheeks. I'll never forget that. He was so sad. I don't ever want to be out of diapers again. I want a job so that the whole wall is lined with boxes of diapers so I never feel that desperate again." It was a passionate story of her father's despair and her own determination. Dee went on to remember when they had no heat and huddled in bed together, all five of them, and played inside with their coats on to keep warm. "We had fun, then, Debbie! It wasn't all bad." she exclaimed. I knew that my task was to hold the good and the bad stories as Dee wrapped them into one strand and recovered what she had lost—her family. It was important for me to remember that in the intimate presence of her baby, many thoughts and feelings were aroused, sometimes pleasant, but also uncomfortable, frightening, and disturbing ones. Dee could have shut down, turned away from her baby, distanced herself so not to feel so much at any one time—the old hurts or the discomfort with separation or longings to be close. She could have gotten rough and hurtful with Darrell; she could have left him in someone else's care as her mother had done. Within the shelter of our relationship, Dee could remember many things that had happened and share them with me. She could observe her baby, too. I could provide "the envelope," the "safe place," the supportive adult presence that she so badly needed.

The Red Coat

Darrell was just waking up when I arrived. Dee took him out of his crib and set him on the floor. The room felt cold, and he was wearing a very lightweight cotton wrapper that was too small. How odd, I thought, and wondered to myself if he was a little cold; I was. Dee didn't seem aware of the cold or Darrell and went on to tell me that she might drop out of school. It was Mrs. Hill's idea to go to school, anyway, and she didn't have to do what she said. "She's just a mean old lady! And she has all my winter clothes. She won't give them back to me. I had a beautiful red wool coat that she gave me last Christmas. I have nothing to wear now, and I'm cold." I responded, "You need a warm winter coat to wrap around you. I know that you really want that red wool coat. Have you asked her to look for it?" "She says she can't find it. She probably gave it to somebody else." "It's not fair, Dee. I know you loved the coat she gave you. It's hard to go without it. You do need a coat. Would you wear a coat if I can find one?" "You just want me to go to school!" Dee teased. "No, it's getting cold and you need a coat to keep you warm." I said firmly. "Can I pay something for it?" "Of course." By now, Darrell was crawling very competently between us. She noticed him, touched his legs and exclaimed, "You're cold! You need a warmer outfit on." She quickly found a clean, heavier stretchy suit. "I don't want my baby to get sick!"

There are many ways this scene might have been played out. I might have noticed that it was cold and asked if Darrell was cold. I could have suggested a warmer outfit right away. I could have asked if she was cold. But, then, would Dee have told me what she needed me to know about the coat and Mrs. Hill and keeping warm and feeling cold and angry and forlorn? I did get her a coat, a donation from our program. In addition to keeping her warm, it was a gesture of caring, an acknowledgment that she should not be cold and that I had the capacity to help her restore a feeling of warmth that she had once had when in the care of Mrs. Hill.

Dee held Darrell in her arms as I got ready to leave that day. "Mommy loves her little man. Mommy loves Darrell. I tell him every day that I love him." Then she kissed him sweetly. Her voice shifted. "Mama never said she loved me. Maybe once, but I'm not sure." I said, "It is very important to know that someone loves you." Dee said softly, "Mrs. Hill never said she loved me, either." "It is difficult to want so much to have your mother and, also, Mrs. Hill say they love you. How important it is for Darrell that you can tell him each day, 'I love you!' when you have missed those words yourself. You are giving him what he needs and what you needed, too. It is a great gift, Dee."

It was a very powerful moment for me. If the truth be known, I had to resist saying that I loved her, for I felt very close to her and very motherly. But I didn't say that. I did put my hand on her shoulder as a gesture of affection, instead. Because Dee sometimes felt unloved and, often, unlovable, it was miraculous to me that she was so able to love her child. Darrell helped, of course. His ready smile and dancing eyes drew his mother to him and fueled her capacity to provide loving care. What was it that I really did there? How could I have handled the visit differently? In terms of attachment theory, Darrell had established a safe haven in his mother's arms and heart. Secure in this relationship, he was able to explore his world. At 10 months, he was playful and increasingly communicative—important outcomes.

The Calm

When Darrell was 12 months old, Dee and Darrell moved to the other side of town, into a two-family flat with her mother and sister. The house was hidden from the street by overgrown trees. Inside it was empty, except for a mattress on the floor and a table in the kitchen. I was startled and saddened by their poverty. The contrast for me was particularly difficult, as my life was full and comfortable. However, I observe: Darrell's smiles were broad and frequent, his laughter was infectious, his cleverness was a delight. He had two new teeth and three new words: "Mama," "bye-bye," and "Nana." His spirit, miraculously, was not impoverished.

Dee was eager to tell me that she was going to get hard-soled shoes so he could walk! She stood him up, held one hand and invited me to take the other. He walked across the living room floor. "I am so proud!" Dee said. I responded excitedly, "You are both taking steps! You, into a new house; Darrell almost walking on his own!" Then Dee's mother came into the room. We exchanged greetings. She recalled, "Dee was a smart baby—just as bright as Darrell." Darrell seemed to enchant his Nana, and they played a few games, "pick me up" and "walk me." The talk turned to another grandchild, a boy, then 5 years old, who was "bright, too, until he fell off my bed and hit his head. He's crazy now." The details of the injury were chilling. Nana brought me a picture of Samuel and then returned to her room upstairs. By then, Darrell had fallen asleep on Dee's shoulder, quieted by her and comforted as usual. She set him down carefully on the mattress on the floor. Dee talked a little more to me about the time she had chicken pox, when she was about $2\frac{1}{2}$ years old, and remembered that her mother rubbed her with calamine lotion. She also told me about the time that she had pneumonia and her mother stayed with her at the hospital. The stories were of much earlier care, when Dee's mother was available and comforting. "I wish I had a mother who was able, now, to take care of me," she said longingly. I replied, "It's been so long since she was able to do that. You've missed your mother's comfort for many years. What you do have are the memories. I imagine they are what help you now to take such good care of Darrell." Dee nodded and stroked his back softly.

The power of the home visit was especially acute that day. I was aware of the importance of babies, the promise they bring to families, and also the pain when they are hurt or mistreated or removed. I was also startled by the word, "Nana." I called my own grandmother by that name, and I had also spent my toddler years in her house with my mother when my father was overseas. I had not thought of her or that period in quite a long while. The use of the word, "Nana," later sent me into deeply personal reminiscence as I drove back to my office. It is one of the gifts we get from this work with families, the gift of remembering.

The Storms

Things change, of course. By the time Darrell was 15 months old, when he was up and running, Dee often erupted into angry tirades. She stormed and yelled and threw words across the room when I was there. She was angry about her sister Zeta, "who cries and gets what she wants from Mama." She was angry with her father, "the old goat who ruined everything," and her mother, "who pays more attention to Zeta and Danny than Darrell and me!" When Darrell whimpered, Dee picked him up abruptly and sent him into the other room. "I always got it when Zeta went whimpering to Daddy!" She remembered standing by the window with Zeta, watching and waiting for their mother to come back. It was a hot summer day. She didn't come back, and Zeta whined and carried on so. "You were both so little, Dee. Two little girls who missed their mother's care." She nodded. "I think we just fell asleep crying, sometimes." "I'm sorry, Dee. None of that was fair. You have a great deal to be angry about." She quieted.

I had a hunch that there was more to her outbursts. There were Darrell's development and increasing independence; his relationship with his Nana; Dee's own longing for her mother's attention, and her continuous rivalry with Zeta, who lived upstairs; her disappointment with how things were. But I couldn't get to any of that, that afternoon. I was frightened and overwhelmed by the depth of her anger. It had stopped me in my tracks, effectively silencing me. I felt helpless and ineffective. It was not until I discussed this visit in supervision that I realized that what I was feeling might explain what Dee was feeling: frightened and overwhelmed. I also remembered another mother, angry, and another baby, silenced by her rage. I struggled with this memory, too.

In the next visit, Dee asked, "Why did I come back here to live anyway? What did I want to find, Debbie?" She continued. "Mama will always favor Zeta. My father—we all know who's his 'pick.'" Her brothers, very cruel when she was younger, also wanted to move in. "I have a baby now! I can't have them messing with him." I agreed, saying, "It is important for you to protect him, Dee. You are his mother. He needs you to keep him safe." Dee knew that she needed to find a place of her own but felt quite stuck, unable to get ahead. As we talked, Darrell played with the sweeper, and it got stuck. He struggled, pushed, and pulled at it to get it free. He started to pout. "He's going to have a fit, Debbie." I leaned toward him and put my hand on the sweeper to help him get it freed. "There! You just needed a little help." He got it out and grinned. "He's so stubborn," Dee said. "He works so hard to get what he wants. He just doesn't give up." She looked and smiled as if she already knew what I was going to say. "I think he's like his Mommy, determined and not ever going to give up," I said, smiling. She laughed, "I'll be in a new place, maybe by next month!"

Building Blocks

By summer's end, Dee and Darrell had moved again. This time they were on their own. For Dee, it was the first time she had not lived with anyone. Of equal importance, she left her family because it was time to leave, not because of the child welfare system. It was a protective move for herself and her child. At 18 months, Darrell looked sturdy; his language was rich. He used words and gestures to describe what he wanted and needed, was playful, and solved problems very well. Dee took great pleasure in her child and was able to allow him to control many playful interactions.

Good-bye

We approached the last phase of our work together with a plan. Dee enrolled in a job training program where there was child care. The days were long. They had to catch the bus at 7:00 a.m. and were home by 4:00 p.m. Darrell was taken care of by caregivers who could nurture, protect, and challenge him to play and learn. Dee was in the building next door. We set up a 3-month schedule for our good-bye. I visited late in the day, every week for the first month, then every other week, and then once at the end of the month. It seemed carefully thought out, but I wasn't prepared for how much I would miss them. They had taken up a big emotional space in my clinical life for almost 2 years.

Postscript

Now, many years later, Dee and Darrell remain together in a small house. Darrell goes to a city magnet school. They have returned to the church where Dee had been active for many years as an adolescent. Darrell has won trophies for his "speaking voice." They are proudly displayed in the small living room. How do I know this? I heard from Dee the spring that both her mother and foster mother died. She asked if I could come see her and, of course, I did. It was a gift for me to see that Darrell was talkative and lively and creative and clearly attached to her. It was also a gift for me to see that what we did together had meaning. Relationships do last. The other cousins have all been placed, for one reason or another, in foster care. Dee is the only one who has kept her child.

Discussions Questions

1. Dee described a dream where she claims her baby as her own in front of the church membership. The IMH therapist used it as an opportunity to affirm, "He is your baby, Dee." How else could you use a moment like this? What else might someone say that could have taken the discussion in a different direction?

2. When Dee discussed how she loved to rock Darrell, the IMH therapist asked who rocked Dee when she was little. Dee responded, "I think it must have been Mama." The therapist sat quietly. Is there more that could have been said? What was gained by remaining quiet?

3. Darrell's mastery of crawling might have been emotionally charged for Dee. Why is this important developmental task sometimes difficult for a parent? What are some IMH strategies that could be helpful at this time?

4. The IMH therapist recognized the importance of sharing in the pleasure of this baby. Why is this an important IMH strategy? Describe ways this can be done.

5. The IMH therapist holds Dee's difficult stories, as well as the good stories. What does "holding" mean in this context? How are stories "held" and why?"

6. What was the significance of the red coat? How was it pivotal in the IMH treatment described?

Editors and Authors

Editors

Joan J. Shirilla, M.S.W./M.Ed., is supervisor of Parent-Infant Programs at The Guidance Center, a large community mental health program serving children, adults, and families in Southeastern Michigan. She was Special Projects Coordinator for the IMH Program at the Merrill-Palmer Institute at Wayne State University, and she has worked with vulnerable infants and families for more than 15 years.

Deborah J. Weatherston, Ph.D., is the director of the IMH Program at the Merrill-Palmer Institute at Wayne State University in Detroit, where she co-developed the interdisciplinary graduate certificate program in IMH. She is Executive Director of the Michigan Association for IMH and was a ZERO TO THREE Mid-Career Fellow from 1999-2000. She has been an IMH specialist, trainer, and consultant for more than 20 years.

Authors

Kathie J. Albright, Ph.D., is a clinical psychologist in the Child and Adolescent Division of the Department of Psychiatry at the University of Michigan. She has provided IMH services to infants, toddlers, and families for over 20 years.

Carla Barron, M.S.W., is an infant mental health specialist and a supervisor in a child welfare program, Parents and Children Together (PACT), at Wayne State University. She has offered IMH services to children and families in the foster care or protective services system for over 6 years.

Aldene "Scruffie" Crockett, M.S.W., is currently the director of a family resource center. She served as therapist, director, and IMH supervisor for the Doula Program for 13 years.

Kendra Curtiss, M.A., is an early childhood educator and works as an early intervention program manager for the Mid-Michigan Community Action Agency. She has provided services to or on behalf of young children for 13 years.

Bonnie Daligga, M.A., is the clinical supervisor of a home visiting program, Healthy Families Oakland. She has worked in the IMH field for over 16 years.

Brooke Foulds, M.A., C.S.W., is a technical assistant and trainer/consultant for Early Head Start. She has more than 25 years of experience working in the field of early childhood, specializing in IMH services for children birth to 3 years of age and their families.

Sandra Glovak, OTR, is the founder and director of Sensory Systems Clinic, a pediatric therapy clinic. She is certified in sensory integration and praxis testing and has been providing occupational services since 1980.

Sheryl Goldberg, M.S.W., is an IMH specialist, providing direct services to infants and families, as well as clinical supervision, training, and consultation to IMH specialists and birth to 3 and family programs for 20 years. She is adjunct faculty at the College of Education, Wayne State University.

Maureen Nelson, M.S.W., is a Doula home-based specialist providing IMH services within a community mental health family service agency for the past 6 years.

Carol Oleksiak, M.S.W., is the Director of Child and Family Services at The Guidance Center, a community mental health family service agency. An IMH specialist, she has provided services to families, supervision, and training for over 15 years.

Nichole Paradis, M.S.W., is the program manager of a child welfare program, Parents and Children Together (PACT) at Wayne State University. She has specialized in the provision of IMH services within child welfare programs for the past 10 years.

Gregory A. Proulx, Ph.D., is an IMH specialist providing IMH home visiting services, training, and consultation to infant and family programs for the past 18 years. He specializes in the delivery of IMH services in rural and urban communities.

Julie Ribaudo, M.S.W., is an IMH specialist in private practice who has worked with infants, toddlers, and families since 1983, specializing in IMH services to children with regulatory disorders, sensory integration challenges, children in foster care, and post-adoption services. She provides IMH training and consultation to infant and family staff working with children ages birth to 3.

Jan Ulrich, M.S.W., is an IMH specialist in a community mental health agency providing home-based, IMH services to infants, toddlers, and families at risk for neglect or abuse, emotional disorders, and cognitive delays. She has worked within the field of IMH for the past 7 years.